Sufis and Anti-Sufis

CURZON SUFI SERIES

Series editor: Ian Richard Netton

Professor of Arabic and
Middle Eastern Studies,
University of Leeds

The Curzon Sufi Series attempts to provide short introductions to a variety of facets of the subject, which are accessible both to the general reader and the student and scholar in the field. Each book will be either a synthesis of existing knowledge or a distinct contribution to, and extension of, knowledge of the particular topic. The two major underlying principles of the Series are sound scholarship and readability.

BEYOND FAITH AND INFIDELITY
The Sufi Poetry and Teachings of Mahmud Shabistari
Leonard Lewisohn

AL-HALLAJ
Herbert W. Mason

RUZBIHAN BAQLI
Mysticism and the Rhetoric of Sainthood in Persian Sufism
Carl W. Ernst

ABDULLAH ANSARI OF HERAT
An Early Sufi Master
A.G. Ravan Farhadi

THE CONCEPT OF SAINTHOOD IN EARLY ISLAMIC MYSTICISM
Bernd Radtke and John O'Kane

SUHRAWARDI AND THE SCHOOL OF ILLUMINATION
Mehdi Amin Razavi

PERSIAN SUFI POETRY
An Introduction to the Mystical Use of Classical Persian Poems
J.T.P. de Bruijn

AZIZ NASAFI
Lloyd Ridgeon

Sufis and Anti-Sufis

The Defence, Rethinking and Rejection of Sufism in the Modern World

Elizabeth Sirriyeh

CURZON

First Published in 1999
by Curzon Press
15 The Quadrant
Richmond, Surrey, TW9 1BP

Typeset in Horley Old Style by LaserScript Ltd, Mitcham
Printed and bound in Great Britain by
Biddles Limited, Guildford and King's Lynn

British Library Cataloguing in Publication Data
A catalogue record for this book is available from the British Library

Library of Congress Cataloguing in Publication Data
A catalogue record for this book has been requested

ISBN 0–7007–1058–2 (hbk)
ISBN 0–7007–1060–4 (pbk)

For my mother, Grace

Contents

Preface

Opposition to Sufism is not essentially a modern phenomenon. It has been evidenced through much of Islamic history, reaching a notorious early culmination in the brutal torture and execution of al-Ḥallāj, ecstatic martyr of divine love, in 922 C.E. However, some of the harshest criticism has traditionally come from within the ranks of the Sufis, as witnessed in the famous comment recorded by Rūzbihān Baqlī (d. 1209): 'I looked into Hell, and I saw that most of its inhabitants were those donning a patched frock and carrying a food-bowl.'[1] The most distinguished of medieval critics, Ibn Taymiyya (d. 1328), who may or may not have been a Sufi himself, provided an important source of authority for many later reformers, whether Sufi leaders intent on ensuring their followers' conformity with the Holy Law or resolute rejecters of Sufism.[2]

Yet while these currents of dissatisfaction with Sufism had long been present in the *umma*, they were to grow substantially from the middle of the eighteenth century, giving rise to a greater variety of self-questioning among Muslims as well as attacks from outside the Islamic world. This book attempts to explore some of the ways in which Sufism has been challenged over the last two centuries by the forces of anti-Sufism, understood at times as opposition to Sufism in all its aspects, at times as criticism of certain Sufi beliefs and practices regarded as unacceptable innovations with no authentic basis in Qur'ān and Sunna and no laudable purpose.

Many studies of Islam in the modern period have been concerned with the attempts of Muslim 'modernists', and more recently 'fundamentalists', to come to terms with Western modernity and, in the process, traditional Sufis have often appeared to be sidelined or placed in a separate compartment. It is often remarked how many of the so-called modernists or fundamentalists were at some time in their lives Sufis or at least had Sufi contacts in their upbringing. This is hardly surprising in view of the fact that the Sufi *ṭarīqas* so permeated the lives of Muslims in most parts of the *umma* until well into the present century, and in a number of areas continue to do so. It would, therefore, appear to be of some consequence to examine the interaction of the defenders and rejecters of Sufism in their efforts to adapt to modernity or even in their refusal to make such adaptation. The present study makes a preliminary attempt to explore this interaction without in any way claiming to be comprehensive.

The actors selected for scrutiny here are but a few of the many individual thinkers, movements, organizations and states involved in the debate. They have been chosen for the influential nature of their contributions and to afford some idea of the variety of the positions taken. Geographical coverage has of necessity been limited and covers principally the Middle East and North Africa, attention being given also to the Indian subcontinent, West Africa (Chapters 1 and 6) and the North Caucasus (Chapters 2 and 6).

Chapter 1, 'Sufis and Their Critics Before the Impact of Europe,' looks at the context of eighteenth and nineteenth century Islamic revivalism with its concerns over Sufi decline and approaches to its reform, mostly from within Sufism but also by the anti-Sufi movement of the Wahhābis.

Chapter 2, 'The Challenge of European Anti-Sufism,' discusses the nineteenth century European colonialist assault on the ṭarīqas and Sufi strategies for survival, with special reference to Algeria, Sudan, the North Caucasus and India.

Chapter 3, 'Traditional Sufism or a Religion of Progress?' examines the conflict between Western and Sufi thought in the late nineteenth and early twentieth centuries and considers the efforts of early Muslim modernists and Sufi traditionalists to deal with the new situation without compromising their faith.

Chapter 4, 'The Sufism and Anti-Sufism of the Salafis,' traces the development of the critique of Sufism by the Egyptian reformer Muḥammad ᶜAbduh (1849–1905) and his close associate, Muḥammad Rashīd Riḍā (1865–1935), and the growth of anti-Sufism in the movement of the Salafiyya, in Syria pre-World War I and in North West Africa in the 1920s to 1940s.

Chapter 5, 'Strengthening the Soul of the Nation,' focuses on the bold efforts of Turkish poet-sociologist Ziya Gökalp (1876–1924) and Muḥammad Iqbāl (1876?–1938) to rethink the role of Sufism in harmony with the nationalist aspirations of their peoples.

Chapter 6, 'Contemporary Sufism and Anti-Sufism,' surveys the experience of the ṭarīqas since the 1950s and the effects on them of the contemporary Islamic revival, before examining state anti-Sufism in the same period, with reference to the Soviet North Caucasus, Turkey and Saudi Arabia. Finally, the study concludes with an assessment of the radical revivalist thought on Sufism of the Sunni Pakistani Abū'l-A^c^lā Mawdūdī (1903–79) and Shī^c^ī Iranian ^c^Alī Sharī^c^atī (1933–77).

Foreign language words, mainly Arabic, are italicized for the first two or three occasions of use in each chapter. In the case of some more common words, the English form of the plural is used in preference to the Arabic, e.g. *ṭarīqas* rather than *ṭuruq*. The system of transliteration is generally standardized except for quotations and some well-known place names or names in the less frequently-cited languages.

I am grateful to a number of friends and colleagues at the University of Leeds for their part in enabling this project to come to fruition: to Ian Netton as editor of this series for inviting me to undertake it and for constant encouragement along the way; to Adrian Hastings, Haddon Willmer, Neal Robinson and colleagues and students in the Islamic Research Group of the Department of Theology and Religious Studies with appreciation of their support and discussion of parts of the manuscript. Finally, I owe a special debt of gratitude to my husband, Hussein, and daughter, Ala, my most persistent supporters, and to Reema for keeping me alive to the world beyond academic research.

August 1997

Elizabeth Sirriyeh
Department of Theology and Religious Studies
University of Leeds

Notes

1 Quoted in Annemarie Schimmel, *Mystical Dimensions of Islam* (Chapel Hill: University of North Carolina Press, 1975), 21.

2 In support of the view that Ibn Taymiyya was a Sufi, see George Makdisi, 'Ibn Taimiya: a Sufi of the Qādiriya Order,' *AJAS* 1 (1974): 118–29, reprinted in idem, *Religion, Law and Learning in Classical Islam* (Hampshire and Vermont: Variorum, 1991); against Ibn Taymiyya's being a Sufi, Fritz Meier, 'Das sauberste über die vorbestimmung. Ein Stück Ibn Taymiyya,' *Saeculum* 32 (1981): 74–89; for an overview of Ibn Taymiyya's critique of certain aspects of Sufism, M. Abdul Haq Ansari, 'Ibn Taymiyah's Criticism of Sufism,' *IMA* 15 (1984): 147–56.

Abbreviations

AJAS	*American Journal of Arabic Studies*
BSOAS	*Bulletin of the School of Oriental and African Studies*
CAS	*Central Asian Survey*
EI 2	*Encyclopaedia of Islam, New Edition*
IJMES	*International Journal of Middle East Studies*
IMA	*Islam and the Modern Age*
IQ	*Islamic Quarterly*
JAAS	*Journal of Asian and African Studies*
JRA	*Journal of Religion in Africa*
MEJ	*Middle East Journal*
MES	*Middle Eastern Studies*
MW	*Muslim World*
TWQ	*Third World Quarterly*
WI	*Die Welt des Islams*

1

Sufis and their Critics Before the Impact of Europe

The eighteenth century has commonly been viewed as a dark age for the world of Islam, a time of political, economic and cultural decline in the three great Islamic states: the Ottoman Empire, Safavid Iran and Mughal India. Writing in the early 1970s, Marshall Hodgson lamented: 'Though the eighteenth century was not without its interesting and creative figures, it was probably the least notable of all in achievement of high-cultural excellence; the relative barrenness was practically universal in Muslim lands.'[1] Yet from the viewpoint of religion, and more especially of the Sufi spiritual tradition, it was not all dark and barren. There was a widespread sense of decline and concern over the debasement of Sufism among the masses, sunk in superstition and entranced by the extravagant claims of wonder-working charlatans. But this apprehension led also to vigorous reform efforts, both by individuals and mass movements, gaining momentum into the nineteenth century. Such efforts would have far-reaching results for the revitalization of Islamic spirituality within the central lands of Islam. They would also work for the spread of the faith into those peripheral areas only superficially Islamized and, in some cases, not previously reached: in Africa South of the Sahara, South East Asia and on the northern borders in the Caucasus and the steppes of Central Asia and across into China.

Most of this struggle for religious renewal would come from within Sufi ranks, whether from scholarly shaykhs noted for their intellectual achievements in other branches of Islamic learning or from those noted solely for their devotion to the spiritual life, or indeed from the many ordinary members of Sufi ṭarīqas that espoused the reforming cause. Occasionally, however, discontent with the prevailing abuses of Sufism ran too deep for any reform of the orders to constitute an acceptable solution. Virulent anti-Sufism then erupted, taking its most famous organized form in the Arabian movement of the Wahhābīs, ideological forerunners of many modern Muslim opponents of the Sufis.

It is proposed here first to note the nature of the anxieties about Sufi decadence in this period before examining some of the attempts to counter it. After exploring the contributions of two pivotal figures in the Sufi reforming thought of the eighteenth century, there follows an examination of mass reform within the Sufi orders with special focus on nineteenth century Africa, before a final consideration of the Wahhābī radical rejection of the ṭarīqas.

The Mood of Decline

In 1950 A. J. Arberry launched a savage attack on the later manifestations of Sufism, but especially that of the eighteenth and nineteenth centuries.[2] He strenuously denounced the decay in Egypt and generalized beyond it across the world of Islam. The picture presented is one of outrageous violation of the Sharīʿa, open immorality and fraudulent opportunism. Witchcraft is remarked as taking the place of reason with the calculated aim of deluding and exploiting the ignorant masses.

> Every village or group of villages acquired its local saint, to be supported and revered during his lifetime, worshipped and capitalized after his death. Few indeed were the voices that dared protest against this ruinous order of things, for politician and theologian alike feared to oppose the true masters, and found it easier and more profitable to share in the swindle.[3]

The 'true masters', the Sufi orders, are thus categorized as a vicious power in Egypt, conspiring to defraud the people, with the understanding that the same situation prevailed everywhere. Arberry proceeds to quote a 'brave spirit of the eighteenth century', al-Badr al-Ḥijāzī, but suggesting that his criticism is an isolated case:

> Would that we had not lived to see every demented madman held up by his fellows as a "Pole".[4]
> Their ulema take refuge in him; indeed they have even adopted him as a Lord, instead of the Lord of the Throne;
> For they have forgotten God, saying, "So-and-so provides deliverance from suffering for all mankind."
> When he dies, they make him the object of pilgrimage and hasten to his shrine, Arabs and foreigners alike:
> Some kiss his grave, and some the threshold of his door, and the dust –.[5]

Allowing for the exaggerations of Arberry's account, he, nevertheless, reflects the concerns of Sufism's critics of the period, who were somewhat more numerous than he seems to suggest. The poet was by no means alone in his distress at corruptions to the faith through popular innovations (*bidaᶜ*), especially those associated with local pilgrimages to the tombs of supposed Sufi 'saints', 'God's friends' (*awliyā' Allāh*). The image of the mad 'saint' (*majdhūb*), robbed of his sanity by an overwhelming experience of the Divine, would become all too familiar to eighteenth and nineteenth century European travellers. The concerns about the exaltation of such men and belief in their powers of intercession were indeed widespread among Muslims, whether Sufi or non-Sufi.

Among those who felt particularly deep revulsion were the Arabian Wahhābīs, who shared a passionate conviction of the urgency of purifying and revitalizing the faith. The voice of the Wahhābīs' founder, Muḥammad b. ᶜAbd al-Wahhāb (1703–92), is one of the earliest and most strident, seeing his own age as another *Jāhiliyya*, but darker and more decadent than the pre-Islamic age of ignorance of true religion:

> The idolaters of our own time are worse in their idolatry than the ancients because the ancients were worshipping God in times of affliction and associating others with Him in times of prosperity, but the idolaters of our own time are always guilty of associating others with God whether in prosperity or affliction.[6]

Not only were they guilty of association, but there was even greater harm and sinfulness in the act because those that they associated with God were immoral and corrupt Sufi shaykhs. Ibn ᶜAbd al-Wahhāb's son, Shaykh ᶜAbd Allāh, expanded on the disastrous state in mid-eighteenth century central Arabia before his father's reforming campaign.[7] Criticizing exaggerated popular devotion to Sufis, he noted that, for the masses, attendance at Sufi gatherings had become more important to them than regular prayers and that they flocked to saints' tombs, decorating them with gold and silver and marble, while avoiding the mosques. Listening to Sufi poetry, they wept with emotion, but recital of the Qur'ān was treated casually by them and aroused no such feelings. Some even told stories of calling upon God in vain, but calling upon a dead Sufi and being answered and assisted. False Sufism had even corrupted their view of the Prophet and relationship to him. Such people made Islamically unacceptable claims for the Prophet's knowledge and powers, and even for those of Sufi saints, so as to approximate the Christians' belief in the Messiah. He comments: 'The

Messiah for them (the Christians) is a name denoting divinity and humanity combined and this is what some extreme Sufis and Shīʿīs say, speaking of the union of divinity and humanity in the prophets and holy men, just as the Christians say of the Messiah.'[8]

However, the voices of criticism also came from within Sufism. Thus a letter from a prominent shaykh, Aḥmad b. Idrīs (1760?–1837), to his disciple travelling to the Sudan warns him of the dangers to his spiritual state from the ordinary people around him:

> Know, my son, that the people of your time, even if they flatter you outwardly, yet they are faint-hearted and this will bring them no benefit with God. And what God, may He be praised and exalted, ordered the Prophet was that he have patience only with "those who call upon their Lord morning and evening desiring His face" (Qur'ān 18.28). The companionship of rabble, who in their companionship have no desire for God and His Prophet, is a lethal poison which instantly destroys faith unless God preserves it. So be wary of the people of your time, for they are not sincere in their love of God. And may God preserve you from the people.[9]

It seems that the shaykh has a low opinion of many African Sufis, although he recognized the existence of the genuinely pious among the Sufis of the Sudan.

In North Africa similar feelings are expressed by his contemporary Aḥmad al-Tijānī (1737–1815) in a letter to one of his disciples in Fez: 'And know that nobody in these times can keep away from sin since it falls on human beings like heavy rain.'[10] On another occasion he lamented: 'This time is one in which the bases of divine ordinance have been destroyed...; and it is beyond the capacity of any person to carry out God's command in every respect in this time....'[11]

The mood of the times is one of gloom, for the common people, in the reformers' eyes, were failing to achieve true spirituality. The picture is less black than that painted by the Wahhābīs, but it is black enough and the understanding is that illumination is rare, that this age is particularly sinful and the unenlightened masses bear a heavy burden of shame owing to their inability to live up to Sufi ideals.

Sufi Reformers: Shāh Walī Allāh and Aḥmad b. Idrīs

Among the most forceful voices pressing for change were two outstanding eighteenth century Sufis: Shāh Walī Allāh of Delhi, a major Indian intellectual Sufi whose influence has been deeply felt to the present among the Muslims of South Asia and more indirectly further afield, and Aḥmad b. Idrīs of Morocco, already noted, who was to play a key role in inspiring the foundation of new reforming orders in Africa.

Shāh Walī Allāh of Delhi (1703–62)

A critical event that shaped Shāh Walī Allāh's commitment to reform took place in 1731–32. This was his journey from India for a fourteen-month stay in the Holy Cities of Mecca and Medina. Once in the Ḥijāz, he studied Ḥadīth with some of the senior scholars of his day and received guidance in Sufism and initiation into four Sufi orders from the noted mystic Abū Ṭāhir Muḥammad (d. 1733).[12] But in addition to his exposure to different legal schools and a variety of scholarly views on religious questions, he experienced visionary dreams which were to affect the pattern of his life. On 14 August 1731, he records how the Prophet's grandsons, Ḥasan and Ḥusayn, appeared to him in a dream:

> Ḥasan carried in his hand a reed-pen, of which the point was broken. He stretched out his hand to give it to me, and said: "This is the pen of my grandfather, the Messenger of God." Thereupon he (withdrew his hand and) explained: "Let Ḥusayn mend it first, since it is no longer as good as when Ḥusayn mended it the first time." So Ḥusayn took it, mended it and gave it to me.[13]

Ḥusayn then proceeded to clothe him in the Prophet's mantle. Through this and other dreams Shāh Walī Allāh developed a deepening spiritual relationship with the Prophet, spending much time in Medina in contemplation at his tomb and on his return journey to India underwent a vision of him, in which the Prophet personally clothed Shāh Walī Allāh in a mantle.

Through his experiences, his external journey to the Ḥijāz and his internal spiritual journey, he was awaking to an awareness that not all was well with the contemporary state of Islam, as symbolized by the broken reed-pen of Prophet Muḥammad, but also that he had a major role to play in rectifying that state of affairs, being the recipient of the mended pen and the Prophet's mantle. His belief in his own very special position is in ample evidence from his writings, for he understood himself to be entrusted by God with the reform of religion in his age as a renewer (*mujaddid*), as the Prophet's plenipotentiary (*waṣī*) to command worldwide obedience and as the pole of the age (*quṭb*), the head of all God's saints on earth. Perhaps it is understandable that those who did not share his convictions would find him almost insufferably conceited and be shocked by some of his claims, which would appear to go well beyond those of even Ibn al-ᶜArabī. Nevertheless, Shāh Walī Allāh's image has survived remarkably well and he has won respect among many in the twentieth century subcontinent and beyond as a great pioneering reformer, presenting the acceptable face of Sufism and paving the way for a much broader renewal with a modern tinge. He has seemed to mark a clear break with the medieval past and with the perceived corruptions of his own day. However, a large part of his endeavours for which he has earned this kind of reputation has little or nothing to do with his Sufism. It concerns his radical efforts for the overhaul of Islamic jurisprudence, where he seems to foreshadow modern juristic reforms in his calls for a new systematic comparison of the four Sunni legal schools with the Qur'ān and Sunna, his demands for a fresh independent interpretation (*ijtihād*) in opposition to the imitative following (*taqlīd*) of medieval authorities. It emerges also in his bold attempt to provide an annotated Persian translation of the Qur'ān for an educated Indian readership, despite the opposition of the religious scholarly establishment. Finally, Western observers have been particularly attracted by his revolutionary and distinctly modern-looking social and economic ideas.

But our concern here is with the specifically Sufi aspects of his career. Much of his initial training in early life was undertaken by his father, a specialist in jurisprudence, but also a noted Sufi. It was his father who initiated him at the age of fifteen into the widespread Qādirī and Naqshabandī ṭarīqas, and also into the Chishtiyya, one of the great orders of medieval India. Two years later he died, but this was not the end of his spiritual guidance as far as Shāh Walī Allāh was concerned. The son continued to visit the father's tomb in the years preceding his journey to the Holy Cities of Arabia, seeking communion with his spirit as practised in the Sufi tradition. This time may be seen also as a period of preparation for the dramatic experiences of that journey which would cause him to perceive serious problems within the Sufism of his own time, as also in other branches of the faith.

Shāh Walī Allāh was disturbed by the popular regard for wonder-working Sufis, admiration for their ecstatic poetry to the neglect of the

Qur'ān and Sunna and obsession with the visitation of tombs for purposes other than the pursuit of spiritual progress. His position in this respect was not, however, new, but is evidently very close to that of the great Ḥanbalī jurist Ibn Taymiyya (d. 1328), whom he admired and whose views he shared on a number of issues, including the dangers of shrine cults. Where Ibn Taymiyya had been troubled by corruption of the faith through Jewish and Christian contacts in Syria, Shāh Walī Allāh was similarly anxious to eradicate Hindu influence in the Indian context. He agreed with Ibn Taymiyya also in his concerns over the potentially pernicious influence of Ibn al-ᶜArabī's theosophy but differed from him in retaining a high regard for the Greatest Shaykh and locating the real difficulties in certain misguided interpretations of the 'unity of existence' (*waḥdat al-wujūd*) and popular misunderstanding of it that led to a perception of God and the world being identical, rejected human accountability and denied God's forgiveness and punishment. He held the fifteenth century poet Jāmī to be one of those especially blameworthy. However, he claimed to support those interpreters who understood Ibn al-ᶜArabī as maintaining that the Universal Existence proceeds from the Divine Essence but is not to be identified with it. Thus he was anxious to uphold the uniqueness of God and also His readiness to forgive and punish. Much of Walī Allāh's reputation for reform rests on his presumed success in revising and modifying the concept of *waḥdat al-wujūd*. Unfortunately, it is by no means clear that he was sufficiently consistent and convincing to claim such a success for his efforts.[14]

His deep concern for the broader reform of religion drove Shāh Walī Allāh to insist that 'Sufis without knowledge of Qur'ān and *Sunna*, and scholars who are not interested in mysticism are brigands and robbers of the *dīn* (religion).'[15] His stress on the need for Sufism to have an underpinning of essential Islamic learning and for scholars to appreciate the value of the direct personal experience of the mystic is certainly not novel, but points in a direction increasingly favoured by subsequent reform-minded Sufis.

Where he is perhaps at his most forward-looking and a harbinger of change is in his desire to overcome the differences and divisions among the ṭarīqas and his position here would bear comparison with his wish to resolve a similar situation in relation to the Islamic legal schools. Before his return from the Ḥijāz, he showed a definite preference for the Naqshabandiyya, describing it as 'the most illustrious and pure and the least heretical *ṭarīqa*.'[16] Later he was more ready to recount the virtues of other major orders in India, the

Qādirī, Chishtī and Suhrawardī, noting with respect the latter's strict adherence to the Qur'ān and Sunna. However, the culmination of the process of bringing together many competing visions, as exemplified in the many orders and sub-orders, is closely tied to Shāh Walī Allāh's conviction of his own special role in ushering in a new and better age of mysticism. In his own words:

> God blessed me and my contemporaries by granting a path (*ṭarīqa*) which of all paths affords the closest proximity to God.... And my Lord revealed to me: "We appoint you as leader (*imām*) of this path and We will show you its most lofty aspects. "Because of the introduction of this *ṭarīqa* all other *ṭarīqas* and methods of traversing the path (*madhāhib*) can be abolished. This will produce a beneficial effect, since the existence of various *madhhabs* in mystical practice gives rise to factionalism among the people.[17]

In this way he reflects growing trends from this period towards exclusive allegiance to an order as well as the urge to build a super-ṭarīqa to be witnessed in the obvious spectacular case of the Sudanese Mahdiyya. Shāh Walī Allāh's vision for the new mystical order inspired a line of distinguished followers, although the dream of his new way superseding all other ṭarīqas remained unrealized.

Aḥmad b. Idrīs (1750 or 1760–1837)

Unlike Shāh Walī Allāh, Aḥmad b. Idrīs might not be classed as an outstanding intellectual Sufi. He was not a prolific scholarly writer and would surely not claim attention for any brilliant theosophy. Yet recent scholarship has focused on him as a seminal figure for the emergence of the new dynamic Sufi organizations that would come to prominence in the nineteenth century.[18] Three of his closest students would go on to become the founders of such orders: the North African Muḥammad b. ᶜAlī al-Sanūsī of the Sanūsiyya in Libya, the Meccan Muḥammad ᶜUthmān al-Mīrghanī of the Khatmiyya in the Sudan, the Sudanese Ibrāhīm al-Rashīd of the Rashīdiyya and its offshoots in the Sudan and Somalia.[19]

Ibn Idrīs seems to have made his greatest impact through his personal contacts and oral communication rather than through his writings, which are mainly compilations of his students' lecture notes and survive in the form of short Sufi treatises and fragments of commentary on Qur'ān and Ḥadīth. To the followers of those ṭarīqas influenced by him, he is most familiar through his prayers and litanies. The following short prayer is characteristic of his style:

> O God, cleanse me of every impurity, every error, every malady, every sickness, every sin, every act of disobedience, every negligence, every transgression, every veil, every estrangement; indeed, of everything of which Thou cleansed Thy Prophet, Muḥammad, May God bless him and grant peace to him and his family, outwardly and inwardly, O Lord of the Worlds.[20]

Many particulars of Ibn Idrīs's long life remain unknown, despite the substantial efforts to investigate them.[21] His date of birth is uncertain, but he was probably born at Maysūr near Fez in Morocco in either 1750 or 1760. At an early age he seems to have been noted for his piety and renunciation of worldly affairs and to have been taught within the family by two of his brothers. At about the age of twenty, he moved to Fez to begin higher education in the famous Qarawiyyīn Mosque and remained in the city for the next twenty or thirty years until his journey to the East around 1798 to 1800.

The reason for Aḥmad b. Idrīs travelling to the East was ostensibly to perform the *ḥajj*, but resulted in his permanent settlement in Arabia, for fourteen years in Mecca and the last part of his life in Yemen. During his stay in Mecca he was aided by the friendship of the Hāshimite Sharīf Ghālib, ruler of the Holy City until its conquest by the Wahhābī religious reformers in 1803. Ibn Idrīs's relationship with the anti-Sufi Wahhābīs is a matter of some interest. Despite his position as a prominent Sufi, he remained in Mecca under their rule and only moved to Yemen in 1827–8, after the Wahhābīs lost control of the Holy City to the Egyptians and Ibn Idrīs experienced rising opposition from the Meccan *ᶜulamā'*. They resented his criticism of the fanaticism and factions of the law schools and his insistence on returning beyond the medieval formulations of the jurists to the original Islam of the Qur'ān and Sunna. Whatever the exact circumstances occasioning his departure from Mecca, Ibn Idrīs was to spend the last ten years of his life in Yemen, for a short while in Zabīd before taking up residence in the village of Ṣabyā in ᶜAsīr where the local ruler was an enthusiastic Wahhābī. Not long after he arrived there, a famous debate took place between him and the Wahhābī scholars, who were allegedly worsted in the encounter. Questioned about his regard for Ibn al-ᶜArabī, whom the Wahhābīs classed as an unbeliever, he maintained his acceptance of Ibn al-ᶜArabī's writings only in so far as they were in agreement with the Qur'ān and Sunna. When asked about Muḥammad b. ᶜAbd al-Wahhāb, he recognized his good intentions in seeking to purify the faith, but held that he had been too harsh in his attacks on those Muslims with whom he had differences. The local Wahhābī ruler was apparently impressed by Ibn Idrīs and he lived in peace until his death, probably in his late eighties, on 21 October 1837.

Aḥmad b. Idrīs was actively concerned with spiritual reform and sufficiently convincing in his fundamentalist approach, it seems, to counter Wahhābīs suspicious of him as a Sufi shaykh and to enable him to reach some form of accommodation with them. Perhaps part of his success in this may be owing to his lack of interest in becoming the founder of any rival mass movement that could provide a serious threat to Wahhābī authority in Arabia. Instead he concentrated on individual purification and the development of total dependence on God (*tawakkul*), operating consciously within the classical Sufi tradition. How far was he simply continuing this tradition and how far heralding the advent of a new age in Sufism?

In certain respects he appeared to be pointing the way towards trends that were to become the hallmark of many modern reformers and yet some of these trends may also be seen as having a long history within the faith. He was concerned with proper exoteric understanding of the Qur'ān and Ḥadīth before embarking on esoteric interpretation in a manner described by an author from within the Idrīsī tradition:

> If Ibn Idrīs was asked anything concerning the Koran, he would look at the inside of his hand and then give his commentary from divine knowledge; if he was asked about the noble Tradition, he would look at the outside of his hand and then explain it from the divine secrets and gnosis of God.[22]

In this way he was acting in the style expected from a Sufi master receiving inspiration from the unseen (*al-ghayb*). But he was also anticipating a demand that would increase in modern times by his insistence on undertaking *ijtihād*, speaking on his own authority without recourse to past masters, despite his extensive knowledge of them.

While noting that he had no obvious pretensions to establish any large-scale movement, Ibn Idrīs displayed a deep concern for mission, especially to those areas that were on the frontiers of Islam. This is reflected in his training of disciples from such areas or those who were ready to travel to them as missionaries and Africa was surely central to his plans for the extension of Sufi renewal. It is there that his influence has been most acutely felt through the new orders in the Idrīsī tradition.

The Spirit of Mass Reform Within the Ṭarīqas

Much has been written of the eighteenth and nineteenth centuries as a time of 'neo-Sufism', a term apparently coined by Fazlur Rahman in 1966 and widely used since, despite some more recent questioning of its applicability. Rahman had posited radical changes in the nature of Sufism in this age, seeing it as being shorn of its ecstatic and metaphysical characteristics and assuming in their place the features of orthodoxy. He went on to state, 'This fact cannot be over-emphasized, since through it Sufism was made to serve the activist impulse of orthodox Islam and is a ubiquitous fact in all the major forms of pre-Modernist reform movements'.[23] However, a serious distortion may be seen to result from such an over-emphasis on a pruning process that is by no means 'a ubiquitous fact' and, if so carried out, would have reduced these movements to little more than benevolent associations, effectively destroying their spiritual *raison d'être*. Sufism would have ceased to be Sufism. Rahman's proposition, inherited from Sir Hamilton Gibb (1948), that Ibn Idrīs and the Idrīsī tradition substituted the ultimate goal of passing away in God (*fanā'*) for a union with the spirit of Prophet Muḥammad has been shown to be highly dubious, as has its extension by J. S. Trimingham (1971) to apply to Aḥmad al-Tijānī.[24]

If the concept of 'neo-Sufism' as involving substantial changes at the very core of its nature is to be rejected, are there ways in which it is still meaningful to speak of new directions in Sufism at this time? Without suggesting total novelty, it is possible to note some features which appear to acquire greater importance with the advent of the new nineteenth century Sufi orders or the appearance of activist reformers within old orders. Firstly, although consciousness of this world as a preparation for the next remained essential and central, there appears to have been a heightened awareness of the need to struggle for the socio-moral reform of society entailing this-worldly and not only otherworldly benefits. Linked to this, movements were often characterized by political activism, where the achievement of a state modelled on that of the Prophet continued to be the ideal goal.

Furthermore, it is often noted that the Sufi reformists were anxious, as was Shāh Walī Allāh, that the Sufi path should be combined with strict adherence to the Sharīᶜa and this is apparent in numerous cases. It could be argued that this is not really a new phenomenon and that many Sufis throughout the centuries had also been jurists. Yet there was a newness perceptible in the forceful and widespread insistence on Sharīᶜa in the community, even when it was not understood in precisely the same way as by those practitioners of the medieval legal schools who were not Sufis and who, therefore, would not claim any mystical insight in their efforts to comprehend God's law. Finally, there is an evident novelty in the growth of ṭarīqas as organized mass movements. Some, such as the Qādirī, had achieved a considerable expansion in preceding centuries, but could be seen as loose-knit associations, generally with little in the way of a rigid, hierarchical structure. The spirit of mass reform brought increasing demands for improved central organization in certain orders that could sometimes lead to a highly developed bureaucracy.

What lay behind such changes that are observable in many areas as isolated from one another as Senegal and Bengal? Some allowance should be made for the fact that geographical distance did not necessarily mean total lack of contact, since patterns of cross-fertilization of ideas have been detected through the networks of scholars travelling for study and spiritual enlightenment to the Holy Cities of the Ḥijāz and other major centres of learning such as Cairo, Damascus, Fez or Zabīd in Yemen.[25] No doubt, such inter-relations served as a stimulus for reinvigorating Sufism on their return to their home areas, imparting perhaps a shared sense of the urgency of reform.

Yet there must be much in the wider common experience as well as in the particular circumstances of individual regions and districts and their traditions to help account for the new features. Loss of political power and economic collapse may be perceived as consequences of a loss of God's favour through failure to live as true Muslims and thus breed a heightened awareness of the need for the community as a whole to regain this lost favour through a programme of moral reform. The achievement of this would frequently be seen to necessitate efficient mass organization, implementation of Sharīᶜa and the pursuit of the ideal Islamic state.

This type of linkage between spiritual and material well-being is apparent in the thinking of Sayyid Aḥmad Barēlwī (1786–1831), a dynamic model of the Sufi activist reformer intent on the creation of a purified Islamic society in northern India in a land liberated from the unbelieving British. They, for their part, dubbed his Ṭarīqa Muḥammadiyya as Wahhābī, although it probably owed most of its inspiration to Shāh Walī Allāh, whose son, Shāh Ismāᶜīl, was closely associated with Sayyid Aḥmad and who left a record of his teaching. He notes his view that all kinds of blessings in this world will result from their struggle,

> such as timely downpour of rain, abundant vegetation, growth of profits and trade, absence of calamities and pestilences, growth of wealth and presence of men of learning and perfection. . . . (These blessings) will likewise and in the same manner materialize, even a hundredfold more, when the majesty of the Religion of Truth (is upheld), when pious rulers govern in the different regions of the earth, when the righteous community (gains) military strength and when the principles of the *Sharīᶜah* are being propagated in villages and towns.[26]

A Qādirī Reformer in West Africa: Usuman dan Fodio (1754–1817)

The perception of righteous behaviour assuring earthly prosperity and sinfulness bringing ruin also appears relevant in certain cases in nineteenth century Africa for an understanding of the summons to establish a pious and purified community with a mass following of the Sharīᶜa. In Hausaland and Bornu (northern Nigeria and southern Niger) the mid-eighteenth century witnessed severe drought affecting some areas for as much as ten years and, around 1790, a famine that brought serious hardship and large-scale movement of population. In such circumstances hopes abounded for the coming of the Mahdī to bring an end to the time of troubles. The Qādirī Sufi reformer known in Hausa as Shehu Usuman dan Fodio and in Arabic as ᶜUthmān b. Fūdī (1754–1817) presented himself as 'the wind heralding the raincloud', preparing the way for the Mahdī. He offered the Fulbe and Hausa peoples the opportunity to rebuild their society, modelled on the ideal of the early Islamic *umma* of the seventh century and purified of un-Islamic accretions and immorality. It was to be a society whose combined repentance and efforts in pursuit of an Islamic life would hopefully earn God's pleasure and with it relief from worldly suffering. Such a message must have exercised a powerful appeal. And yet there was always the acknowledgement that the end time was not far distant, that Usuman dan Fodio was the last of the renewers of the faith to bring a sinful community back into the right path. This-worldly benefits would be assured, but there was also preparation for the Day of Resurrection.

How did Usuman dan Fodio come to receive and implement his vision for these West African communities? He had been born in northern Hausaland in 1754 into a family from a Fulani clan with a tradition of religious scholarship. His younger brother, Abdullahi, wrote of their early education with their father, uncles and other teachers: Qur'ānic studies; the biography of the Prophet and poetry in praise of him, including the famous *Burda* of the Berber poet al-Buṣīrī popular with Sufis; jurisprudence of the Mālikī rite predominant in West Africa; astronomy but not religiously disapproved astrology; poetic composition; Sufism.[27] Usuman was to be initiated into three ṭarīqas: the Qādirī, Shādhilī and Khalwatī. However, it was the first with which he was to be most closely associated, culminating in his reception of dream visions of the great saint ᶜAbd al-Qādir al-Jīlānī in the company of the Prophet. His sense of being chosen came to him at the age of forty in 1794 after a period of meditative retreat, perhaps in expectation of such a spiritually important occasion. He wrote of this experience:

> When I reached the age of forty, five months and some days, God drew me to Him. I found there Our Master Muḥammad with the companions and the prophets and the saints.... Then came the intermediary, the Lord of Men and Jinn, ᶜAbd al-Qādir al-Jīlānī, bringing a green robe embroidered with the phrase, "There is no god but God and Muḥammad is His Messenger..." He tied around me the Sword of God (or Truth) to draw against His foes.[28]

Such visions convinced him of the necessity of *hijra* away from unbelieving rule in the Hausa state of Gobir, a move to be followed by preparation for the military *jihād*. It was to be a struggle lasting several years until final victory in 1810. The new state that resulted was to be under the Islamic rule of his brother Abdullahi and son Muḥammad Bello, but for Usuman it would mean renewed dedication to the greater *jihād* of the Sufi path. He died in April 1817 and, despite his personal opposition to grave cults, his tomb soon became a place of pilgrimage.

Given that Usuman dan Fodio had a profound personal commitment to the Sufi life, and at the same time to the mass reform of his society, one might expect that he would encourage or demand popular participation in Sufism and especially in the Qādiriyya. Yet it is not at all evident that this was the case. It has been remarked that Usuman dan Fodio's Sufism 'was personal and devotional, and only marginally social or organizational.... Indeed there is no evidence that the Shaykh ever perceived the hierarchical structure of *ṭarīqah* membership as a model or means for social and political organization.'[29] Sufism as practised in the Qādiriyya might indeed be seen to provide the inspiration for the top leadership in this instance without its being confirmed as the ṭarīqa for the masses. Even when all were included in the mission to raise the level of piety in the community, Shehu Usuman appeared to recognize that not all would necessarily be capable of the deep inner spiritualization demanded of aspirants on the Way. Therefore, his vision of a reformed society was of one in which the great majority would be Muslims with a basic understanding of the externals of the religion, avoiding immorality and syncretism with Hausa religion. A minority of the spiritually-minded would then pursue the perennial goals of Sufism.

This two-tiered approach to reform is evident from his writings, some of which are concerned with elementary instruction of the people in their religious duties, others directed to a scholarly readership. In a small treatise on the difference between the government of Muslims and of unbelievers he outlined the essential reform needs:

> An example of bringing about reforms in religious and temporal matters is that the governor of every town should make an effort to repair the mosques and establish the five prayers in them and command the people to endeavour to recite the Qur'ān and teach the art of reciting it and to acquire learning and impart it. He should also make an effort to reform the markets, care for the poor and needy and order all that is beneficial.[30]

There is nothing here of an esoteric nature, but the stress is certainly on a this-worldly socio-moral improvement which is described as 'the way of Paradise'.

In a work composed in 1792–3 and perhaps intended for the use of those engaged in mission (*daᶜwa*), Usuman outlined his intention to restore the Sunna in the lives of ordinary people.[31] He stated that he had no wish to pursue them for their faults or to shame them, but to revive the Prophet's practice and eliminate innovations in order to save the community. His concentration, therefore, was essentially on the Sharīᶜa and he remarked the dangers for a lay person engaging in theology; it could lead to fanaticism, to involving the common people in specious arguments about religion, to the adulteration of Islamic beliefs and unnecessary indulgence in the philosophers' mysteries. It is thus clearly marked as the preserve of *ᶜulamā'* and he was opposed to those who made such knowledge a requirement for all believers.[32] The treatment of Sufism is also brief and, while the common people are not discouraged from it as from theology, the stress is very much on moral improvement and drawing nearer to God through concentration on religious duties and avoiding prohibited and undesirable acts, such as wrongly declaring someone to be a saint, depending on a dream after praying for guidance, and consulting fortune-tellers. There is no suggestion that any mass adherence to the Qādiriyya is to be urged or indeed that much devotion to the Path is expected. That would appear to be a matter for the spiritual élite. The promotion of Qādirī ṭarīqa membership to achieve widespread reform belongs rather to the period after the Shehu's death.

A New Order for Mass Reform: the Tijāniyya in North and West Africa

By contrast, leaders in other new orders, or reformers within old ones, would not infrequently encourage active membership in the ṭarīqa to which they belonged. The order would then become a potent vehicle for reform on a mass scale rather than the focus of spiritual allegiance and inspiration for the select few committed to a wider and more basic reform of Islam in the lives of the people. The Tijāniyya, founded by the North African Aḥmad al-Tijānī, was one of the most dynamic new orders to realize its potential as an instrument for reviving the faith through calling for all sections of society to join the ṭarīqa.[33]

Aḥmad al-Tijānī was born in the oasis of ᶜAyn Mahdī in southern Algeria in 1737, but journeyed to Fez as a young man in search of religious learning and spiritual guidance. It was there that he joined three Sufi orders, including the Qādiriyya, before withdrawing to a Sufi *zāwiya* on the edge of the desert. In 1772–3 he set out for the pilgrimage to Mecca, seeking contacts with a number of Sufi shaykhs, especially those of the Khalwatiyya, being given particular recognition in the Holy City by ᶜAbd al-Karīm al-Sammān, chief of the reformed Sammāniyya branch, and Maḥmūd al-Kurdī in Egypt, who authorized his preaching of the order in North Africa. It was not until about five years after his return to Algeria that he began to claim that he had received a waking vision of Prophet Muḥammad who taught him the litanies for his new order. From this time in 1781–2 al-Tijānī began the propagation of the Tijāniyya, seemingly viewing it from the beginning as a movement of outreach to the people, 'the dregs of the Berbers and the Arabs' in the opinion of a contemporary critic.[34] Tijānī and non-Tijānī sources give very different interpretations of the reasons for al-Tijānī's final move to Fez, Tijānīs recording it as a mark of his growing success, non-Tijānī critics alleging that he was actually expelled by the authorities, perhaps because he was seen as a threat to public order. In Fez he was favourably received by the sultan of Morocco, Mawlay Sulaymān, a ruler generally noted for his disapproval of Sufi orders and support of the Arabian Wahhābīs.There al-Tijānī is portrayed as living a life of considerable comfort, building up his order with wealthy backing, but little scholarly approval, until his death in 1815.

Following its founder's death, the new ṭarīqa spread widely in North Africa and with special success in West Africa, whether peacefully or through armed jihād. Al-Ḥājj ᶜUmar Tal (1794–1864) was to be its most famous propagator in mid-nineteenth century Senegal, Guinea and Mali, actively summoning to Tijānī membership all classes, regardless of educational background and welcoming women and slaves. ᶜUmar Tal eventually established a Tijānī-organized Islamic state, enforcing the Sharīᶜa as understood by him with mystical insight and not only through exoteric juristic study. He remained conscious of the moral dangers of over-attachment to temporal power and practised frequent Sufi retreat in his efforts to overcome temptations. He died in fighting against fellow-Muslims, mainly Qādirīs, some reports indicating a possible suicide, blowing himself to pieces with a barrel of gunpowder. His sons continued to run the state on Tijānī lines until 1893, when finally conquered by the French.

What distinctive features in the Tijānī doctrines and propagation methods can be seen as enabling the ṭarīqa's development as an agent of reform? Firstly, and perhaps most obviously, the exclusive demands made on the individual have been observed as particularly effective in promoting allegiance to the Tijāniyya. On joining the order, a Tijānī would be expected to renounce all commitments to other orders, being assured that they were all inferior and that no harm could come to one who abandoned them. However, abandonment of the Tijāniyya was held to be extremely dangerous, leading to death as an apostate. Tijānī preachers stressed the great benefits in this world and the world-to-come as a result of adhering strictly to all the practices of the order, including regular recital of the Tijānī litanies (*awrād*). By contrast, failure to perform them or speaking ill of Aḥmad al-Tijānī would end in the same fate as abandonment of the ṭarīqa. Exclusiveness was further ensured by a prohibition on visits to the tombs of dead Sufi 'saints'.

Non-Tijānīs have generally been sceptical of the founder's motivation in requiring exclusive attachment to his order and this has tended to cast doubts on his sincerity. It is possibly too easy for a cynic to see the obvious advantages of building a mass belief in the Tijāniyya as the only true path to worldly prosperity and heavenly bliss. Yet it is surely not difficult to appreciate the rationale behind such demands in a North African society deeply imbued over many centuries with the love of the Prophet and taking very seriously the possibility of communicating with him through dreams and waking visions. Tijānī gnostic theory has been seen to build on a long heritage of 'a corpus of ideas that had circulated in North Africa, no doubt changing from time to time in detail and emphases, ever since the Muḥammadī *ṭuruq* began to emerge under the influence of Muḥyī al-dīn b. al-ᶜArabī and the writers of *madīḥ* (panegyric of the Prophet), in the eighth/fourteenth century.'[35] Within such a context it is not so extraordinary to find that Aḥmad al-Tijānī could have arrived at a firm belief that the Prophet had appeared to him and that, having the perfect master, he should consequently break ties with all other masters and expect the same from his followers.[36] The exclusiveness of the order and its exceptional claims may well have contributed greatly to its success, but probably all the more so because the ground was already prepared over a long period for the reception of such authority.

Aḥmad al-Tijānī's achievement of earthly riches has also bred scepticism among critics of the ṭarīqa, who question the reasons for his rejection of traditional Sufi asceticism (*zuhd*), perhaps another key factor in expanding membership. Instead of the strict exercises of physical renunciation, he encouraged his followers to develop a spirit of thankfulness (*shukr*) for God's bounty in this world. It might be noted that the rich did not need to give up their luxurious lifestyle, but could use their wealth in the service of the order. The poor were not urged to make their lives still harder through further abstinence and could hope for an improvement in their lot. Sufis hostile to the Tijāniyya could interpret such an approach as a dilution of Sufism for sale to the mass market. Critics of Sufism in general could find in it further evidence to back their arguments regarding the corrupting influence of Sufis. Yet, even if there were attractions in the setting aside of a severely ascetic life, it does not seem that al-Tijānī intended the acceptance of the ṭarīqa to be effortless. Those joining would ordinarily be expected to fulfil their religious duties as well as the additional Tijānī litanies and prayers and to undertake the responsibilities of work, not to beg or depend on charity. They were to concentrate on freeing the heart of all worldly attachments and cultivating a state of love for God's gifts and gratitude for them under all circumstances, whether rich or poor. They were not to seek to be marked out from the rest of humankind, not to be noted as righteous on account of any extraordinary fasts or vigils, but to live like anyone else, while seeking to avoid sinfulness. It was a practicable way for a wide range of people to give attention to both worldly and otherworldly concerns, to save themselves and their families from hardship in this world at the same time as saving their souls in the next. For many in Africa the visible prosperity enjoyed openly by Aḥmad al-Tijānī and a number of his followers would also appear as an endorsement of righteousness and an assurance of being on the right path that would help to encourage membership.

However, the sanctioning of wealth and its appreciation was not unique to the Tijānīs among African Sufis of the nineteenth century. A close contemporary of al-Tijānī, Sīdī al-Mukhtār (1729–1811), proclaimed a very similar message in this respect during his career as a distinguished Qādirī shaykh among the Kunta of the southern Sahara. They had a long history of involvement in the long-distance trans-Saharan trade and Sīdī al-Mukhtār stressed the religious value of this commercial activity and the importance of work and self-sufficiency.

> He placed great emphasis upon the accumulation of wealth, and insisted that there was a clear link between economic success and religious piety. Wealth, he said, was an indication of one's *jah* (dignity and status).[37]

The teaching of the new nineteenth century Sanūsī order is also remarkably similar with regard to the encouragement of a work ethic. The founder, Muḥammad b. ᶜAlī al-Sanūsī (1787–1859), has already been noted as one of the close disciples of Aḥmad b. Idrīs, but he also seems to have had some contact with his fellow-Algerian Aḥmad al-Tijānī, when he was in Fez in 1814 and possibly initiated into the Tijāniyya.[38] Al-Sanūsī clearly advocated the benefits of work in the building of a broad network of Sanūsī lodges extending from the present-day area of Libya deep into central and western Africa, proclaiming that 'God helps those who help others' and that the builders and carpenters engaged in the enterprise would themselves benefit from them. He also urged military training to bring peace and Islamic order to the tribes and gave encouragement to the active practice of agricultural and commercial pursuits. Where he differed from al-Tijānī, and indeed from Sīdī al-Mukhtār, was in his disapproval of luxury.

The Sanūsiyya was probably the best-known of several orders in Africa and Arabia founded in the nineteenth century following the example of Aḥmad b. Idrīs. Among the leaders of orders within the Idrīsī tradition in the Sudan, the founder of the Khatmiyya 'disliked the exaggerated dress and asceticism (*taqashshuf*) of the dervishes.' The order had a noted success among middle class traders.[39]

The discouragement of asceticism and commitment to a work ethic look distinctively modern. However, these tendencies could already be observed in the medieval Shādhilī tradition in North Africa and Egypt. It may be no coincidence that both Aḥmad b. Idrīs and Aḥmad al-Tijānī were initiated into the Nāṣiriyya branch of the ṭarīqa early in their careers. The influence of the Shādhiliyya may yet be discovered at the root of these trends in the new African orders. But it does not explain the frequent readiness to receive such teachings in nineteenth century Africa. This readiness seems to derive in part from a compatibility between the doctrines of the new orders and existing African religious attitudes and in part from their perceived relevance to the particular circumstances of those seeking to maintain, or aspiring to improve, their condition and status. A world-denying message, emphasizing preparation for the world-to-come to the exclusion of earthly considerations, had drawn a limited following by comparison with the great upsurge in recruitment to the new mass organizations.

Questions have been raised as to how far the experience of socio-economic dislocation, notably that caused by the slave trade, may have increased receptivity to the teaching of the Sufi movements and hence their success.[40] It is still unclear as to whether the areas suffering most severely responded most warmly to the ṭarīqas. Conversely, the very success of Muslim trading and agricultural enterprises may be highlighted as a stimulus to large-scale membership. The message would be well-received both by the prosperous entrepreneurs themselves and by those wishing to gain access to opportunities offered by association with them. The more closely-structured Sufi orders afforded such an association for the rank and file and, at the same time, could operate as an effective mechanism of control for the leadership, especially with the growth of requirements for exclusive adherence to a single order.

All this is not to discount the spiritual appeal, the conviction among the adherents of the orders that their founders and leading figures are gifted by God with remarkable powers and guided in the right path through visionary contacts with the Prophet and major Sufis of the past. Without a widely-shared belief in the authenticity of their mystical experience and role as guides, the most efficient organization would have remained a hollow shell and unable to win any substantial acceptance. The real key to sustained vitality in the African ṭarīqas seems to lie in their able combination of response in both the spiritual and material fields. In the words of Donal Cruise O'Brien, discussing African religious leadership and its popular reception:

> The miracle-working saint or prophet could bring supernatural assistance to bear in support of his disciples' endeavours, whether in trade or in war. And the miracle was taken as proof that here was a leader who could intercede for his disciples on the Last Day, who could deliver on his promise of paradise in the hereafter. Success in business, success in war, with a guaranteed paradise as the bottom line: who might not have been tempted by such a charismatic contract?[41]

Many in Africa were so tempted.

Attention here has been focused on Africa, but not with the understanding that the African situation was unique within nineteenth century Sufism. The urge to mass reform is clearly visible throughout the worldwide umma, especially in reformed branches and offshoots of the Naqshabandiyya in Asia, the Middle East and eastern Europe. However, African Sufis have been singled out as exemplifying this spirit of renewal in a noticeably vital and effective manner, giving rise to significant new ṭarīqas with a high degree of organization and commitment to mission. Building on a long tradition of Sufi spirituality, owing much to the medieval Qādirī and Shādhilī orders in particular, they appeared to have developed characteristics that distinguished them from their medieval heritage. At the same time they did not cut themselves adrift from its foundations. While aiming to preserve spiritual values, their organization, work ethic and development of political and economic power provided them with a strong basis of support from which to expand in the twentieth century. Certainly in Africa, but also in a number of other areas, such revitalized Sufism would have evident accomplishments, but the voices raised in criticism would also grow louder.

Rejection of the Ṭarīqas: the Arabian Wahhābīs

The most frequent reformist responses to the dilemmas of eighteenth and nineteenth century Sufism remained essentially within the Sufi tradition, however much change they might involve. The Wahhābī movement affords an exceptional example of a stern and total rejection of Sufism and its organized expression in the orders. The severe distress of early Wahhābīs at the state of popular Sufi practice remains perhaps their best-known characteristic, but their relationship to reform efforts by Sufis themselves is much less clear, as evidenced by the apparent compromise reached with Ibn Idrīs and by the early contacts of Ibn ᶜAbd al-Wahhāb himself with Sufi reform tendencies in the Holy Cities.

Muḥammad b. ᶜAbd al-Wahhāb was born into a family with a strong scholarly tradition as Ḥanbalī jurists and it is this side of his heritage which has commonly been stressed, especially the influence on his thought of Ibn Taymiyya. Yet Ibn Taymiyya was not only influential in Ḥanbalī circles. Shāh Walī Allāh's admiration for him has already been remarked, so that he can also be seen as affecting the outlook of Naqshabandī Sufi reformists and not only non-Sufi critics of the abuses of Sufism. Furthermore, Ibn ᶜAbd al-Wahhāb has been shown to have been made aware of these Naqshabandī reform trends during a period of study in Medina. One of his main teachers there was an Indian Sufi, Muḥammad Ḥayyā' al-Sindī, who, in common with Shāh Walī Allāh, had studied under the prominent Naqshabandī Abū Ṭāhir Muḥammad. It has been suggested that the teaching of al-Sindī was to lend encouragement to the young Ibn ᶜAbd al-Wahhāb in his struggle against popular 'saint' cults.[42] However, such strains of influence do not necessarily have to be opposed to others coming from the Ḥanbalī tradition as mediated by Ibn Taymiyya. There appears to be considerably more cross-fertilization in the reformists' heritage than has often been assumed.

In various respects the religious reform movement inspired by Muḥammad b. ᶜAbd al-Wahhāb would seem to have much in common with some of the vigorous new or reformed ṭarīqas. There is the urge to remodel the community on the lines of the earliest Islamic community at Medina, to encourage conformity with the Sharī^{c}a and the elimination of the corrupt innovations of later ages; in this return to an original Islamic state, rigid imitation of medieval jurists is discarded in favour of the effort to undertake fresh individual interpretation of the law (ijtihād). Many of the concerns are the same; for example, that regular prayer is to be encouraged, and both Ibn ^{c}Abd al-Wahhāb and Ibn Idrīs would regard the one who neglected prayer as an unbeliever.[43] The Wahhābīs, although often viewed as harsher and more committed to the enforcement of religious duties, were not always necessarily so much more severe than some of the nineteenth century Sufi reformists who were a little later than them in gaining the opportunity to implement their visions politically.

The Wahhābīs were, for their part, able to realize their goals quite quickly through the alliance forged in 1744 between Muḥammad b. ^{c}Abd al-Wahhāb and the temporal power of Muḥammad b. Su^{c}ūd, local ruler at Dar^{c}iyya in the central Arabian region of Najd. Together they launched their campaign of continual jihād against all those supposedly in the umma, but whom the Wahhābīs regarded as non-Muslim because of their refusal to respond to the summons to repent and join the one true unitarian community. Following the death of Ibn ^{c}Abd al-Wahhāb in 1792, the jihād fervour continued with Wahhābī attacks deep into Iraq, targeting Shī^{c}ī holy sites and culminating in the sack of Karbalā' and the destruction of the tomb of Ḥusayn in 1801. By 1805 Mecca and Medina had been brought under Wahhābī rule and the new state had extended to include much of the eastern coast of Arabia and, for some while, the island of Baḥrayn.

Yet this dedication to jihād was also shared with many Sufi reformers. Where the Wahhābīs differed most significantly from the Sufis was in their denial of mystical insight as a valid means to guide the true community of Muslims. The call was to follow again the original revealed message of Islam and attention was diverted away from the personality of the spiritual leader in the enterprise. Even those Sufis with strong reformist credentials were on this account judged guilty of the serious sin of *shirk*, associating others with God, because of their excessive veneration of the Prophet and too high a regard for the powers of their shaykhs beyond those allotted to the ordinary creation.

Why did the Wahhābīs take up such an extreme rejectionist position with regard to Sufism? One obvious answer might seem to lie in their debt to Ibn Taymiyya and his harsh critique of so many manifestations of late Sufi innovation. But Ibn Taymiyya's view of Sufism in general is summed up by him as follows: 'The right attitude towards sufism, or any other thing, is to accept what is in agreement with the Qur'ān and the Sunnah, and reject what does not agree.'[44] In effect, it is a position which would be quite consistent with that of the Naqshabandī reformers or of Ibn Idrīs. So were there other factors in the Arabian situation which made Muḥammad b. ʿAbd al-Wahhāb and his movement adopt a stronger, more uncompromisingly anti-Sufi stance? It is possible that they did not see the moderate Sufi reformism of Medina as capable of purifying Islam in the Arabian tribal society of Najd, where only the most corrupt forms of popular Sufi practice were seen to be present. Perhaps, if there had been some tradition of a higher level of Sufism in the region, the movement of the Wahhābīs might have built on it constructively instead of seeking to uproot every vestige of the Sufi outlook. As it was, they provided a striking precedent for those sufficiently disenchanted with Sufi deviations to demand a total rejection of Sufism.

Notes

1 M. G. S. Hodgson, *The Venture of Islam* (Chicago: Chicago University Press, 1974), 3: 134.
2 See A. J. Arberry, *Sufism: An Account of the Mystics of Islam* (London: George Allen and Unwin Ltd., 1950), Chapter 11 'The Decay of Sufism'.
3 Ibid., 121.
4 Arabic *quṭb*, 'the pole, axis', at the apex of the saintly hierarchy, around whom the world appears to revolve.
5 Arberry, *Sufism*, 121.
6 Muḥammad b. ʿAbd al-Wahhāb in *Majmūʿat al-rasāʾil waʾl-masāʾil al-najdiyya*, ed. ʿUthmān b. Bishr (Cairo, 1928), 1: 74–5.
7 For ʿAbd Allāh b. Muḥammad b. ʿAbd al-Wahhāb's criticisms of Sufis see his treatise *al-Kalimāt al-Nāfiʿa fiʾl-mukfirāt al-wāqiʿa* in *Majmūʿat*, vol. 1.
8 Ibid., 1: 288.
9 My translation from a letter of Aḥmad b. Idrīs to Muḥammad al-Mīrghanī in *The Letters of Ahmad Ibn Idrīs*, eds. Einar Thomassen and Bernd Radtke (London: Hurst and Co., 1993), 52. The editors provide Arabic texts and translations.
10 Aḥmad al-Tijānī quoted in Jamil Abun-Nasr, *The Tijaniyya* (London: Oxford University Press, 1965), 42.
11 Ibid.
12 Abū Ṭāhir Muḥammad was the son of Ibrāhīm al-Kūrānī (d. 1690), also a revered Sufi. The orders into which Shāh Walī Allāh was initiated were the Shādhiliyya, Shaṭṭāriyya, Suhrawardiyya and Kubrawiyya.

13 From *Fuyūḍ al-Ḥaramayn*, quoted in J. M. S. Baljon, *Religion and Thought of Shāh Walī Allāh Dihlawī 1703–1762* (Leiden: E. J. Brill, 1986), 17. I am indebted here to this account of his work. Baljon notes the broken pen as 'presumably indicating that in the Muslim world production of inspired religious writings had stopped' (17, n. 8).

14 See further the discussion of Abdul Haq Ansari, 'Shah Waliy Allah's Attempts to Revise *Waḥdat al-Wujūd*,' *Arabica* 35 (1988): 197–213.

15 From *Risāla muqaddima saniyya fi'l-intiṣār li'l-firqa al-Sunniyya*, quoted in Baljon, *Religion and Thought*, 78.

16 From *Tafhīmāt-i Ilāhiyya* in ibid., 85.

17 Ibid.,18, n. 5.

18 The Department of History, University of Bergen, has been active in organizing seminars on Aḥmad b. Idrīs since 1984, drawing on an international network of scholars. The account of Ibn Idrīs's career here is based especially on R. S. O'Fahey, *Enigmatic Saint: Ahmad Ibn Idrīs and the Idrīsī Tradition* (London: Hurst and Co., 1990) and Ali Salih Karrar, *The Sufi Brotherhoods in the Sudan* (London: Hurst and Co., 1992).

19 The Dandarāwī branch of the Rashīdiyya spread subsequently South to Zanzibar and the Tanzanian coast and North to Egypt and Syria.

20 Trans. and quoted in O'Fahey, *Enigmatic Saint*, 205.

21 O'Fahey notes the problems with Ibn Idrīs's biography (1990: x–xi) and acknowledges the pioneering attempts by Ali Salih Karrar of the National Records Office in Khartoum, drawing on previously unexplored materials in the NRO and from descendants of Ibn Idrīs in the Sudan for his M.A. thesis, 'Athar al-taᶜālīm al-Idrīsiyya fi'l-ṭuruq al-ṣūfiyya fi'l-Sūdān,' University of Khartoum, 1977.

22 The source here is from the Rashīdiyya, M. al-Hajrasi's *al-Qaṣr al-mashīd fi'l-tawḥīd wa-fī ṭarīqat sayyidī Ibrāhīm al-Rashīd* (Cairo, 1896–7), trans. and quoted in O'Fahey, *Enigmatic Saint*,198.

23 Fazlur Rahman, *Islam*, 2d ed. (Chicago: University of Chicago Press, 1979), 206.

24 See the arguments of R. S. O'Fahey and Bernd Radtke, 'Neo-Sufism Reconsidered,' *Der Islam* 70 (1993): 52–87.

25 On these scholarly networks see John Voll, 'Muḥammad Ḥayyā al-Sindī and Muḥammad b. ᶜAbd al-Wahhāb: an analysis of an intellectual group in eighteenth-century Madina,' *BSOAS* 38 (1975): 32–9; idem, 'Ḥadīth Scholars and Tariqahs: an ulama group in the eighteenth century haramayn and their impact in the Muslim World,' *JAAS* 15 (1989): 264–73.

26 Trans. and quoted in Rudolph Peters, *Islam and Colonialism* (The Hague: Mouton, 1979), 47–8.

27 Mervyn Hiskett, *The Sword of Truth* (London: Oxford University Press, 1973), 33–41 for an account of this education, based largely on Abdullahi's writings.

28 Quoted in B. Martin, *Muslim Brotherhoods in Nineteenth-Century Africa* (Cambridge: Cambridge University Press, 1977), 20.

29 Louis Brenner, 'Muslim Thought in Eighteenth-Century West Africa: The Case of Shaykh Uthman b. Fudi,' in *Eighteenth Century Renewal and Reform in Islam*, eds. Nehemia Levtzion and John Voll (New York: Syracuse University Press, 1987), 55–6.

30 My translation is from the edited Arabic text of Mervyn Hiskett, '*Kitāb al-Farq*: a work on the Habe kingdoms attributed to ᶜUthmān dan Fodio,' *BSOAS* 23 (1960): 559–65. A full English translation follows, 565–72.

31 *Iḥyā' al-sunna wa-ikhmād al-bidᶜa*, ed. I. A. B. Balogun in a Ph.D. thesis, SOAS, London, 1967.

32 See further Brenner, 'Muslim Thought,' 42–9 and n. 12 for a list of some works in which the issue of *kalām* is treated.

33 Details of Aḥmad al-Tijānī and Tijānī doctrines are drawn from Abun-Nasr, *Tijāniyya*.

34 The criticism was that of the Moroccan historian Muḥammad b. al-Qāsim al-Zayānī (d. 1833).

35 Mervyn Hiskett, *The Course of Islam in Africa* (Edinburgh: Edinburgh University Press, 1994), 39.

36 R. S. O'Fahey and B. Radtke also find al-Tijānī's demands unsurprising in this light. See their comments on the significance of the 'Muḥammadan Way' (*ṭarīqa Muḥammadiyya*) in 'Neo-Sufism,' 64–71.

37 Louis Brenner, 'Concepts of Ṭarīqa in West Africa: The Case of the Qādiriyya' in *Charisma and Brotherhood in African Islam*, eds. Donal B. Cruise O'Brien and Christian Coulon (Oxford: Clarendon Press, 1988), 38–9.

38 Abun-Nasr, *Tijāniyya*, 50.

39 Ali Salih Karrar, *Sufi Brotherhoods*, 69. He compares the Ṣāliḥiyya in Somalia with the Sanūsiyya in its establishment of agricultural settlements. It also combined religion and trade with some success.

40 See comments of Nehemia Levtzion, 'The Eighteenth Century Background to the Islamic Revolutions in West Africa' in *Eighteenth Century Renewal*, eds. Levtzion and Voll, 21–38; Donal Cruise O'Brien, 'Introduction' in *Charisma and Brotherhood*, 9–11.

41 Ibid., 2.

42 On this question of influence and the scholarly Sufis of the Holy Cities see n. 26 for John Voll's studies of their connections.

43 For Ibn Idrīs's denunciation of the neglecter of prayer as an unbeliever see *Letters*, 20–1. He cites ḥadīths to this effect and the opinion of Aḥmad b. Ḥanbal as well as a Mālikī juristic authority.

44 Quoted in Abdul Haq Ansari, 'Ibn Taymiyah's Criticisms of Sufism,' *IMA* (1984): 147.

2

The Challenge of European Anti-Sufism

In the years since the collapse of Communist régimes in the Soviet Union and eastern Europe, it has become a commonplace to perceive a new 'Islamic threat' to the West. But it is all too often forgotten that the last time such fears were expressed was at the height of the European colonial enterprise, when the Sufi orders, especially those of the new and reformed variety, were considered a dangerous ingredient in the Islamic opposition to the Great Powers of Europe. They were to be regarded as a major element in a wider and distinctly sinister conspiracy against the imperialists:

> The campaign against Islam became as fierce as ever, fortified as before with arguments dating back to the Middle Ages, but with modern embellishments. As a result, passing references to the satanic foundation of Islam now occasionally appeared. French Catholics, for example, claimed that a conspiracy was uniting against progress and truth (as represented by the Church). Furthermore, the conspirators in this case, were not only Muslims, but Protestants, Englishmen, Freemasons and Jews, all obedient to Satan. *The Muslim religious orders were considered particularly dangerous and were believed to be inspired by a virulent hatred of civilization.* (Italics mine)[1]

Not only French Catholics, whether officials or missionaries, shared in such a vision of fanatical Sufis conspiring to disrupt their 'civilizing mission'. Similar anxieties were aroused among British, Dutch and Italians, who not infrequently saw the orders as a reactionary bulwark against the advance of their own civilization into the deprived regions of Asia and Africa. Some, carrying their concerns to the point of paranoia, even went so far as to assume that the reason for the foundation of certain newer orders was primarily to function as resistance organizations, and this obsession led them to overlook all the Sufis' clearly avowed spiritual purposes. They might even suggest that their religious leadership had abandoned any desire for careful initiation and guidance in order to gain an immediate mass support of fanatical followers.[2]

It seems ironic that such a fear of organized Sufism should have been conceived in a period of notable Muslim weakness, in which Sufis had very little real opportunity to constitute the supposed 'Islamic Peril', although many might engage in vain attempts to defend the *umma*. From their side and that of all Muslims, the deep fears of a Western, identified with Christian, threat were much more realistic and indeed realized with increasing dismay, as the nineteenth century progressed and more and more lands of Islam fell under non-Muslim domination. It was a process which had, of course, started very much earlier and could be traced back to the latter part of the seventeenth century and the beginnings of Ottoman weakness following their second unsuccessful siege of Vienna in 1683. A critical point might be identified in their failures against the forces of the Austro-Hungarian Empire and its allies, culminating in the treaty of Karlowitz in 1699. On that occasion most of Hungary, Slovenia, Croatia and Transylvania were lost and the long, ultimately useless, struggle for eastern Europe was under way. By 1774 the Ottoman armies succombed to a disastrous defeat by the Russians and were forced to cede the Crimea with a loss of largely Muslim-occupied territory. Further across in Asia, the British merchants of the East India Company extended their control over Bengal in the 1750s and 60s with the aid of local interested parties, both Muslim and Hindu. However, the brief invasion of Egypt by the forces of Napoleon Bonaparte in 1798 is often seen as the moment marking the beginning of the stampede by Europeans to occupy by force the intensely vulnerable lands of Islam. The significance of Bonaparte's expulsion from the Middle East owing to British naval intervention, not Ottoman or local arms, would not be lost on Muslim observers. Throughout the following century and well into the twentieth the assault would continue, largely by the Christian powers of Britain, France, Holland, Spain, Italy and Russia.

> By 1920, when the moribund Ottoman government signed a treaty with the Allies, only the Anatolian hinterland was not under the direct control of a Christian power. Neighbouring Iran, whose neutrality had been violated by British, Russian and Ottoman forces, was in chaos, with Britain now the dominant presence since both the Russian and Ottoman empires had

> collapsed. British influence was likewise paramount, though less directly applied, in Afghanistan and most of Arabia. There was scarcely such a thing left as a Muslim state not dominated by the Christian West.[3]

With loss of independence came the collapse of vital Islamic institutions. Islamic government was destroyed and Islamic law would be deposed from its wide-ranging role in the regulation of an Islamic lifestyle and at best be confined to family matters, such as marriage, divorce and inheritance. Frequently Muslims would witness the destruction of effective Islamic education, a dearth of trained *ᶜulamā'* and severe decline in their status, while Muslim populations would begin to be educated in Western secular systems. The European occupation was thus to extend far beyond the physical takeover of land and launch a devastating attack on all aspects of Muslim identity. In this process Sufism, as a central feature of this identity, was to be challenged more severely than at any point in its history. By contrast with this worldwide European assault, all previous internal Muslim anti-Sufism pales almost into insignificance.

The Lesser *Jihād*

For numbers of Sufis their first encounter with Europeans was a violent one. In areas without other effective armed forces, where larger Islamic state control was weak or non-existent, it was often they who formed the front line of Muslim resistance, engaging in the traditional religiously-approved strategy of jihād against the unbelieving enemy. This physical armed struggle had commonly been termed among Sufis the 'lesser jihād' (*al-jihād al-aṣghar*), the 'greater jihād' (*al-jihād al-akbar*) being the struggle for the interior spiritualization of the individual, a battle waged against the base self rather than exterior armies.[4]

Yet there was much debate during the nineteenth century as to the justification for this 'lesser jihād' and under what circumstances it would become a duty for the believer. When, if at all, was it essential to migrate away from lands under occupation by non-Muslims, emulating the Prophet's example in his *hijra* from the rule of the unbelievers in Mecca? Should a latter day hijra lead on to jihād?

British-occupied India became an important arena for such debates as Indian Sufi reformists in the line of Shāh Walī Allāh had proved active in anti-British jihād, waging especially vigorous campaigns in the early nineteenth century. Sayyid Aḥmad Barēlwī and his Ṭarīqa Muḥammadiyya have already been noted in this context. They might be seen as struggling on three fronts in the 1820s and 1830s against decadent forms of Sufism, against the Sikhs and against the British. Even after their original leaders, Sayyid Aḥmad and a grandson of Shāh Walī Allāh, were killed in battle with the Sikhs in 1831, the order continued to attack the British from its base on the North-West Frontier into the 1880s. The same reforming order fought against Hindus and British in West Bengal until defeated by the British army in 1831, and adherents were also involved in the Indian Mutiny (First War of Independence) in 1857. When armed resistance failed, they were forced to adjust to the realities of non-Muslim occupation. The reforming wing of Sufism formed one aspect of the multi-faceted rethinking around the problem of how to reconstruct a purified Islamic society, able to counter the dangers of contamination by the ways of unbelief. At the same time they found themselves still fighting a rearguard action against the plethora of 'unreformed' Sufis in India and increasingly open to attack by those for whom no reform of Sufism could be radical enough.

Algeria: Divided Struggle, Quietism and Collaboration

Algeria presents a case where Sufis assumed a variety of positions with regard to the demands of jihād against non-Muslim occupation of their lands; these range from complete dedication to the struggle through degrees of quietism to outright collaboration with the French invaders. Inadequate resistance or the failure to resist has left a bitter legacy of resentment against Sufism in general or particular forms of it. Algeria may also seem to merit closer examination as a Muslim country subjected to one of the earliest and longest-enduring colonial occupations by a modern Western power, an experience where Sufis were immediately challenged and continued for a long time to have an active role to play in Algerian-French relations.

The Tijāniyya had faced difficulties from the Ottoman Turks since its beginnings in the 1780s in southern Algeria. Aḥmad al-Tijānī may have been expelled by them to Morocco and he prayed for an end to Turkish government in Algeria. The Tijānīs subsequently maintained determined opposition to Ottoman rule under two sons of al-Tijānī who returned to their homeland after their father's death and provided a focus for anti-Turkish activities. Religiously, they had, of course, their special status, giving them claims to the exclusive allegiance of their followers and they sought to put this to use by calling on them to refuse obedience to the Ottomans, including the withholding of tribute and taxes. Burdensome Turkish taxation and heavy-handed collection methods, along with the natural disasters of bubonic plague and locusts, served to drive the people of southwestern Algeria to placing their hopes for salvation in the Tijānī leadership. Among the Tijānīs' allies, from about 1826, were the tribe of Banū Hāshim, despite the fact of their allegiance to the Qādiriyya. It was to this tribe and order that ᶜAbd al-Qādir belonged, who would be future jihād-leader against the French. In 1827 the allied tribes attacked a Turkish garrison at Mascara (al-Muᶜaskar) on the plain of Gharīs behind the western coastal city of Oran. A part of the Banū Hāshim had succombed to bribes by the Ottomans and their treachery contributed to the defeat of the tribal forces. Aḥmad al-Tijānī's eldest son, Muḥammad al-Kabīr, was taken prisoner and executed by the Turks. The resulting bitterness of the Tijānīs towards both the Ottomans and the Qādirīs of Banū Hāshim had important repercussions on their dealings with the French and their role in future resistance to occupation. Initial Tijānī reaction to the arrival of the French troops and their overthrow of the Ottoman government was to regard such an event as an answer to their founder's prayer. ᶜAbd al-Qādir, although away on pilgrimage and in no way involved in the 1827 catastrophe, was to be treated with suspicion.[5]

On 2 March 1830 Charles X of France informed the Chamber of Deputies of the decision to invade Algeria. The decision came as the climax to a prolonged financial crisis dating back to the Napoleonic period. In the 1790s wheat had been bought from Algeria for the French army with Jewish merchants acting as middlemen. Unfortunately, the merchants were never paid and found themselves in debt to the *dey* of Algiers. Apart from the problems caused by the cycle of unresolved debt, other pressures had been mounting for the French to undertake the invasion of Algeria, whether for the aggrandizement of the French monarchy or in pursuit of more pragmatic commercial interests. French policy in the occupation fluctuated with changes in the government and senior command, following the fall of Charles X and accession of King Louis-Philippe in August 1830. For the next ten years the plan would be for a 'limited occupation' of major towns, changing to a policy of total occupation in the 1840s. The chief executor of this policy was General Bugeaud, who assumed command of operations from February 1841 to June 1847. His cruel efficiency has been noted by historians of North Africa.

> The war, he (Bugeaud) felt, could only be won by creating a climate of terror by the destruction of villages, the burning of fields, and wholesale slaughter. There was an implacable logic in Bugeaud's theory and a cruel determination in his officers to put it into practice. A French officer, Saint-Arnaud, informs us in his chatty letters that according to orders received: 'I shall burn everything, kill everyone' . . . and that is precisely what he and his fellow officers and men did, as official reports testify.[6]

The harshness that characterized Bugeaud's early campaign has been observed as continuing with remarkable effectiveness:

> There are also records of four incidents occurring between 1844 and 1847 in which French officers ordered the burning of defeated groups of Muslims in caves even after they offered to surrender. The morality of war apart, the method proved effective in demoralizing the Algerian Muslims, and continued to be used by the French army until the conquest of Algeria was completed with the subjugation of Kabylia in 1857.[7]

In the midst of this devastating French onslaught, much of the Algerian population looked once again to the traditional Sufi leadership for protection. Not that it was Sufis alone who provided leadership in the resistance; al-Ḥājj Aḥmad Bey, a senior official of the old Turkish régime, rallied the eastern province of Constantine in warfare against the French from 1833–1837 and even later maintained a more limited struggle in the South until 1848. However, Sufis were very actively involved in jihād, at first through the Moroccan-dominated Ṭayyibiyya with support from the Moroccan sultan until pressured by the French to abandon the conflict in 1832. Following this, the Ṭayyibīs retreated into a quietist policy of patiently awaiting the *Mahdī* to achieve victory on their behalf.[8]

It was the Amīr ᶜAbd al-Qādir from a Qādirī holy lineage who became the focal point of Algerian resistance between 1832 and 1847. ᶜAbd al-Qādir occupies a notable place in the annals of reformist Sufism. His grandfather had studied in Egypt with al-Zabīdī, a prominent disciple of Shāh Walī Allāh, who also figures in the scholarly connections of Ibn Idrīs. This influence may well have been disseminated through the family of ᶜAbd al-Qādir. A further line of contact with Sufi reforming thought can be established from the mid-1820s when he set out on pilgrimage with his father and encountered on his travels Shaykh Khālid al-Shahrazūrī (1776–1827).[9] This shaykh was of major importance as a renewer of the Naqshabandiyya in the nineteenth century, such that his name was given to a new branch, the Khālidiyya, which spread widely in the Ottoman Empire and up into the Caucasus and Central Asia. Of critical importance for this new development in Sufi reform was Shaykh Khālid's stay of several months in India in 1809, when he studied in Delhi with a son of Shāh Walī Allāh. ᶜAbd al-Qādir and his father are said to have spent several weeks in the company of Shaykh Khālid and during this time ᶜAbd al-Qādir was initiated by him into the Naqshabandiyya.

While it is not clear how much importance should be attached to this initiation, there is some evidence of a shared outlook between Shaykh Khālid and Amīr ᶜAbd al-Qādir. Both show a very strong concern for strict implementation of the *Sharīᶜa* to the extent that their critics might find them at times harsh and rigid. ᶜAbd al-Qādir was anxious to establish a firm legal basis for all his actions as leader in the jihād against the French. Thus he assiduously sought *fatwās* from jurists to endorse his calls for Algerian Muslims to migrate to areas under his control, performing hijra away from lands under the domination of the infidel enemy. He endeavoured to gain scholarly sanction for his view that those who failed to offer him support were, in effect, unbelievers themselves, who might with a clear conscience be killed, their women and children captured and their property confiscated. Shaykh Khālid, for his part, adopted a position of extreme hostility towards Christians and all who did not conform to his demanding vision of what it meant to be a true Sunni Muslim. ᶜAbd al-Qādir seems very similar in his outlook, although with more obvious justification and his attitude need owe nothing to Shaykh Khālid's example. Yet both men were notable among their contemporaries for a deep inner spirituality that enabled them to survive the cruellest vicissitudes of life, Shaykh Khālid the enmities of rival shaykhs and the loss of his young son through plague, ᶜAbd al-Qādir the years of struggle and later of imprisonment. Both could be seen to suffer from an inability to win the backing of other Sufis. In ᶜAbd al-Qādir's case the Tijānīs remained bitter over their earlier betrayal to the Turks, while the Darqāwīs and Ṭayyibīs were too closely linked to the Moroccan sultan, who proved an unreliable source of support. The Sufi leaders were thus unable and unwilling to form a unified resistance to the occupation. Despite popular regard for his heroism, ᶜAbd al-Qādir ultimately failed and with his failure went the dream of an Islamic state run according to the ideals of nineteenth century Sufi reform. He surrendered in 1847 and was subsequently imprisoned in France until October 1852, when he was granted safe passage and a pension to end his days in Damascus, where he was accompanied by a number of still devoted followers.

On the religious level, the failure of the Sufi leadership in the initial resistance to the French could be perceived as having serious implications. Widespread belief in their spiritual power to protect their people and to work miracles with God's permission was deeply shaken. Their powers assumed to exist through their special relationship to God had been tested and found wanting and questions would then be asked as to the validity of their respective *ṭarīqas.* Perhaps they were not indeed all they had set themselves up to be and were not actually the recipients of true guidance in Islam, equipped to serve as the best guides of their community. Although Sufis of the Raḥmāniyya[10] were to play an active role in the major popular uprising of 1870–71, from the later nineteenth century the orders were increasingly to be regarded as the decadent tools of French colonialism. The Tijānīs, in particular, came under attack from nationalists, who considered them heavily infiltrated by the authorities and effectively allies of the French. Thus Sufi credibility, both spiritual and temporal, entered the twentieth century in Algeria severely damaged.

Mahdism and Sufi Resistance

As the nineteenth century wore on, many became convinced that non-Muslim acquisition of so many Islamic territories heralded the coming of the end time. A spread in unbelief of this nature was recognized as one of the signs of the last days to be accompanied by natural disasters such as drought and famine. With the approach of the Islamic year 1300/1882–3 it was presumed that the *Mahdī's* arrival was imminent, and the Sudanese *Mahdī,* Muḥammad Aḥmad, provides the most prominent example of a wider phenomenon. Various Sufi leaders were acknowledged in this role: notably Sayyid Aḥmad Barēlwī (d. 1831) in India, whose followers believed he had gone into concealment and would return as the Mahdī to lead them to victory; and Sayyid al-Mahdī (d. 1902), son of the founder of the Sanūsiyya in Libya, who came of age in the critical Islamic year 1300.

While both Sayyid Aḥmad Barēlwī and Muḥammad Aḥmad of the Sudan were actively involved in armed struggle against the British, Sayyid al-Mahdī adopted a position of guarded neutrality in his relations with Britain, France and Russia and carefully refused to be brought into any confrontation on behalf of the Ottomans in opposition to any of these powers.

Just as acceptance of a mahdī's appearance did not necessarily cause Sufi leaders to adopt an activist militant approach to dealing with the invading unbelievers, so also the response of the rank and file was not always to take up arms. In some cases the expectation of the Mahdī led them to passive acquiescence in the face of European dominance. It was the Mahdī who would set all to rights without the need for their engagement in the task. No action was expected on their part to usher in the new Golden Age on the pattern of the earliest Islamic community. Frequently, however, the announcement of a mahdī would elicit active Sufi support for his struggle to establish the age of righteousness. Frequently, even with no such announcement, disciples of the Sufi orders would hasten to obey a summons to hijra and jihād to retain or regain the territories of Islam.

Muḥammad Aḥmad, the Sudanese Mahdī (1844–85)

On 29 June 1881 at Abā Island in the White Nile, Muḥammad Aḥmad b. ᶜAbd Allāh, a Sufi shaykh of the Sammāniyya, revealed himself to be the long-awaited Mahdī. Like Muḥammad b. ᶜAbd al-Wahhāb, he perceived his age as one of evil and injustice, but that the time had come for this to end with a return to the model of the original Islamic state of the Prophet. However, whereas Ibn ᶜAbd al-Wahhāb's task could have been performed by any dedicated Muslim religious scholar, the task of Muḥammad Aḥmad could not. As Mahdī he was convinced of his uniqueness; but not as the Mahdī of the Shīᶜī tradition, an infallible immortal who would institute new and perfect prescriptions to supersede all previous revealed law, whose community would transcend that of the Prophet Muḥammad. Rather, as Mahdī within the Sunni tradition, he believed himself to be the supreme renewer of the faith, appointed and guided by God to restore the Sunna of the Islamic community, to lead the erring back to the true path. In order to do this he would need to sweep away the accretions of centuries, the whole edifice of jurisprudence (*fiqh*) erected by the four Sunni law schools and the many Sufi ṭarīqas. He alone was in a position to recreate the ideal time of the earliest umma because of his direct visionary contact with the Prophet, who, he claimed, had appeared to him and informed him of his new status as the Mahdī.

Being assured of such high authority for his special role, and with much popular support, Muḥammad Aḥmad began his struggle to rid the Sudan of its Egyptian administrators whom he held to be unbelievers on account of their corrupt and sinful ways, their unjust rule and alteration of the Sharīʿa. The occupation, begun in 1820, had been much extended by the forces of Khedive Ismāʿīl (1863–79), ostensibly with the aim of suppressing the slave trade. Yet another province was thus added to the Ottoman Empire, with the Egyptian government ruling the Sudan in the name of the sultan. Not only 'Turks', but all supposed Muslims, including Sudanese, who failed to recognize Muḥammad Aḥmad as Mahdī and come to his support were dubbed as unbelievers. Hence the Mahdī's response to a letter accusing him of killing fellow-Muslims:

> Your contention that we have unjustly and wrongly killed a group of Muslims that had settled in this region, is untenable since we have only killed the inhabitants of the [Djabal] al-Djarādah after they had called us a liar and attacked us. The Prophet and all possessors of gnosis (*ahl al-kashf*) have informed me that those who question my Mahdī-ship and deny and contradict it, are unbelievers who can lawfully be killed and whose property is booty.[11]

The unbelief of the Mahdī's enemies was compounded by their readiness to associate themselves with the Christian British, especially in the form of Charles George Gordon, the British general who had first been appointed by the khedive to high administrative office in the Sudan in 1873, assuming the governor-generalship from 1877–80. Following the British occupation of Egypt in 1882, Gordon was sent back to the Sudan in 1884 to arrange for the withdrawal of the Egyptian army and administration, the British government having no wish to become embroiled further in the disturbed state of affairs there. To the Mahdī, Gordon was another unbeliever whom it was his duty to call to Islam and with whom no friendship or compromise was possible. He, therefore, returned Gordon's gifts and rejected his offer of the sultanate of Kordofan, saying that as the expected Mahdī and successor to the Prophet, he had no need of 'the kingdom of Kordofan or elsewhere, nor of the wealth of this world and its vanity.'[12] The scene was set for the final struggle to establish the Mahdī's authority and it was only a matter of time before Khartoum was besieged and fell to the forces of the Mahdiyya on 25 January 1885, Gordon being beheaded during the capture. A few months later the Mahdī was dead, leaving his designated successor, the Khalīfa ᶜAbdallāhī, to run the Mahdist Islamic state until his death in battle with the British in 1899.

Many of the Mahdist reform concerns appear to be shared with the Wahhābīs and indeed with many other traditional reformers in Islam. Prominent and basic is the emphasis on *tawḥīd*, contained at the beginning of the Mahdist oath of allegiance, and the determination to root out all false innovations that might compromise this principle and reduce the sense of God's transcendence. Hence there is the need to avoid excessive reverence for any human, including the Mahdī himself and Muḥammad Aḥmad insists that his position is not due to any personal worth, but to God's choice of him to fulfil His purposes. In common with the Wahhābīs also is the firm rejection of any compromise with moral lapses. A strict position is maintained with regard to immodest behaviour of women in public and prostitution, homosexuality, drinking of alcohol and smoking, music and dance. The views of Muḥammad Aḥmad and Ibn ᶜAbd al-Wahhāb clearly coincide regarding the necessity of jihād against all those 'unbelievers' who do not support their cause.

Both Wahhābīs and Mahdists have an uneasy relationship to Sufi shaykhs, but the character of the relationship is very different in the two cases. The Mahdī saw himself as superseding the Sufi orders that had first drawn him into the reformist path to become a shaykh of the Sammāniyya, the earliest of the reforming orders to enter the Sudan c.1764.[13] While the Sammāniyya seems to have suffered from internal disputes and fragmentation with some Sammānīs being absorbed into the old, unreformed ways, Muḥammad Aḥmad was not willing to do the same. He had been impressed by Ibn Idrīs's teachings, which had already permeated the Sudan with so much success. He could have founded yet another new Sufi ṭarīqa, had he not been convinced of his special mission. Early in 1884 he announced the ban on all the ṭarīqas and declared that their adherents should abandon them and join his Way. His mahdīship did not deny the truths of Sufism, but made its previous organizational form obsolete. The new orders with their centralized administration and efficient cross-tribal networks had laid the basis for a brief-lived 'super-ṭarīqa'.

It is hardly surprising that such an accomplishment should be of short duration, when its viability depended so closely on the individual and unique personality of the Mahdī. After the demise of the Mahdist state, the ṭarīqas reasserted their position and the successors of the original Mahdiyya found their movement coming to terms with an existence alongside the orders and with no sharp differentiation from them.

The North Caucasus: Resistance and Revitalized Sufism

On the northern borders of Islam in the Caucasus, Naqshabandī and Qādirī shaykhs were prominently engaged in leading jihād against Russian advances. Here, in a long period of resistance with very little room for compromise, Sufis apparently gained not only in long term prestige, but especially in consolidating reformed varieties of Sufism in an area only fully Islamized with the conversion of the Ingush quite late in the nineteenth century. The 1990s campaign for the independence of Chechnya from Russia has been merely the latest phase in what has been described as an 'epic struggle, in comparison to which even Abdel Qadir's resistance to the French conquest of Algeria pales'.[14] Epic indeed it was, having extended with some interruptions from 1783 when the Russians launched a major offensive on the North Caucasus until the present.

The early period of jihād is associated with the Naqshabandiyya, although some confusion remains about the legendary inspirer of the late eighteenth century resistance, Shaykh Manṣūr Ushurma. Caucasian oral tradition and Russian historiography have combined to mystify rather than enlighten. He has been variously described: as a Naqshabandī initiated in the Central Asian city of Bukhara or by a Bukharan shaykh travelling in the Caucasus; as a Central Asian himself, a Tatar of the Orenburg steppes; as an agent of the Ottoman Empire sent to rouse the Chechens and Daghestanis against the Russians; even as an Italian Jesuit. More recent studies are satisfied that he was a Chechen from a family background in the North Caucasian village of Aldy.[15] Whether or not he was a Naqshabandī is still uncertain, but his preaching has been described as very similar to that of later Naqshabandī leaders. In common with many other Sufis, a dream of the Prophet appears to have had a decisive effect in convincing him to undertake his jihād against the Russian offensive on his homeland. His certainty that he was carrying out direct orders of Prophet Muḥammad seems to play an important part in his mission to unite the tribes of the region in their resistance. In 1785 he achieved a major victory over the Russians on the Sunzha river, eliminating a full brigade and cementing his control over a wide area of the North Caucasus until his capture in 1791 and subsequent death in prison.

Shaykh Manṣūr was remembered in song and legend as setting the pattern for future jihād, but he is not regarded as having established the Naqshabandiyya in the region. After his death there is no record of its existence for another twenty or thirty years and it is not known whether he was ever an initiating shaykh or whether his disciples were simply obliterated in the Russian repression.

The Naqshabandiyya was more firmly introduced into the Caucasus in the 1810s–20s by a deputy (*khalīfa*) of Shaykh Khālid al-Shahrazūrī, also the initiating shaykh of the Algerian Amīr ᶜAbd al-Qādir.[16] It is thus the reformed Naqshabandiyya-Khālidiyya with its strong Sharīᶜa-consciousness and antipathy towards 'the enemies of religion, the cursed Christians' from Shaykh Khālid's viewpoint.[17] Perhaps because of these features, Russian, and later Soviet, sources frequently failed to identify the order as Sufi and regarded it as a totally distinct movement of an anti-Sufi nature. They termed it *Miurdizm* (Murīdism).[18]

The effects of the Russian occupation in Daghestan and Chechnya created a climate favourable to the reception of the reformers' message. Both areas had suffered considerable social and economic disruption from the Russian presence. Particularly devastating for the economy was the Russians' ban on the slave trade and raiding in furtherance of it. The capture of Christian Armenians and Georgians for sale as slaves in the Middle East had previously been a major source of support in the region and the Russians were perceived to be violating their Islamic legal rights to enslave non-Muslim captives, although Muslims were forbidden to be taken as slaves. In addition, the Russians made heavy tax demands on the Daghestani and Chechen population as well as forcing them to supply food, horses and other requisites to sustain the occupation. They were further forced into the construction of roads by a *corvée*. In Chechnya farmers were violently dispossessed and Cossacks were settled on much of their fertile land.

On the social level, Muslims witnessed what was for them an intolerable violation of the Sharīᶜa through the Russian importation of alcohol and gambling and through the abuse of Muslim women. General Ermolov, governor of Georgia and the Caucasus from 1816 to 1827, would long be remembered for his extreme brutality, the slaughter of women and children, elsewhere the selling of Chechen women into slavery or the bestowing of them on his officers. Such actions would call in question the declared humane objectives of the Russian abolition of Caucasian participation in the slave trade. When rebuked for his cruelty by the Tsar, Ermolov declared, 'Gentleness, in the eyes of Asiatics, is a sign of weakness, and out of pure humanity, I am inexorably severe. One execution saves hundreds of Russians from destruction and thousands of Muslims from treason.'[19] But it was not one execution and did not apparently have the desired effects of saving either side in the confrontation.

Local rulers were seen as flouting the Sharīᶜa by their dissolute lifestyle and association with the hated Russian occupiers. A typical picture is of indulgence in drinking bouts and brutally ill-treating their own people with a total disregard for the maintenance of justice. Perhaps, in view of the double sufferings of the people from the Russians and from their own overlords, it is not surprising to find an enthusiastic reception for the Naqshabandī-Khālidī concern with support for the Sharīᶜa and hostility to the Christian Russians. When Ghāzī Muḥammad came to prominence among the leaders of the order and was declared the first *imām* of Daghestan in 1829, his objectives were first to implement the Sharīᶜa before launching jihād. His disciples were seen to 'go around the villages in order to return sinners to the right path, to straighten up the crooked and to crush the criminal leadership of the villages.'[20] By 1830 the *imām's* authority had been greatly extended, not only among Daghestanis, but also among the Chechens, Ingush and other peoples of the region. With such strong popular support, a short period of jihād was launched with some success, but faltered when Ghāzī Muḥammad, with about fifty of his close followers, was killed by the Russians on 29 October 1831.

The imāmate of his successor, Ḥamza Bek, was short-lived, as he was assassinated due to internal quarrels, but was followed by the renowned third imām, Shamīl. It is the time of Shamīl's imāmate, 1834–59, that marks the high point of sustained successful resistance and an attempt to operate an independent Islamic state based on Naqshabandī principles.

Imām Shamīl, like his predecessors, was openly determined to promote the Sharīᶜa and himself performed the role of chief judge within his state. Where judicial authority was delegated, religious jurists were compelled to adopt Shamīl's interpretations of Islamic law. While the imām was observed to be respectful towards the *ᶜulamā'* and to involve them in consultations, he was also significantly guided by mystical experience. In personal life he was extremely devout, often going into retreat (*khalwa*) before undertaking any critical action. During this time he would fast, pray and conduct the silent Naqshabandī *dhikr*. After some days he would sometimes fall down unconscious and, on recovering, announce before the people that the Prophet had appeared and commanded him to take certain action. This could lead to the adoption of measures which might actually seem contrary to the exoteric understanding of the Sharīᶜa. However, they were justified by this resort to higher authority. When the Prophet commanded in person, what need was there to refer to the collections of Ḥadīth and their interpretation by past generations of jurists?

In some matters Shamīl introduced harsher regulations than would have been demanded by the traditional law. For example, in cases of drunkenness, offenders were flogged in excess of the forty stripes decreed in Sharīᶜa and habitual offenders were sentenced to death. Tobacco was strictly banned in Shamīl's state. Smokers were publicly humiliated by being seated on donkeys, facing the tail and with pipes through their noses. The severe position taken on this issue bears close comparison with that of the Arabian Wahhābīs and Sudanese Mahdists, as does Shamīl's equally firm ban on dancing and music except on the occasion of weddings and circumcisions. This contrasts with the more widespread Sufi advocacy of both music and dance for spiritual purposes. Shamīl's severity reportedly alienated some Chechens and Daghestanis, who were, furthermore, exhausted by the long years of jihād against the Russians. However, the Russians themselves remarked a great improvement in morality among the population under Shamīl's control in the 1840s. The majority of his followers remained devoted, appreciative of his piety and justice and his unrelenting struggle also against their own local rulers who were seen to have no legitimate right to rule because of their neglect of Sharīᶜa.

The imām was finally forced to surrender to Prince Baryatinsky on 25 August 1859 and left for a prolonged exile in Russia. Only in 1870 was he at last permitted to depart for the Holy Cities and died in Medina on 4 February 1871.

For many years after the collapse of Shamīl's state the Naqshabandiyya was harshly suppressed and its effective functioning in the North Caucasus severely limited. But this did not signify a decline in Sufi activity. On the contrary, a new pattern of Sufi renewal was in progress, that represented by the Qādiriyya.[21] A branch of the order was first established by Kunta Haji Kishiev, a Daghestani shepherd living among the Chechens. In the 1850s, supposedly following his initiation in Baghdad on a visit to the tomb of the founding saint, ᶜAbd al-Qādir al-Jīlānī, Kunta Haji returned home and was met with hostility by the jihādist Naqshabandīs. His message was one of traditional Sufi quietism and renunciation of the evils of the world by ascetic withdrawal. Only after performing *ḥajj* and returning in 1861, did he find a more receptive atmosphere for his teachings among people weary of constant warfare. The new order then spread rapidly, particularly in those areas which had suffered harshly from the Russian presence. The loud dhikr, ecstatic dancing, singing and music were very different from Shamīl's austere prescriptions and brought enthusiastic participation. Many former Naqshabandīs joined the Qādiriyya, but its introduction also led to the conversion of Ingushetia to Islam by the 1870s.

However, it would not be long before Kunta Haji's quietism was abandoned under the pressure of general discontent with Russian repressive measures. In a climate of growing tension in the early 1860s, the Russians feared renewed jihād and took what they hoped would be preventative action by arresting Kunta Haji and his closest disciples in January 1864. By May 1867 he was dead in prison. Despite further Russian efforts to limit the influence of the Qādiriyya by banning their loud dhikr and encouraging emigration of Qādirīs to Turkey, the order continued to expand. In 1877–78 it actually joined forces with the Naqshabandiyya in yet another jihād, once again crushed with great severity. The cycle of jihād followed by harsh repression and further jihād only contributed to the strength and prestige of the Sufis. By the time of the Russian Revolution of 1917 almost the entire adult population of Chechnya-Ingushetia were members of the Naqshabandiyya or Qādiriyya. The situation in Daghestan was somewhat more mixed, but still with very substantial numbers of Sufis.

Implications of the Lesser Jihād

A very varying picture emerges of Sufi involvement in the lesser jihād against the European onslaught. In the majority of cases, it coincided with the height of the European imperialist enterprise in the nineteenth and early twentieth centuries, ending repeatedly in failure.

In some cases the whole undertaking was deeply damaging to those Sufi orders involved, when Sufi leadership was discredited and questions were asked within their communities, not simply about their military incapacities but about the validity of their spiritual perceptions and powers. If they lost, it was often judged to be because they were not true to the faith, and this view was reinforced in situations where they were seen to collaborate with the European occupiers following the jihād or even during it. Where collaboration was evident, they would be especially vulnerable to the challenges of rising secular nationalists or anti-Sufi religious leaders. However, the effects of collaboration were not always negative, but could help to produce a favourable environment for the spread of Sufism under the protection of a colonial régime or even for primary conversion to Islam in a Sufi form. Occasionally, the jihād itself could lead to such expansion and even its failure be judged merely as a passing ordeal for God's elect, whose spiritual and temporal status would only be enhanced by the experience.

The Greater Jihād and Wordly Constraints

Despite the obvious widespread dedication of Sufis to the lesser jihād against the Europeans, many more did not participate. As noted earlier, there were those who adopted a quietist approach in the face of European dominance, believing that the coming of the Mahdī would set all to rights or that personal engagement in this form of jihād was not a vital religious duty by comparison with the greater jihād, in effect that: 'The true Flight or Hijrah is the flight from evil, and the real Holy War or Jihād is the warfare against one's passions.'[22] For those orders with a long eirenic tradition this would hardly be a surprising stance, although it could be radically altered in the face of a sufficiently serious challenge. This is evidenced by the experience of the Caucasian Qādirīs.

Many, of course, were never so directly challenged and the whole issue of whether or not to join in militant jihād remained irrelevant. Others did not present the obvious bodies to resist a challenge from Europe. This applies clearly to those with very little in the way of organization and no experience of an armed jihād tradition. It also applies to those living within Islamic states with regular armies, although particular Sufi orders might have adherents among the armed forces. Within the Ottoman Empire the Bektāshiyya is remarkable in this respect for its close connection with the élite corps of the Janissaries.[23] By the early nineteenth century this officially Sunni, but actually very heterodox order, incorporating extremist Shīʿī, Christian and Turkic elements, presented a force intensely opposed to Ottoman efforts at introducing Western-style military reforms. In 1826 Sultan Maḥmūd II determined to move against the Janissaries and the ṭarīqa to which they were attached. A massacre of Janissaries was followed by a general assault on the Turkish Bektāshīs, many of their lodges being destroyed and properties confiscated. Officially, it was declared, despite centuries of previous state support, that they had now gone beyond the bounds of acceptable belief and were guilty of heresy as well as immoral behaviour through their consumption of alcohol and mingling of men and women in their gatherings. Their potential as a jihādist force was eliminated and they, along with Sufi orders in general, were brought increasingly under the watchful eye of the state.

With the operation of these restraints, it is perhaps no surprise that the Ottoman Naqshabandiyya, even in its Khālidī reformed version, contained many bureaucrats who bore little resemblance to their brothers active in the Caucasian resistance. They even included those in favour of the Westernizing measures opposed by the Bektāshīs and who, in their turn, were suspected by Sultan Maḥmūd, despite his espousal of the noted reforms. Although they were members in the same branch of the ṭarīqa, they were very different from Imām Shamīl with his rigid rejection of all Western influences. Nor were they all stridently opposed to music and dance, as some also belonged to the Mevleviyya (famous in Europe as the Whirling Dervishes). In fact, many appear to have followed a more tolerant strain of Naqshabandism and not the strict reformism of Shaykh Khālid.[24] Similarly relaxed attitudes seem to have been characteristic of Naqshabandīs in eastern Europe. In Bosnia they were noted for the quietism characteristic of most Bosnian Sufism, being remembered for their peaceful promotion of spiritual welfare through their lodges in and around Sarajevo.[25]

Thus the pattern of non-participation in lesser jihād can be seen to be highly varied and to cut across ṭarīqas, involving reformists as well as arch-traditionalists, those with a close association with the state and those with no political connections, the highly orthodox and the extremely heterodox. Whatever their degree of resistance activity, the reality by the late nineteenth to early twentieth centuries was that most Sufis found themselves living in states ruled by Europeans or deeply influenced by contacts with them. It is proposed here to examine some of the ways in which Muslims in British India adjusted to the experience and sought to retain a place for Sufism as a relevant *modus vivendi* or to discard it in the new conditions.

Surviving the British Raj

In India European rule came early and lasted longer than in many regions of the Islamic world. After the suppression of the Mutiny in 1857, the lesser jihād was no longer a realistic option for the great majority of Indian Muslims. Delhi itself suffered severely in the wake of the Mutiny. For some time the British expelled the entire population, occupying mosques and destroying institutions of Islamic learning in the city. ᶜUlamā' were dispersed into the smaller towns of the surrounding countryside. Amidst the general climate of despair and with no hope of regaining an Islamic state by force, many turned inward to the spiritual life, pursuing strategies to aid the survival of a true, morally upright Islamic society. The greater jihād had a major role in this, as did its extension to wider sections of the community.

Retreat into a privatized Islam, seeking a conscious separation from the state, already had a long pedigree in Sufi practice. It was a familiar theme in the teachings of the major Indian ṭarīqa of the Chishtiyya,[26] which can be seen as having an important influence on the nineteenth century Sufi reformists. Even the Suhrawardīs, noted for their readiness to consort with rulers, had retained a certain ambivalence towards such associations with worldly power, following the sentiments of their reputed founder, Abū'l-Najīb al-Suhrawardī:

> One must obey him (the ruler) except in disobedience to God or violation of traditional law. One should pray for the ruler and avoid slandering him. It is meritorious to visit a just ruler; but one should stay away from an unjust ruler except in case of necessity or in order to reprove him. He who has to visit them should pray for them and exhort them and reprove them according to his capacity. Some eminent Sufis used to approach the rulers for the welfare of their people.[27]

Given such a cautionary view of Muslim rulers, how much more problematic did the relationship between Sufis and rulers become when the ruler was not a Muslim, not even an unjust Muslim, who might reasonably be reproved with some hope that he might repent and be guided. It was not impossible to 'pray for the ruler', and some did later pray for Queen Victoria in her last illness, but, without hope of exerting influence, there seemed little alternative but withdrawal into a society apart from their rulers.

The Deobandī Sufi Reformers

At Deoband, a small town about ninety miles to the North of the abandoned city of Delhi, a group of religious scholars came together in an effort to continue the Sufi reform tradition in India.[28] They saw themselves consciously as the successors of Shāh Walī Allāh. They appear to have taken very seriously his attempts to achieve a new superior school of Sufi teaching, extracting the very best from the major ṭarīqas present in the subcontinent: the Chishtīs, Suhrawardīs, Qādirīs and Naqshabandīs.

In 1868 the Deobandī shaykhs founded their own famous school, destined to become one of the most important centres of traditional Islamic training in the world. Large numbers of Deobandī schools were subsequently affiliated to it. Education was given a central place in their programme in order to create a body of scholars trained to disseminate their reform thought and hopefully build a purified community able to withstand the occupation of unbelievers with all its perceived pernicious influences. There was a heavy concentration on the study of Qur'ān and on Ḥadīth in particular, with a study of a much wider range of Sunni collections than were normally taught in India at this period. Jurisprudence (*fiqh*) was also taught at the school, the Deobandīs being much respected and consulted for their Ḥanafī interpretation of Sharīᶜa. Here they did not follow in Shāh Walī Allāh's footsteps, but sought to adhere closely to the rulings of previous jurists and not to surmount and unify the law schools as they did the ṭarīqas. However, they might be seen to follow Walī Allāh in the legal field through the number of fatwās that they issued outlining acceptable and unacceptable practices in Sufism. They condemned as *bidᶜa* most of the popular customs associated with saint cults. In addition, the school taught logic and philosophy, but was less noted for these fields. Arabic and Persian were given some importance, but Urdu was promoted as the main teaching language and this has been considered a significant step in popularizing its use as an academic language in North India.

It is very noticeable that all Western studies were carefully avoided at the school and English was not among the languages taught. Yet even in this bastion of Islamic tradition there were innovations under British influence in the organization and teaching methods, apparently modelled on Christian mission schools and on Delhi College before the Mutiny.

Nevertheless, the deep-seated attitudes and aims of the project were less easily won over to a British system, although they also might be held to contain some degree of innovation. Essentially the purpose of the Deobandī scholars was not simply to impart book learning (*ᶜilm*), but to guide their students towards insight through mystical gnosis (*maᶜrifa*), knowledge on a different plane. Some level of innovation may be discerned in this extraordinary nature of the teacher-student, *shaykh-murīd* relationship observable in the Deoband school. In this way the deepest personal bonds of allegiance developed directly between a student and an individual teacher rather than through an initiation into a single ṭarīqa. A single master might teach a combination of approaches derived from more than one ṭarīqa or he might train one student in a loud Qādirī recitation of dhikr, another in a silent Naqshabandī dhikr. This pattern seems to owe a great deal to Shāh Walī Allāh, but the way in which it was institutionalized stands out as a particular achievement of Deoband.

The Deobandīs might also be regarded as innovatory in the ways in which they sought to promote their Sufi reformist teachings in the wider community. They were quick to appreciate the advantages of the printed word for spreading their training beyond the immediate circles of the master and students. The printing of fatwās on Sufi questions was one successful method already noted. Others were the translation of religious texts from Arabic and Persian into Urdu and the writing of works intended for a more popular readership. One of the most influential in this category was the *Bihishti Zewar* (Heavenly Ornaments), written early in the twentieth century by Ashraf ᶜAlī Thānawī (1864–1943), 'widely considered the prominent Sufi of modern India'.[29] It is remarkable as a book of guidance directed specifically to Muslim women and, in its Sufi aspects, seeking to develop their spirituality to the same level as that aspired to within the community of Deobandī male shaykhs and their disciples. It is revealing of Thānawī's attitude that, when asked to write a guidebook for men, he declared this to be unnecessary, as they could equally well benefit from the same guidance, and he merely added an appendix.

Bihishti Zewar was intended to reach women of all ages and levels of educational background, including the illiterate, to whom the book could be read aloud within the household. Its lessons were to be repeated and discussed with the aim of effecting a complete reform of the heart. The seventh section of the book is devoted strictly to Sufi concerns. The goal is nothing less than to wean women away from reliance for their salvation on the intercession of holy men and participation in all the customary practices of folk Sufism. Instead they were to take responsibility for working towards such ultimate salvation by constant struggle in the greater jihād. They are reminded:

> There are two causes that disrupt one's ability to distinguish good from evil and to secure the reward described above. The first cause is your own lower soul, which at every moment is sitting right in your own lap. The lower soul suggests all sorts of things; it invents pretexts to oppose doing good; it rationalizes the necessity of doing evil. If you frighten it with the fear of torment, it reminds you that God is the Forgiver, the Merciful. On top of this, Satan lends it his support. The second cause of disruption involves those people with whom you have some relationship, whether relatives, acquaintances or neighbours.[30]

The women, therefore, are counselled to restrict their social circle to a few trusted, pious people, to remain at home engaged in their religious duties and pursuit of the Path and to seek to guide others along the same lines.

> It is clear that it is not good for women to go to mosques. You should weigh the fact that although nothing is the equal of prayer, it is not considered good to go out even for that. Surely, then, to go out of the house for foolish gatherings or for carrying out customary practices must be very bad indeed.[31]

Should they be in any doubt about the desirability of this life of pious and modest seclusion, they are constantly reminded of the horrors of Hell awaiting those who do not repent and dedicate their lives to the greater jihād.

Very often the Deobandī reformers were labelled 'Wahhābīs' on account of this extremely austere approach and their harsh condemnation of much popular Sufi practice in India. Such a label obviously did not apply to them with any accuracy, but the defenders of traditional Sufism believed that it did. The label has often stuck and given rise to erroneous perceptions of the Deobandīs as a totally anti-Sufi movement.

The Barēlwī Defenders of Traditional Sufism

The most vociferous defence of the Sufi *status quo* came from the tendency known as Barēlwī after its founder, Aḥmad Rizā Khān Barēlwī (1856–1921).[32] However, 'Barēlwī' was not the term that they used for self-identification. They regarded themselves as being true Sunnis in opposition to all deviations by Deobandīs and other reform-minded Muslims, whom they saw as constituting as much of a threat to Islam in India as the British unbelieving rulers. Consequently, they became the ardent champions of all the manifestations in their day of Muslim customs built up over the centuries: elaborate ceremonies for the Prophet's birthday (*mawlūd*); celebration of the death days (*ᶜurs*) of Sufi saints,[33] especially that of the saintly founder of the Qādiriyya, ᶜAbd al-Qādir al-Jīlānī; pilgrimage to saints' tombs to seek their intercession for sin or their aid to cure disease or infertility or relieve debt; the widespread use of amulets (*taᶜwīz*) and of divination by examining animal entrails. Among the beliefs strenuously defended by the Barēlwīs were those connected with the exaltation of the Prophet: the Sufi doctrine of the Light of Muḥammad, held to be derived from the Divine Light at the beginning of creation, such that the Prophet was considered to be light without a shadow, human but not exactly as other human beings; the claim that the Prophet had full mystical knowledge of the unseen world (*ᶜilm al-ghayb*); and the conviction that he had full powers to intercede with God for those who called on him.

Aḥmad Rizā Khān and his followers spent much time and effort in countering criticisms of all the above, issuing numerous fatwās in which, like their Deobandī opponents, they drew on traditional Ḥanafī jurisprudence to reach very different conclusions. They also shared with the Deobandīs a deep concern to build a Muslim community in India, spiritually strengthened and able to resist the experience of British rule. However, their methods were different and more in line with the medieval Sufi tradition. Their appeal was very strong among the rural and uneducated, but was not without an ability to attract an educated Sufi élite. The founder himself was noted for his exceptional scholarship as well as his spiritual advancement.

Anti-Sufi Reformists: Ahl-i Ḥadīth

Both Deobandīs and Barēlwīs encountered opposition from those who refused to tolerate even the most restrained and reformist tendencies in Sufism. In this period the most forcible expression of anti-Sufism came from the movement known as Ahl-i Ḥadīth ('People of the Tradition'), although their influence was never so widespread as that of the other two groups. They were also commonly styled 'Wahhābīs' and with somewhat more reason, although it was not an accurate description of their doctrinal position.

Originally Ahl-i Ḥadīth consisted of families of high status who had suffered a visible decline as a result of British rule and were extremely discontented in the aftermath of the Indian Mutiny. Although they also claimed to follow Shāh Walī Allāh, they only appeared to do so in their insistence on looking afresh at Qur'ān and Ḥadīth and in the great stress they placed on personal understanding of the Ḥadīth. Every member was expected to make decisions on the basis of a close examination of these fundamental texts. The judgments of the legal schools and all mystical insights were rejected. It was a system which placed heavy demands on the individual to interpret and undertake right action, effectively undercutting the authority of the religious scholar and Sufi shaykh in their roles as mentors for the Muslim community. Understandably, the traditional religious leaders vigorously opposed such a potentially dangerous trend and Ahl-i Ḥadīth for their part were highly confrontational in their approach. The result was frequent violent disputes and the development of an exclusivist body, setting itself apart from other Muslims in separate mosques with distinctively different prayer practices.

The preaching of Ahl-i Ḥadīth was never likely to undermine the hold of the Sufi shaykhs over the mass of the population. Its appeal was limited to those with sufficient traditional religious education to study Qur'ān and Ḥadīth for themselves and with the confidence to make judgments that this was the right way to proceed without need to resort to the specialist guidance of a holy man. Nor was the embattled and élitist nature of the movement capable of attracting the same breadth of following as the larger Sufi tendencies. When a breakaway section formed Ahl-i Qur'ān, asserting only the Qur'ān as a source of guidance, the new group was marked by an even more exclusivist stance with less popular appeal than Ahl-i Ḥadīth.

In India the responses of Sufi leaders and their opponents to the actualities of non-Muslim rule are among the most consciously and systematically thought-out anywhere in the umma. No doubt, this is partly due to the very length of the experience, but it is also presumably owing to the rich heritage of Sufi thought in the subcontinent and a strong tradition of intellectual reformism. In other regions some similar rethinking would be undertaken, although often not displaying the same level of development and variety as in India. In some cases, new local orders or new reformed sections of older orders would arise in response to the challenges of European colonial rule. However, organized anti-Sufism was frequently a later development than in India and gained ground only with more extensive exposure to modern Western as well as traditional anti-Sufi thought.

Notes

1 Maxime Rodinson, *Europe and the Mystique of Islam* (London: I. B. Tauris, 1988), 66.

2 One of the prime examples of this attitude to the orders is to be found in O. Depont and X. Coppolani, *Les Confréries religieuses musulmanes* (Algiers, 1897). R. S. O'Fahey and Bernd Radtke provide a helpful discussion of this *littérature de surveillance* in 'Neo-Sufism Reconsidered,' *Der Islam* 70 (1993): 61–4.

3 Edward Mortimer, *Faith and Power: the Politics of Islam* (New York: Vintage Books, 1982), 86.

4 For discussion of the Sufi significance of 'greater jihād' see John Renard, '*Al-Jihād al-Akbar:* Notes on a Theme in Islamic Spirituality,' *MW* 78 (1988): 225–42.

5 Sufis of the Darqāwiyya founded by al-ᶜArabī al-Darqāwī (1760–1823), a contemporary of Aḥmad b. Idrīs and Aḥmad al-Tijānī, also played a part in opposition to Turkish rule in Algeria. See B. G. Martin, *Muslim Brotherhoods in Nineteenth-Century Africa* (Cambridge: Cambridge University Press, 1976), 43–5.

6 Magali Morsy, *North Africa 1800–1900: a Survey from the Nile Valley to the Atlantic* (Harlow: Longman, 1984), 141.

7 Jamil M. Abun-Nasr, *A History of the Maghrib in the Islamic Period* (Cambridge: Cambridge University Press, 1987), 259.

8 See Rudolph Peters, *Islam and Colonialism* (The Hague: Mouton, 1979), 42. The North African Ṭayyibiyya derived from the major Shādhilī order in the late seventeenth century and acquired its name from its fourth shaykh, Mūlay al-Ṭayyib (d. 1767). It also became known as the Wazzāniyya after its place of origin at Wazzān, Morocco or Tihāmiyya after al-Tihāmī, a grandson of its founder.

9 On Shaykh Khālid and the Naqshabandiyya-Khālidiyya see Albert Hourani, 'Sufism and Modern Islam: Mawlana Khālid and the Naqshabandi Order,' in *The Emergence of the Modern Middle East* (London: Macmillan, 1981), 75–89; Butrus Abu-Manneh, 'The Naqshabandiyya-Mujaddidiyya in the Ottoman Lands in the Early 19th Century,' *WI* XII (1982): 1–36. David Commins, 'ᶜAbd al-Qādir al-Jazā'irī and Islamic

Reform,' *MW* 78 (1988): 121–31 includes discussion of his connection with the Naqshabandī-Khālidī reform movement.

10 The Raḥmāniyya was another of the orders to develop in the early nineteenth century, as a North African offshoot from the Khalwatiyya, an order of major importance in the Ottoman Empire.

11 The Mahdī's reply to Yūsuf Pasha Ḥasan al-Shallālī, commander of an ill-fated Egyptian expedition against the Mahdist forces in 1882, quoted in Peters, *Islam and Colonialism*, 68. For details see P. M. Holt, *The Mahdist State in the Sudan, 1881–1898* 2d ed. (Oxford: Oxford University Press, 1970), 55–8.

12 The Mahdī's words quoted in Holt, *The Mahdist State*, 93.

13 The Sammāniyya was founded by Muḥammad ᶜAbd al-Karīm al-Sammān (1718–75) and was an offshoot of the Khalwatiyya. The new ṭarīqa was first propagated in the Sudan by Aḥmad al-Ṭayyib b. al-Bashīr (1742/3–1824). See Karrar, *Sufi Brotherhoods*, 43–9.

14 Marie Bennigsen Broxup, ed., *The North Caucasus Barrier: The Russian Advance towards the Muslim World* (London: C. Hurst and Co., 1992), ix.

15 See Paul B. Henze, 'Circassian Resistance to Russia,' in *The North Caucasus Barrier*, 75; Chantal Lemercier Quelquejay, 'Sufi Brotherhoods in the USSR: A Historical Survey,' *CAS* 2 (1983): 5–6.

16 The spiritual genealogy of the Caucasian Naqshabandiyya is traced back through Shaykh Khālid to the Delhi line of Shāh Walī Allāh.

17 Shaykh Khālid's words quoted in Abu-Manneh, 'The Naqshabandiyya-Mujaddidiyya': 15.

18 A name derived from *murīd*, a Sufi disciple. However, there was often Russian misunderstanding of the spiritual *murīd-shaykh* relationship and the term *murīd* came to be applied to all those who fought under Naqshabandī leadership. The Russian concept of Murīdism was taken up by some Western historians and persists.

19 Ermolov's words quoted in John F. Baddeley, *The Russian Conquest of the Caucasus* (London, 1908; reprint, New York: Russell and Russell, 1969), 97. More recently on Ermolov see Moshe Gammer, 'Russian Strategies in the Conquest of Checnia and Daghestan, 1825–1859,' in *The North Caucasus Barrier*, 45–9; idem, *Muslim Resistance to the Tsar: Shamil and the Conquest of Chechnia and Daghestan* (London: Frank Cass and Co. Ltd., 1994), 29–38.

20 Ibid., 50.

21 On the Qādiriyya in the North Caucasus see Chantal Lemercier Quelquejay, 'Sufi Brotherhoods': 8–11.

22 A ḥadīth quoted by al-Ghazālī in *The Beginning of Guidance* in *The Faith and Practice of al-Ghazāli*, trans. W. Montgomery Watt (London: George Allen and Unwin Ltd., 131.

23 The classic study of the Bektāshiyya is J. F. Birge, *The Bektashi Order of Dervishes* (London: Luzac, 1937; reprint, Luzac Oriental, 1994). For recent studies see J. L. Lee, 'Bektashiyya Sufism of Turkey and the Balkans' (Birmingham: Centre for the Study of Islam and Christianity Papers, No. 11, 1994); H. T. Norris, *Islam in the Balkans: Religion and Society between Europe and the Arab World* (London: Hurst and Co., 1993), 89–100.

24 See Abu-Manneh, 'The Naqshabandiyya-Mujaddidiyya' on these tendencies in the ṭarīqa.

25 The first Naqshabandī lodge was established in Sarajevo in 1463 by Iskender Pasha, a governor of Bosnia, but no longer exists. A new lodge was built there in the nineteenth century. On the Naqshabandiyya in Bosnia see Hamid Algar, 'Some Notes on the Naqshabandi Tariqat in Bosnia,' *WI* 13 (1972): 168–203.

26 The Chishtiyya is one of the oldest ṭarīqas, noted for its commitment to extreme asceticism and avoidance of involvement in political affairs. Its name is derived from Muᶜīn al-dīn Chishtī (c. 1142–1236), whose tomb at Ajmer became a major pilgrimage site.

27 Abū'l-Najib al-Suhrawardī, *A Sufi Rule for Novices (K. Ādāb al-Murīdīn)*, trans. Menahem Milson (Cambridge, Mass.: Harvard University Press, 1975), 58. Al-Suhrawardī (d. 1167) was originally from Suhraward in Iran, but spent most of his active career in Iraq. The order named after him was introduced into India in the thirteenth century, where it became especially influential.

28 See Barbara Metcalf, *Islamic Revival in British India, Deoband 1860–1900* (Princeton, N.J.: Princeton University Press, 1982) on the development of the Deobandī movement, including their role as Sufis.

29 Ibid., 157. *Bihishti Zewar* has been translated by Barbara Daly Metcalf under the title *Perfecting Women* (Berkeley, Los Angeles and Oxford: University of California Press, 1990).

30 Ibid., 233.

31 Ibid., 182.

32 For further details see Metcalf, *Islamic Revival*, 296–314.

33 *ᶜUrs*, literally meaning 'wedding', a term used to describe the commemoration of a Sufi's death day, being the occasion on which his final existence in the world and separation from the Divine would be regarded as coming to an end.

3

Traditional Sufism or a Religion of Progress?

By the second half of the nineteenth century it was becoming ever more difficult for Muslims to prevent not only the physical, but also the intellectual, invasion of the *umma* from the West. It was increasingly impracticable to insulate the spiritual life of Muslim communities from all contact with modern Western thought. In the Ottoman Empire the ideas of the French Enlightenment had been seeping into the circle of Westernizing bureaucrats and technocrats from soon after their inception and had become common currency, despite a spirited religious opposition that included many Sufis. In India, while both Sufi and anti-Sufi reformers endeavoured steadfastly to reject the language and culture of the British rulers, it became harder for many educated Muslims to avoid all influence, when they received more secular education and worked in the imperial administration. Elsewhere different levels of exposure produced varying degrees of concern to contain the dangers to Islam seen to be presented by the penetration of European ideas.

Sufism and European Thought in the Nineteenth Century

The process of interaction between Islamic thought and the European thought of the nineteenth century was frequently painful. Challenges arose to traditional methods of thinking about Islam and about the place of Sufism within the faith. Often the European values of the age seemed directly opposed to those of the Sufis. Modern European exaltation of rationalism conflicted with faith in mystical insight leading to a deeper apprehension of the Truth (*al-Ḥaqq*), the ultimate Reality of the Divine unknowable through the exercise of human reason alone unaided by Qur'ānic revelation and gnosis. Classical Sufism had been able to survive the earlier challenges from the Greek intellectualism that invaded Islamic thought from the eighth to tenth centuries and was expressed theologically by the Mu^{c}tazilites as well as by a distinguished line of Hellenized philosophers. The mystics found a niche for Neoplatonism within their own theosophy, most systematically rendered in the synthesizing work of Ibn al-^{c}Arabī in the thirteenth century. But it was also a two-way process in that some philosophers absorbed elements of Sufi teachings and their rationalism was leavened by the yeast of mysticism. Whatever doubts and suspicions might linger and resurface concerning this medieval interaction between mysticism and rationalism, yet it had involved a fairly equal exchange of influence. By the nineteenth century the inequalities of political and economic power appear too great, the divisions of outlook too deep for a harmonious reconciliation of the Sufi heritage and Western rational method. Western observers of Sufism in this period often highlight the irrational and visibly bizarre, as when the French novelist Gustave Flaubert on his journey in Egypt in 1849–50 details the nauseating degradation of false Sufis, idiotic and mad 'saints'.[1] Sufis, or rather the abusers of Sufism, make an excellent target to contrast with the reasonable civilization of Western Europe. At best they may be purveyors of the entrancingly exotic, the living embodiment of Occidental fantasies of the Orient.

Ernest Renan, eminent Orientalist philologist, had experienced a crisis of faith which led him to reject Christianity and, from 1845, to dedicate his life to the pursuit of a scholarship that he judged suited to the modern, post-Christian mind. For him philology represented a thoroughly modern development, sharing with the natural sciences in promoting rational, critical, liberal thinking. Writing in 1848 of his vision of a scientific future, he recognized with satisfaction the threat posed to the traditional religions of the East:

> The youth of the East, in coming to the schools of the West to drink from the fountainhead of European science, will take away with it its inseparable corollary, the rational method, experimental spirit, sense of reality and the impossibility of believing in religious traditions evidently conceived without any criticism.[2]

Sufism would be understood to figure prominently among those 'religious traditions' whose passing away was so confidently predicted by Renan, when the rising Muslim generations adopted Western scientific approaches. Renan's perceptions were clearly very different from those of the Sufis, for not only would they question the attainments possible through the spirit of free scientific enquiry, but also the intrinsic value of his 'sense of reality'. To them it would be Renan and the materialists who had no 'sense of Reality', the only Divine Reality behind the world of material forms veiling the Godhead from humanity. The miracles (*karāmāt*) of saints were regarded by Sufis as manifestations of God's grace to His 'friends' (*awliyā'*) and not seen as amenable to scientific explanation; such Sufi belief in the miraculous was to be strenuously attacked by those advocating Muslim acceptance of modern European scientific understandings of the world.

When Renan wrote of 'criticism' and the lack of a critical approach to 'religious traditions' in the East, Sufis were prominent among those exemplifying the uncritical faithful. Modern critical method conflicted with the Sufi requirements for a disciple (*murīd*) to submit completely to the absolute authority of the shaykh responsible for his spiritual guidance in the Way. This attitude of total unquestioning obedience contrasted sharply with the modern Western emphasis on the need for the individual to interpret and analyse and make decisions on the basis of personal judgment. For the Sufis, even the most intellectually gifted disciple would be expected to defer to the judgment of the spiritual master and the failure to do so would be looked upon as a sign of presumptuousness leading to dangerous delusions. Many a cautionary tale would be told to illustrate the risks of the disciple who thought and acted independently of his shaykh, supposing himself to be sufficiently spiritually advanced. Whatever role reformist Sufis might envisage for *ijtihād*, it was still a traditional tool in the hands of a traditionally-trained élite and did not equate with Western demands for a rigorous critical sifting of centuries of accumulated Islamic heritage. At first sight the anti-Sufi Ahl-i Ḥadīth appear more ready than the Sufis to assign individuals a personal decision-making role in asking them to assess Qur'ān and Ḥadīth for themselves rather than submitting to the established views of earlier authorities. However, by nineteenth-century Western standards, this process of reassessment did not constitute 'criticism', as the sect favoured narrow and literalist understanding of the texts, not a full critical re-examination.

In 1859, just over a decade after Renan's ponderings on the future of science, the English naturalist Charles Darwin published *On the Origin of Species*, to be followed in 1871 by *The Descent of Man*. Darwin's theory of a continual process at work in the natural world, by which one species would evolve from and might eventually replace another, heightened growing tensions between science and religion in its challenge to religious beliefs in the creation of every living thing by separate divine acts. Evolutionary theory was as contradictory to the Qur'ānic revelation of God's creation by speech as it was to the Biblical account taken literally. It was also directly opposed to popular Sufi notions of the nature and status of Prophet Muḥammad. The concept of the Prophet as the recipient of the Divine Light (*Nūr Muḥammad*) existent from the beginning of creation gained credence at some point during the ninth century among the Shīᶜa and in Sufi circles and is first recorded in the thought of Sahl al-Tustarī (d. 896). At the same time there emerged the claim that it was for Prophet Muḥammad that the world was created and that it was his light that shone through the other prophets. These ideas had reached their fullest development in the theorizing of Ibn al-ᶜArabī, for whom the Prophet assumed the role of the Perfect Man (*al-insān al-kāmil*) through whom God could be known and manifested in the world as in a mirror. By the nineteenth century such beliefs had long since come to permeate traditional Sufism, as evidenced among the Indian Barēlwīs. Consequently, for Sufis it was inconceivable for the Prophet to arise out of a humanity evolved from a lower species.[3] The concept of natural selection contained in Darwin's theory, and made famous as the 'survival of the fittest', was almost equally repugnant from an Islamic viewpoint. In its cruder development, unsanctioned by Darwin himself, it entailed a commitment to constant struggle for presumed superior races to assert themselves over inferior ones. While it would be used by Europeans as a justification for imperialism, for Muslims it ran contrary to the regulation of the world, including human lives, by God's decree; in opposition to Sufi values, it might be seen to glorify and strengthen the worst elements in the *nafs* (the base self) that they sought by spiritual struggle in the 'greater *jihād*' to overcome.

The arguments for social development based on evolutionary theory became closely linked with a rigid view of progress, most influentially disseminated by the English social theorist Herbert Spencer. His first efforts, in the 1850s, to apply to social systems laws supposedly governing biological systems actually predated Darwin's work and drew upon earlier nineteenth century evolutionary theory, subsequently discredited.[4] In 1857 he produced a paper entitled 'Progress: its Law and Course' which posited a universally applicable law of progress governing solar as well as biological and social systems. With the Eurocentrism characteristic of his time he saw the peak of social evolution as having been achieved within the Western society of the latter half of the nineteenth century. Spencer's major work of the 1870s–90s endeavoured to support his ideas of the universal evolutionary process and gained a wide currency.

For those Muslims bent on modernization, the Spencerian vision of 'progress' was not without its fascination. For Sufis, however, it held few attractions, partly because most of what was valued as progress would be considered mere worldly delusions impeding real spiritual progress. More fundamentally, they would question the very existence of social evolution, seeing that perfection was present in the beginning when the Divine Light entered into Prophet Muḥammad. The passage of time brought only further separation from God, unless the mystic could travel on the Path of return to that ideal primordial state before all that was created in time, when God alone was. In that state, with all earthly attributes annihilated, it would be possible to bear witness most fully to the Absolute Unity of God. Progress in Sufi terms might come about through constant spiritual struggle and through God's grace. It was not a passage from a condition of savagery and barbarism to civilization and enlightenment as exemplified by nineteenth-century Europe, and it could not be realized by continual national or racial struggle including warfare or by the development of strong industrialized economies or by the will to dominate another culture. That it should involve moral advancement was one point on which the two sides might be seen to agree, but Sufis would be bound to disagree with Spencer's claim that this had happened in the case of his own society and was a necessary result of obeying laws of social progress, which, from a Sufi perspective, were non-existent.

While Sufism had frequently shown itself able to integrate ideas garnered from other religious traditions within its belief system, the ideas of Europe in the mid-nineteenth century proved much harder to integrate. Crucial aspects of the European outlook, as illustrated above, seemed irreconcilable with Sufism's essential 'truths'. Moreover, in the cases where Sufism met, for example, with Indian or African religions, the meeting was commonly on equal terms or in situations where the Sufis were part of a dominant culture. In the new situation where the Sufis were among the colonized, European thought was projected by the colonialists as consciously superior, the mark of real 'civilization' and fit to replace that of Islam, and manifestly of its Sufi forms.

Nevertheless, Westernization of thought could not easily be turned back in the circumstances of visible European success in the domination of Islamic territory. With the growth of Westernized classes, key elements of the rulers' thought were absorbed more or less consciously and transmitted with varying degrees of adaptation to indigenous thought patterns. Those who attempted a constructive integration of these ideas with Islam have generally been described by Western, and by some Muslim, scholars as 'Muslim modernists', although among Muslims the label is often used disparagingly. For Sufism acute problems were to arise out of the modernists' efforts, when they experienced grave difficulties in reconciling such opposing views on fundamental questions of the nature and purpose of human existence. The result was generally a new critique of Sufism, or of much of its traditional content, the arguments of the indigenous anti-Sufism being combined with new anti-Sufi intellectual tools imported from the Christian, and post-Christian, West. An attempt will be made here to examine the process of formation of this new critique. Sufi defence of their position will also be considered with special reference to the arena of the Ottoman Empire, the last great Islamic state that might serve for a while as a bastion of Sufi perspectives.

But it was in India that the impact of emergent modernism was felt with full force in the years after the 1857 Mutiny and it is there that the critique begins.

Early Islamic Modernism and Sufism

Sayyid Aḥmad Khān (1817–98)

Sayyid Aḥmad Khān, one of the founding fathers of Islamic modernism, was born in 1817 into an upper-class family of Delhi. Both his parents were mystically inclined. His father followed the reformist path of the Naqshabandiyya-Mujaddidiyya, while his mother revered the son of Shāh Walī Allāh, Shāh ᶜAbd al-ᶜAzīz (1746–1823), and his family. The influence of this background on Sayyid Aḥmad was substantial and, had he not been thrown into close contact with the British rulers, he might have grown old in the reforming school of Sufism that they represented. As it was, after his father's death in 1838, he found himself compelled by his circumstances to seek employment in the judiciary of the East India Company. The nature of his career involved him in regular moves, as he worked his way up through the lower levels of judgeships open to an Indian Muslim of his period until his final retirement in 1877.

However, Sayyid Aḥmad was never so preoccupied with his legal career as to be prevented from a series of other pursuits, literary, theological, scientific, political and educational. His wide-ranging interests as a young man included a concern with the reform of Sufism, evidently in the tradition of the Walī Allāhīs, and expressed in several of his writings of the 1840s and 50s. In 1849 he published a treatise denouncing abuses and sharply critical of *shaykh-murīd* relationship. A year later a better known work, *Rāh-i Sunna dar Radd-i Bidᶜa* (The Path of the Sunna in Rejecting Innovation), is urging reforms within the same framework, calling for the elimination of un-Islamic innovations and restoration of the Sunna; in substance it could have been authored by any of the eighteenth to nineteenth-century Sufi reformers.[5] He apparently continued to share essentially in their religious outlook until some years after the tragic events of the Mutiny of 1857, from which his own family suffered and which led him to strive for a rapprochement between the Muslims and British as a means of reinstating the Indian Muslims in the eyes of the rulers and enabling them to compete with the Hindu majority, who were increasingly favoured by the British in government appointments.[6]

In the 1860s closer association with the British brought Sayyid Aḥmad into contact with the Western scientific and social thought of his day and in the process gradually distanced him from the Walī Allāhī school. In 1864 he founded the Scientific Society with the aim of translating English scientific works into Urdu and thus disseminating a knowledge of Western sciences among Indian Muslims. But his major efforts in the educational field were to be devoted to the establishment of modern schooling and higher education based on English models, yet keeping in mind the specific needs of India. Also in 1864 he had opened his first school, but in 1869–70 embarked on a journey to Europe, accompanying his son, Sayyid Maḥmūd, who had won a British government scholarship to study at Cambridge. This journey seems to have had a deep effect on Sayyid Aḥmad, giving him the opportunity to examine the English education system at first hand and inspiring him to found a school which later became the Muḥammadan Anglo-Oriental College at Aligarh in 1878, planned as the Oxbridge of India. It was to achieve university status in 1920.[7]

However, although he found much to admire in the course of his visit to Europe, and especially to England, Sayyid Aḥmad was also psychologically disturbed by the encounter. Despite his appreciation of the architecture and city planning of Paris on his travels through

France, he was very much saddened by a painting of the French defeat of Amir ᶜAbd al-Qādir in Algeria and the rape of his *ḥarīm*. In Sayyid Aḥmad's eyes it was a disgraceful and dishonourable theme. He had long respected the great reforming Sufi jihādists, ranking the *amīr* along with the great Indian heroes of the jihād, Sayyid Aḥmad Barēlwī and Shāh Ismāᶜīl. The mingling of emotions experienced in France is symptomatic of the painful adjustments taking place within Sayyid Aḥmad. He feels the attractions of European education and culture and the desire for his fellow countrymen (and women) to share in it, but at the same time recognizes that the mystical religious leaders of the Muslims have mainly failed. If he approves their vision of the faith, yet he emerges from his journey no longer certain that theirs is the right religious path for Muslims of his own age.[8] In England, the home of India's rulers, he was to undergo an even greater ambivalence towards Western achievements and the relationship of Indian Muslims to them. Speaking very little English himself, he was largely dependent on his son to interpret for him. Esteem for the advances made by British science and technology and for widespread education, including female education, caused him to develop an ever-increasing awareness of the great gap between Britain at the height of imperial power and the Muslims of occupied India. For a while he seems to have been overwhelmed with feelings of inferiority vis-à-vis the English, leading him to write: 'The natives of India, high and low, merchants and petty shopkeepers, educated and illiterate, when contrasted with the English in education, manners and uprightness, are as like to them as a dirty animal is to a handsome man.'[9] The tone of such letters naturally enough provoked anger in India. Sayyid Aḥmad at this time presents a lonely figure, on the margins of nineteenth-century English society, but rejected by the traditionalists among his own people.

The journey marks a personal religious turning point. No longer would Sayyid Aḥmad be able to think about Islam, including its mystical content, without reference to the views of Western, especially English, contemporaries. In December 1870 he began publishing the journal *Tahdhīb al-Akhlāq* (The Rectification of Morals), to be an instrument by which the rationalist, critical thought of Europe could be applied to the situation of Indian Muslims. His declaration of aims in the first issue is indicative of the new modernist direction of his thought:

> The aim of this periodical is that the Muslims of India should be persuaded to adopt the best kind of civilisation so that the

> contempt with which the civilised people look upon them should be removed and they may join the comity of civilised people.... It is true that religion plays a great part in making a people civilised. There are, no doubt, some religions which stand in the way of progress. It is our aim to judge where Islam stands in this regard.[10]

Sayyid Aḥmad, acutely conscious of Muslim inadequacy in his own day, appears at this point to jettison any judgment of Indian Muslims according to ideal Islamic standards. Unlike past reformers, he is no longer looking to rebuild Islamic society on the pattern of the earliest Islamic state, but his model is nineteenth-century European, and particularly Victorian British, 'civilisation'. Islam must stand or fall by the degree of its conformity to 'progress', as represented in the non-Islamic terms of an alien ruling élite.

Sayyid Aḥmad's conviction developed that Islam, **if correctly understood**, would be shown to be such a religion of progress and capable of civilizing those Muslims whom, in 1870, he perceived as being regarded with contempt by the 'civilised people' of the West. For him it became a matter of urgent necessity that the true, original Islam be rescued from the obscurantism and superstition that had overwhelmed it. Otherwise, he could see no future for the faith. If religion were to be left in the hands of the traditional *ᶜulamā'* and Sufi shaykhs, it would simply be swept away by the forces of modern materialistic naturalism, as the younger 'Muslim' generation imbibed the latest discoveries of science without a firm faith underpinned by reason. He expressed his doubts about the retention of belief in the interpretations of Islam, including Sufi interpretations, current in India:

> I happen to believe that there is nobody who is well acquainted with modern philosophy and modern and natural science as they exist in the English language, and who at the same time believes in all the doctrines of Islam in present-day understanding.... I am certain that as these sciences spread – and their spreading is inevitable and I myself, after all, too, help and contribute towards spreading them – there will arise in the hearts of people an uneasiness and carelessness and even a positive disaffection towards Islam as it has been shaped in our time. At the same time I believe firmly that this is not because of a defect in the original religion but rather because of those errors

> which have been made, wilfully or not, to stain the face of Islam. . . . The person that states Islam to be true must also state how he can prove the truth of Islam.[11]

According to Sayyid Aḥmad, it would be possible to prove the truth by establishing to what extent Islam is 'in correspondence with the natural disposition of man, or with nature', as God is the creator of the universe and of the natural laws that govern it. Consequently, a religion that is truly ordained by Him would not contradict these laws of nature. In Sayyid Aḥmad's view, Islam in its original form is perfectly suited to human nature. There can be no contradiction between the true divine revelation of God's word in the Qur'ān and the revelation of God in nature, His work. Thus real Islam would not contradict any of the findings of modern science and Muslims should be fully capable of studying the latest science and technology from the West without fear of violating their faith. In a famous statement, Sayyid Aḥmad declared, 'Islam is nature and nature is Islam.'[12] He thus earned himself and his followers the disparaging title of *naychirī* ('naturist') among critics of his new theology. A prominent Sufi opponent was quoted by his son as saying that the modern apostates moved first to Wahhābism before espousing *naychiriyya* ('naturism'), which he equated with unbelief.[13]

Naychiriyya was regarded with scorn not only by Sufis, but by many traditional and some very untraditional Muslims, the most famous critique being that of the celebrated Pan-Islamist Jamāl al-dīn al-Afghānī.[14] For the generality of Muslims, it was a very unsatisfactory, indeed heretical, view of Islam that demanded only that they submit their whole nature to God and, in so doing, dedicate themselves to good acts. Even the most fundamental rituals of the faith were laid open to question. But, in addition, Sufism appeared to be targeted specifically by the new natural religion, which reduced demands on the believer to the minimum and dispensed with the mysterious and miraculous in favour of plain exoteric knowledge available to any intelligent, rational observer and not the preserve of a spiritual élite.

In Sayyid Aḥmad's view, the laws of nature were God's promises to His creation and could not be violated, as God would not break His promises. Therefore, no miracle could occur that entailed a suspension of natural laws, but only those that might be amazing events to humankind without disobeying God's laws. Thus all alleged miracles of the prophets must be rationally reinterpreted. Ironically, the search for such rational explanations could lead Sayyid Aḥmad on occasion to a rethinking of prophetic experience in mystical terms. Thus in the case of Prophet Abraham (Ibrāhīm), in Qur'ān ii, 260, he asks God to show him how He gives life to the dead:

> And when Abraham said, 'Lord, show me how you bring the dead to life.' He said, 'Do you not believe?' He said, 'Yes, but that my heart may have assurance.' He said, 'Take four birds and cut them in pieces. Then put a part of them on every mountain. Then call them and they will come to you walking. Know that God is Mighty, Wise.'

According to Sayyid Aḥmad, this was not an actual dismemberment of the birds, who were then physically brought to life before the prophet's eyes, but a dream in which Abraham received mystical insight into God's creative powers.[15] In rationalizing the miracle, the modernist interpreter has dwelt upon the centrality of mystical knowledge for the prophet's understanding of God's operations in the world.

The interpretation is similar in Sayyid Aḥmad's discussion of the crucial event of Prophet Muḥammad's journey by night (*isrā'*) to Jerusalem and his ascension (*mi^crāj*) through the seven heavens to meet with the previous prophets and ultimately receive the vision of God. He is anxious to deny the event as a physical miracle, but understands it as a dream experience important for the Prophet's spiritual development. Heaven itself is no longer held to be a place, but is regarded instead as representing the higher order of the spiritual world to which the Prophet ascends from the lower order of the physical world. Sayyid Aḥmad's interpretation is consequently closer to Sufi views of the spiritual nature of the *mi^crāj* than to literalist understanding of the traditional miraculous occasion. However, this model of ascension does not become for him a pattern to be imitated by adherence to the Way, ascending through its seven stages in the manner of the Sufis. It is a level of experience acknowledged to exist among the prophets and some exceptional mystics, but not a means to guide the majority of the modern Muslim community, who should pursue rational methods in seeking to understand Islam and keep it alive.

If the great prophetic miracles were to be reinterpreted by reasoning away any violation of the laws of nature, how much more would this be expected to apply to the miraculous charismatic gifts (*karāmāt*) attributed to Sufi 'saints'?

It seems ironical that a marked admiration for the rationalism of Shāh Walī Allāh should have led Sayyid Aḥmad to reject his mentor's vision of a future that would see the birth of a new and better age of Sufism. He may have inherited from his predecessor in reform a sense of tension between the mystical and the rational, but by the late nineteenth century the mystical appears less of a viable option for the younger generations of educated Indian Muslims. If Islam was to prove itself compatible with European ideas of progress, it seemed to Sayyid Aḥmad that Sufism had little part to play in the enterprise of reconstruction necessary for the faith's survival.

Sayyid Jamāl al-dīn al-Afghānī (al-Asadabādī) (1838–97)

A contemporary of Sayyid Aḥmad Khān, the celebrated 'Sage of the East' (*ḥakīm al-sharq*) Sayyid Jamāl al-dīn al-Afghānī, appears to have had much more in common with the Indian modernist than a shared title of *sayyid* marking their common descent from the Prophet. But, as with much else in their lives, the apparent similarity served to mask real differences. Aḥmad Khān's claim to the status of *sayyid* was through a Sunni line of ancestry, Jamāl al-dīn al-Afghānī's through a Shīʿī line. Both were critical of the traditional *ʿulama'* and Sufis of their day and attracted to rationalist interpretations of religion, yet not abandoning totally strains of earlier mystical influence. Both remained committed to the introduction of modern sciences among the Muslims and are commonly spoken of in the same breath as founding fathers of Islamic modernism. But their goals, their hopes and fears, and especially their strategies, were often different and in India al-Afghānī came to attention chiefly as a virulent critic of Khān and of 'naturism'.

Early Influences

While Sayyid Aḥmad's life is a relatively open book, that of Jamāl al-dīn al-Afghānī retains its share of mystery even after the most painstaking modern efforts to uncover its secrets.[16] The claim of his foremost Sufi enemy, Shaykh Abū'l-Hudā al-Ṣayyādī, that he was a *muta'afghin* ('one who claims/pretends to be an Afghan'), and not actually an Afghan, seems to be proved correct.[17] Born probably towards the end of 1838 in the village of Asadabād near the city of Hamadan in North-West Iran, he studied in Iran and at Najaf, the centre of Shīʿī learning in Iraq. He thus imbibed a combination of the traditional Islamic sciences taught throughout the *umma* and philosophical and mystical teachings of the medieval heritage, such as were still available in the Shīʿī schools, including the works of Ibn Sīnā (Avicenna), Shihāb al-dīn al-Suhrawardī and Mullā Ṣadrā.[18] Nevertheless, he was deeply dissatisfied with his early training and disillusioned with his studies under superficial religious scholars, from whom he believed himself to have derived little benefit.

The young Sayyid Jamāl al-dīn was also exposed to a heady fare of the new heterodoxies current in the Shīʿism of his day. He experienced the impact of the philosophical and mystical thought of the Shaykhīs, who owed their inspiration to Shaykh Aḥmad Aḥsā'i (1754–1826) and believed that, in the absence of the Hidden Imām, there would always be present on earth a perfect spiritual guide able to achieve mystical communication with the Imām and interpret his will. This ability is closely comparable with similar communication between Sufi masters and dead 'friends of God' (*awliyā' Allāh*) or perhaps even more directly with the experience of such nineteenth-century religious leaders as Aḥmad al-Tijānī, the Sudanese Mahdī and Imām Shamīl in their claims to communication with the Prophet. Al-Afghānī apparently carried two Shaykhī treatises with him on his travels for a number of years.[19]

He was also very much aware of the Shaykhī-influenced, religious revolutionary activism of the Bābīs, led by Sayyid ʿAli Muḥammad (1819–50), who in 1844 claimed to be the Bāb ('Gateway') to the Twelfth Imām and to have received a new revelation, the *Bayān*, which would supersede the Qur'ān and render the Sharīʿa obsolete. The Bābīs were sharply critical of corruption in ruling circles and among the ʿulamā' and made various demands for social justice, including the better treatment of women and children with an end to polygamy and beating. They also advocated an acceptance of interest-bearing loans with a view to providing economic incentives, hopefully leading to greater prosperity. Bābī revolts between 1848–51 were harshly suppressed by the forces of Shāh Nāṣir al-dīn (1848–96), the Bāb himself being executed by firing squad in 1850. While there is no suggestion that Jamāl al-dīn ever became a committed Bābī, he may well have been stimulated by their activist approach and sympathetic to some of their social reform aims, which are shared with prominent Muslim modernists.

After the death of the Bāb, his followers were divided into two camps, the majority giving their backing to Bahā'ullāh, who in 1863 claimed to be a new prophet and in the process founded the new Bahā'ī faith. A minority supported the Bāb's designated successor, Ṣubḥ-i Azal, and became known as Azalīs, continuing the Bābī tradition of militancy. Azalīs and former Azalīs were among al-Afghānī's close associates.[20] That accusations of Bābī allegiance were levelled at al-Afghānī personally is suggested by some verse of his own composition from the late 1860s, speaking of the conflicting opinions current as to his religious identity:

> Some of the virtuous Imāmites have imagined me a Bābī.[21]

But in the same passage he remarks that he is also variously held to be a Sunni, a Shī^cī, a Wahhābī or even a materialist, an unbelieving sinner. He does not care at this point to set the record straight.

Indeed, the problem of his religious affiliation or lack of one remains an enigma. It appears very probable that his beliefs fluctuated considerably during his turbulent life and that it is not helpful to classify him as being of a particular, consistent persuasion in matters of faith. He spent some time in India as a young man at the time of the Mutiny, and possibly for a few years afterwards in the late 1850s to early 1860s. The experience served to awaken in him an acute sense of the dangers posed by Britain to the East. There also he became acquainted with Western scientific thought and may have succumbed to a loss of faith in Islam, possibly becoming temporarily an atheist. However, this phase of doubt seems to have been followed by one of intense mystical awareness, a new enlightenment in which he saw a truth beyond the empty formalism to which he had been subjected in his youth. He recorded his reawakening in a brief autobiography that he wrote soon after his arrival at Herat in Afghanistan in the autumn of 1866:

> I saw that this world was only an unreal mirage and appearance. Its power was precarious and its sufferings unlimited, hiding a venom in every delight, an anger in every benefit. Thus I was inevitably led to remove myself from these tumults and to break all my ties of attachment. And thanks to God and all those who were near him, I was saved from the world of shadows and penetrated the universe of devotion, resting on the sweetness of the cradle of lights. Today I have chosen for company the Prophet and his companions.[22]

The imagery in which he writes of his salvation from the deceptive world of 'unreal mirage', 'shadows' and 'sufferings' is familiarly

Sufistic. Although it may consciously echo the famous eleventh-century spiritual autobiography of al-Ghazālī, *al-Munqidh min al-ḍalāl* (The Deliverer from Error), it never appears to have been intended for public consumption and there is no reason to suppose that al-Afghānī intended to do more than keep a personal record of a critical religious turning point in his life, which he may privately have felt resembled that of the medieval mystic. Both had come to reject the perceived inadequacies of the religious scholarship of their day in favour of a richly internalized spirituality.

What is less clear in al-Afghānī's case is the extent to which he went beyond the initial illumination, which may be deemed a conversion experience, to sustain such an outlook in later life. From 1866–68 he was still an obscure figure, passing under different names and engaging in shadowy anti-British activities until his expulsion from Afghanistan in late 1868 by the pro-British Amīr Shīr ᶜAlī. After he emerged from the shadows and assumed a more public role, his views on Islam became more exposed to the scrutiny of adoring disciples or sceptical and often hostile rulers and influential religious leaders. It thus becomes a much harder task to unravel the true nature of a possibly shifting faith.

True Philosophy, True Sufism and Actually Existing Islam

Al-Afghānī's wanderings are relatively well-documented from the 1870s onwards. His life is more publicly lived. In 1869 he arrived in Istanbul where he stayed until 1871, associating with known Westernizers and apparently pleading their cause. For the first time he is recorded as giving public lectures, lamenting the decline of Islam and urging the need to learn the secrets of Europe's strength, to grasp the key to the process of self-strengthening for the Muslims so that they may be restored to their former glories. At one time they were the strongest of peoples, but have been weakened before the world through their sinking into ignorance and laziness. If Sayyid Jamāl al-dīn saw the potentialities of true Sufism in Afghanistan, in Turkey a little over three years later he was ready to castigate the Sufis of his own day:

> Later this people sank into ease and laziness. It remained in the corners of the madrasas and the dervish convents; to such a degree that the lights of virtue were on the point of being

> extinguished; the banners of education were about to disappear. The suns of prosperity and the full moon of perfection began to wane.[23]

The Sufis of the 'dervish convents' are linked with the superficial teachers of the madrasas from whom he gained little in his youth. They are not identifiable with the true Sufism of his Herat vision, although this is not openly mentioned. Perhaps it did not serve his purpose at a time when he wished to emphasize the need to Westernize in order to advance along the path of the civilized nations, whom he identified as the European nations.

That he had not abandoned all thoughts of the true Sufism emerges from al-Afghānī's stay in Egypt from 1871–79. It was in this period that he made a deep impression on a close circle of disciples, the most prominent being the distinguished scholarly reformer Muḥammad ᶜAbduh. ᶜAbduh recorded that Jamāl al-dīn introduced him to a deeper knowledge of Sufism, apparently acquainting him and a selected group of students with works not taught in Egypt at that time. These included a commentary by the great fifteenth-century Naqshabandī mystical poet ᶜAbd al-Raḥmān Jāmī, discovered in a collection of al-Afghānī's books with marginal notes by him and five students, in addition to a list of others who had borrowed it.[24] Apart from introducing the group to Sufi writings excluded from the very conservative programme of studies at the ancient mosque-university of al-Azhar, Sayyid Jamāl al-dīn also read with them works by Ibn Sīnā on philosophy and by Nāṣir al-dīn al-Ṭūsī on astronomy. But arguably of greater importance was his insistence that they should reject the habit of rote learning and blind acceptance of the Azhar scholars' teachings and his demand that they should build instead an open-minded approach to debate and the development of rational independent thought.

Expelled from Egypt by Khedive Tawfīq in August 1879, as a result of his political opposition to growing European involvement in Egyptian affairs, al-Afghānī travelled once again to India. It is from his time there that some of his best-known short writings have survived. The message is adjusted to the new environment. It is somewhat less openly Westernizing than in Istanbul, critical of foreign encroachments and of conservative scholars as in Egypt, concerned not only with the defence of Islam but with India also as a great source of civilization, 'a land that was the source of all the laws and rules of the world.'[25] Indians had been the teachers of the Greeks in science and philosophic thought and such valuable knowledge did not belong exclusively to the Europeans who had come as conquerors. On other occasions it was the early Muslims who were mentioned as the sages of old and the superiors of the modern supposed scholars in India, who, like their counterparts in Turkey and Egypt, were actually sunk in ignorance. The need was to recapture the true spirit of Islam and authentic Islamic learning that would be relevant to the present age and open to the absorption of modern science and technology, a veritable religion of progress:

> For religious beliefs, whether true or false, are in no way incompatible with civilization and worldly progress unless they forbid the acquisition of science, the earning of a livelihood, and progress in sound civilization.[26]

The sentiments here expressed might equally well have been penned by Sayyid Aḥmad Khān, who is directly attacked in this article for seeking 'to remove the beliefs of the Muslims . . . to serve others and to prepare the way for conversion to their religion.'[27] Sayyid Aḥmad is being accused of serving as an instrument in the hands of the British, conspiring with them to spread Christianity among the Indian Muslims. This is certainly a misrepresentation of Khān's goals, and al-Afghānī did not hesitate to distort his views and those of his followers in his longer work *Ḥaqīqat-i mazhab-i naychirī va bayān-i hāl-i naychirīyān* (The Truth about the Naychiri Sect and an Explanation of the Condition of the Naychiris), originally written in Persian but better known under the title of its Arabic (adapted) translation, *al-Radd ᶜalā'l-dahriyyīn* (The Refutation of the Materialists).[28] There has been speculation about the genuineness of al-Afghānī's differences with Khān. How far were they owing to deeply felt religious and intellectual disagreements, how far motivated by political disapproval of Khān's pro-British image? The *naychiriyya* dispute illustrates the difficulty of knowing Sayyid Jamāl al-dīn's real opinions, especially during the later period of his life.

In his Indian writings he says virtually nothing concerning Sufism, although he does condemn the damage done to Islam by esotericism in general, and more specifically in allusions to the Ismāᶜīlīs and Bābīs.[29] However, philosophy is a frequent topic of discussion and al-Afghānī's treatment of it may provide some clues as to the nature of his somewhat ambiguous relationship to Sufism and Sufis. The pursuit of philosophy is strongly advocated.

> It is philosophy that makes man understandable to man, explains nobility, and shows man the proper road. The first defect appearing in any nation that is headed to decline is in the philosophic spirit. After that deficiencies spread into the other sciences, arts and associations.[30]

The non-existence of philosophy in the schools of the Ottoman Empire was cited by al-Afghānī as a sufficient explanation of failure to make progress in the new sciences, despite their introduction in these schools from the early nineteenth century. Yet, he could hardly find a better situation in India (or for that matter in his native Iran) where some philosophy had continued to be taught. The problem, he concluded, was in this case owing to wrong approaches to the subject that led to no real benefit. The so-called philosophers had failed to ask the right questions and to seek solutions to the problems of the age. Buried in the study of old texts, 'they do not ask: Who are we and what is right and proper for us? They never ask the causes of electricity, the steamboat and railroads.'[31] The practice of an effective philosophy would have brought about the reform of the umma in accordance with science.

In India the traditional scholars and religious leaders were attacked for their failure to develop true philosophy. Al-Afghānī concentrated on the topic, seeking to promote it as an issue of public concern for the welfare of the Muslim community. He was similarly critical of the traditionalists' narrow understanding of jurisprudence, although he managed to link this to their philosophical inabilities.

Sufism, however, he passed over in silence. Perhaps the cultivation of true mysticism appeared to him less urgent or less relevant to his reforming message of the necessity of this-worldly progress. It could not be so readily applied to the need for railroads and good government. It might moreover have stirred up a hornets' nest of controversy that Sayyid Jamāl al-dīn would have considered judicious to avoid. Philosophy was, after all, a peripheral field of study for Indian Muslim scholars and one in which their shortcomings could be quite easily recognized without striking at their saintly reputations. Al-Afghānī was probably wise to avoid launching an attack on the deficiencies of Indian Sufis. However, from his earlier activities and his later career, it appears that he identified certain similar underlying problems in both philosophy and Sufism as they existed, or failed to exist, in the later nineteenth century. Philosophy had only a limited presence in the umma, but, in the eyes of Sayyid Jamāl al-dīn, it was the wrong kind of philosophy. Sufism was all-pervasive, but it was the wrong kind of Sufism.

For al-Afghānī the Sufis of his day were prominent among the traditional religious leaders who were responsible for the decline of Muslim fortunes. They failed on various counts; they were implicated in false interpretations of Islam that were alien to its true nature and ran counter to reason; they encouraged a fatalistic attitude of passive resignation to God's will, an attitude that led to inactivity and even laziness instead of productive effort; they followed their shaykhs in a spirit of blind obedience and imitation that undermined the capacity for creative and independent thought. There is a call to reject all the negative and degenerate features of popular belief and practice that al-Afghānī associated with the late nineteenth-century Sufis, even when they were not directly specified in his critique, but implied by the nature of the criticism.

By 1883–84 al-Afghānī had moved from India to European exile in Paris. There he continued to work for the cause of Muslim unity and reforms that would ensure the survival of an assertive and progressive Islam. To that end he published (with the help of ᶜAbduh also in exile) the famous, but short-lived, Arabic periodical *al-ᶜUrwa al-Wuthqā* (The Firmest Bond), used by al-Afghānī with reference to the Ottoman Caliphate.[32] From this time on, the stress on Pan-Islamism came increasingly to the fore, combined with the summons to engage in persistent struggle against corrupt Muslim rulers and European interference in the affairs of the umma. In this context the weaknesses of actually existing Islam were brought into focus, including the undesirable aspects of contemporary Sufism from the viewpoint of al-Afghānī's campaign.

However, his wanderings and attempts at more direct interference in politics were not yet over. After a brief period in the service of Shāh Nāṣir al-dīn of Iran, he fell from favour owing to his involvement in the popular agitation against a concession granted by the Shāh to a British company for the sale and export of tobacco. In 1891 Sayyid Jamāl al-dīn was unceremoniously deported, embarking on his final journey to spend the last years of his life in Istanbul under the surveillance of Sultan Abdülhamid II. On his first arrival, he seems to have entertained hopes of influencing the Sultan's own Pan-Islamic policy. Later such hopes receded, as he was viewed with increasing suspicion, much of it stemming from the Sultan's closest Sufi advisers, and in particular Shaykh Abū'l-Hudā al-Ṣayyādī, who accused al-Afghānī of irreligiosity. The assassination of Shāh Nāṣir al-dīn in

1896 by an associate of Jamāl al-dīn made the sayyid even more suspect and isolated.[33] On 9 March 1897 he died of cancer of the jaw after at least two operations and much suffering, although some of his followers spread the rumour that he had been poisoned on the Sultan's orders.

To the end of his life the contradictions remained. Was he an ascetic or a libertine? A man of true faith or an unbeliever? What was his real position with regard to Sufism and did he bear sincere witness to it? The traditional Sufis of the Ottoman court disapproved of his alleged behaviour in frequenting taverns where he drank beer and teased the bar girls. They censured also his recorded visits to Romany fortune-tellers.[34] Such reports are certainly hard to reconcile with his general image of an ascetic figure prepared to sacrifice even the permitted pleasures in order to devote himself to a higher cause. This was the image that he apparently wished to project to his disciples and in public, but there is a disagreement as to how far he sincerely subscribed to a Sufistic view of the virtues of self-denial. His avowed celibacy and rejection of marriage to a beautiful slave-girl offered him by the Sultan have been variously interpreted. Did Sayyid Jamāl al-dīn refuse the gift out of a desire to avoid worldly attachments in a Sufi pursuit of nobler goals? Did he simply want to avoid becoming over-indebted to Sultan Abdülhamid, considering this another of the Sultan's attempts to snare him?[35] The refusal would seem consistent with his also declining decorations and distributing money given to him by the Sultan among poor students, keeping only enough for his basic subsistence. The survival of his Sufi ideals, combined with a determination to maintain independence, would seem an adequate explanation of al-Afghānī's behaviour in his last years, if it were not for the conflicting reports of his 'un-Islamic' lapses and the suspicions of Shaykh Abū'l-Hudā and his circle.

Shaykh Abū'l-Hudā's suspicions about al-Afghānī's ideas do not necessarily indicate that he had departed from and actually rejected all Sufism. The Syrian shaykh seems to have been more concerned about the sayyid's Shīʿī Iranian origins and the way in which he sought to minimize Sunni-Shīʿī divisions, so deeply ingrained in the long history of hostility between the Ottoman Empire and Iran. Shaykh Abū'l-Hudā may also have been disturbed by al-Afghānī's attempts to smooth away the essential differences between Judaism, Christianity and Islam. Points of divergence were owing to ignorant misunderstanding on the part of religious leaders, according to al-Afghānī, and an effort must be made to reinterpret whatever appeared contradictory in the three religions so that it would be possible to recapture the original pure faith of each. In undertaking such a reinterpretation, Sayyid Jamāl al-dīn was consciously drawing on Sufi models, claiming that 'the essential meaning of a text is often different from the apparent (*ẓāhir*) meaning, as the Sufis know.'[36] But his use of Sufi method was a very radical departure from traditional Sufi practice. Similarly, his entirely novel approach to reading the Qur'ān was developed out of a very unconventional adaptation of the Sufi belief in many layers of meanings being contained within a Qur'ānic verse. By an extension of this belief, al-Afghānī argued it would be possible to discover within the Qur'ān meanings previously hidden from Muslim exegetes, through which the Qur'ān would be shown to contain information and guidance relevant for Muslims to make progress in the modern world. It is hardly surprising that Shaykh Abū'l-Hudā and his fellow traditionalists should have been sceptical about the Islamic credentials of a Shīᶜī Iranian pretending to be an Afghan and advancing some highly unusual religious views with a supposed origin in Sufi thought. On a personal note, it would have been all too obvious that they were included in the ranks of the ignorant religious leaders accused by al-Afghānī of creating spurious divisions through their errors and superstitions.

Understandably, Sayyid Jamāl al-dīn al-Afghānī's hostility towards many of the Sufis of his day was to be influential in developing negative attitudes towards Sufi traditionalism among those of a modernist inclination. Increasingly Sufis would be seen as instrumental in bringing about decline in the umma and blocking the path towards Western-style civilization and progress. On the other hand, al-Afghānī manifested his own somewhat eccentric spirituality through much of his life and his first steps towards rethinking the religion of Islam in modern terms owe much to his original Sufi training and studies. As a highly 'unorthodox' pioneer, he would also inspire future efforts to rethink the role of mysticism among modern Muslims and whether it could mean something other than what nineteenth-century Sufis held it to mean.

Sufi Orders and the Ottoman Version of Pan-Islamic Regeneration

Threats to the Islamic identity of the Ottoman Empire had increased during the nineteenth century. The confessional basis of its organization had been steadily undermined by the reforms of the

Tanzimat 'reorganizations' since the *Hatt-i şerif* of Gülhane, a royal decree of 1839, declared equality of all before the law with no distinction between the Muslims, Christians and Jews of the empire. In 1856 the *Hatt-i Humayun* extended the move away from confessionalism by abolishing the civil authority of the religious leaders over their respective communities, declared members of all faiths and denominations to be equally eligible for public office and permitted Christians and Jews to join the army. Such 'reorganizations', promoted by Westernizing reformers and under pressure from the Western powers, were perceived by many devout Muslims as threatening the demise of the Islamic state.

Other threats arose from religious critics of the Ottomans. The Arabian Wahhābīs had for long been prominent as a physical challenge on the empire's southern edge. Even when this was contained, the infiltration of their ideas among the Sultan's subjects remained a constant source of anxiety for the state, since the acceptance of Wahhābism would entail a rejection of the Ottomans' Islamic credentials. The Mahdiyya of the Sudan posed a similar problem in the late nineteenth century with their militant condemnation of un-Islamic Ottoman government.

The Ottoman claim to the Caliphate and pursuit of a Pan-Islamic policy was central to the promotion of positive views of the Ottoman Empire as the Islamic state *par excellence*. The exaltation of the Sultan as Caliph had emerged in the latter half of the eighteenth century at a low point in the fortunes of the empire, apparently 'mainly as a bargaining point in the negotiations with Russia at the end of the war of 1768–74.'[37] The proposal of this new status for the Sultan was then allowed to lapse until the time of Sultan Abdülaziz (r. 1861–76). However, it was Sultan Abdülhamid II (r. 1876–1909) who undertook the systematic development of his position as Sultan-Caliph commanding the allegiance of all Muslims world-wide. This was obviously intended to challenge the authority of European colonial powers over their Muslim subjects and to provide some leverage in any disputes with Russia, Britain and France. But it was especially important in the effort to maintain religious credibility among Muslim subjects within the borders of the Ottoman Islamic state, of whom the largest number were Arabs. Turks continued to be bound by patriotic bonds as the dominant ethnic group in government and the Eastern European Muslims, notably in Bosnia and Albania, formed much smaller constituencies. Therefore, if the Ottoman Empire were to survive with its Islamic legitimacy preserved, it must depend on the allegiance of Arab Muslims, who were exposed to the subversive demands of all those who questioned that legitimacy. If Arab Muslim loyalty were to be assured, the heads of the traditional Sufi orders still seemed particularly well suited to win the necessary support: Shaykh Abū'l-Hudā al-Ṣayyādī among the Rifāᶜiyya in Syria and Iraq; Shaykh Muḥammad Ẓāfir among the Shādhiliyya-Madaniyya in North Africa; Shaykh Faḍl among the ᶜAlawiyya of South Arabian Haḍramawt.[38] Consequently, it was not unreasonable for Sultan Abdülhamid to work through them to aid the growth of these orders in his most vulnerable provinces.

Shaykh Abū'l-Hudā al-Ṣayyādī and the Rifāᶜiyya

Shaykh Abū'l-Hudā al-Ṣayyādī and his fellow Sufi traditionalists in Istanbul have suffered from a mainly unfavourable presentation of their role. They appear most commonly as the arch-reactionary propagandists for Sultan Abdülhamid, opposed to the forces of progress, to constitutional reform and democracy,[39] to the incipient nationalisms of subject peoples in the Ottoman Empire, opposed also to anti-Sufi Wahhābism and the burgeoning of Islamic modernist thought. Shaykh Abū'l-Hudā, as chief defender of the old Ottoman order and a principal opponent of al-Afghānī, has acquired an especially negative image. From a critical viewpoint, he was a self-seeking sycophant, a hypocrite with a pious demeanour, currying favour with the Sultan and enjoying a luxurious lifestyle in his mansion in a superior suburb of Istanbul. Unlike al-Afghānī, he did not decline the Sultan's medals. His understanding of Islam was utterly different also from that of al-Afghānī and his disciples.

> Abū'l-Hudā stood for Islam as it had in fact developed with its traditions, its mystical theology, its Turkish leadership: the *umma* 'cannot agree on an error,' and if it has finally taken this shape then it must be accepted as it is. The modernists wished to proceed up the stream of development to the point at which it had gone wrong, and beyond it to the primitive Islam as they conceived it.[40]

Understandably the modernists and proto-nationalists saw little virtue in the activities of Shaykh Abū'l-Hudā and his circle in support of their older vision of the faith and its organization in the world. When the Sufi shaykhs worked to restrain the development of identity based on ethnicity, language and territory and to foster religion as the primary focus of loyalty, they were widely condemned as the dangerous tools of an autocratic and repressive rule.

It is not an easy task to extract a clear picture of Shaykh Abū'l-Hudā from the hostile legends that surround him and to disentangle any Sufi ideals from the machinations of *realpolitik*. The obscurity of his early life is not surprising in view of his humble origins. He was born in a village in the district of Ma^{c}arra to the South of Aleppo in northern Syria in July 1850 or possibly about five years earlier.[41] His father is described as a travelling tradesman who later settled to become a farmer. Illiterate himself, he was determined to educate his son, Abū'l-Hudā, and sent him to study the Qur'ān and Islamic studies under a local shaykh in Ma^{c}arra. But he was especially concerned to attend to his spiritual training and arranged for his initiation into the Rifā^{c}iyya, one of the oldest popular ṭarīqas with a strong basis in the Syrian countryside and with its fortunes rising also in the city of Aleppo. Shaykh Abū'l-Hudā writes of his early association with an influential Rifā^{c}ī shaykh who, in the 1860s, became Ḥanafī *muftī* of Aleppo, Shaykh Bahā' al-dīn. Abū'l-Hudā relates of his encounter with him:

> He granted me a diploma (*ijāza*) in some Rifā^{c}ī litanies (*awrād*) and Aḥmadī offices (*aḥzāb*) and he was the first to grant me a diploma in the litanies. I heard him reciting the great office (*ḥizb*) and the small office of Imām al-Rifā^{c}ī and I was less than fifteen at the time, so I asked him for the diploma in both and he gave it to me. He also had me listen to much of his and his father's poetry.[42]

Shaykh Bahā' al-dīn was to serve as a valuable protector, when Abū'l-Hudā and his father were ousted from their village as a result of a quarrel and he appears to have been instrumental in furthering the career of the young al-Ṣayyādī.[43] However, it is the spiritual, rather than the worldly, benefits of the connection that Shaykh Abū'l-Hudā would later recall.

His actual initiation into the Rifā^{c}iyya was through two shaykhs, ^{c}Alī b. Khayr Allāh al-Ṣayyādī of Aleppo, whom he describes as a paternal cousin, and Muḥammad Mahdī al-Rawwās, an Iraqi Rifā^{c}ī shaykh, who initiated him during a pilgrimage visit (*ziyāra*) to Baghdad in 1866–67. Shaykh Abū'l-Hudā appears to consider al-Rawwās more significant for the order by the much greater attention he devotes to his biography as against that of his cousin.[44] Like Abū'l-Hudā himself, neither had come from a notable background, despite Abū'l-Hudā's efforts to trace the descent of all of them from Aḥmad al-Ṣayyād, a grandson of Aḥmad al-Rifāᶜī, the ṭarīqa's founder. Otherwise, he is at pains to emphasize the poverty and distress from which his shaykh, al-Rawwās, rose through his spiritual qualities to recognition as a *walī Allāh*. From the lowliest beginnings as an orphan in a southern Iraqi village, he embarked on travels that took him to the holy cities of Arabia to seek knowledge from the religious scholars of Mecca and Medina. But on his way to the Ḥijāz he claimed that a miraculous event occurred. Being affected by sunstroke, al-Rawwās asked to shelter in a tent, but was turned away by its owner because he was poor and ragged. He claimed that a tree had then offered to shelter him, acknowledging him as a *walī*.

After a year in Mecca and two in Medina, al-Rawwās journeyed to Egypt where he 'stayed in the mosque of al-Azhar for thirteen years, studying the Sharīᶜa and the healing arts with the shaykhs of al-Azhar until he excelled in each subject.'[45] Still poor, he returned to Iraq where he was appointed a Rifāᶜī *khalīfa*. He then set out once more for travels that took him even further afield: to India, Khorasan and Persia, Turkistan and Kurdistan, Syria and Turkey including Istanbul, before a return to the Ḥijāz and beyond to Yemen, Najd and Baḥrayn. But by now he was not merely an orphan scorned on account of his poverty. He was treated with respect in meetings with top scholars and shaykhs and, above all, honoured by God with the higher stations of the Path and chosen for His service.

Shaykh Abū'l-Hudā's biographical notice of his spiritual mentor is, on the face of it, a standard piece of hagiographical writing, but it is interesting for what it does and does not stress and that may become more readily understandable when the target audience is considered. The book on the Rifāᶜiyya, in which this account appears, was composed by Abū'l-Hudā in the late 1880s at the height of his power and influence in Istanbul. It was a time when Sultan Abdülhamid was exercising strict control over all Arabic publications and preventing the circulation of any material that might encourage opposition to his policies. However, 'while historical and literary works pertaining to Arabic culture were officially frowned upon, there was an outflow of sufi material.... Abulhuda and his circle alone published about ten books and booklets a year on average; for many people this was their only reading material.'[46] Shaykh Abū'l-Hudā's record of al-Rawwās was, therefore, not simply a fond recollection of his master, but geared to the wider aims of the Sultan's propaganda and aimed at a captive readership. The glorification of the Rifāᶜiyya had an important role in seeking to promote the order among the popular classes of Syria and Iraq and is consequently a common theme in Hamidian propaganda. The figure of al-Rawwās, as presented by Abū'l-Hudā, is also one with whom the public could be expected to identify. His is the classic story of the poor village boy made good, one of themselves who is not barred from the highest achievements, even though he is not born into a family of scholars or notables. The details of his studies and the men with whom he sought knowledge are noticeably absent. He is learned as far as the common people are concerned, but more space is devoted to praise of his spiritual qualities and miracles that provide the proof of his saintly status. It is probably also significant that he is an Iraqi from the area of the ṭarīqa's origins and might help to provide a focus for the Rifāᶜiyya's revival in that province, thus complementing Abū'l-Hudā's activities in Syria. Sultan Abdülhamid provided funds to restore the tomb of Aḥmad al-Rifāᶜī in the marshes of southern Iraq and encouraged its development as a site for pilgrimage visits. The promotion of a more recent 'saint', identifiable as one of their own and with such a close connection to Shaykh Abū'l-Hudā, would hopefully also foster the allegiance of a population easily disaffected in a district notoriously difficult to control.

After the tale of career success and the confirmatory miracle stories, Shaykh Abū'l-Hudā concludes his account of al-Rawwās with an outline of his teachings. Here is the core of the message and it is delivered from one who is a real people's saint. The preaching is not of a complex mystical doctrine, but of the need to adhere firmly to the Rifāᶜī ṭarīqa, and, in doing so, to follow the Sunna, for the morals of al-Rifāᶜī are those of the Prophet. The people are to honour the *awliyā'*, for God favours those who love them and seek their intercession. But, in honouring their shrines, they must not indulge in practices contrary to the Sharīᶜa. Thus it is the Sufis who are the true guardians of the Sunna and the preservers of religion.

Yet however much Shaykh Abū'l-Hudā wished to promote the Rifāᶜiyya, he was also aware of the importance of a unified Sufi position. In a pamphlet of 1892–3 he sought to overcome a rift between Rifāᶜīs and Qādirīs. On the one hand, he asserted the nobility of his order as the way of the respected early master al-Junayd (d. 910) and of strict adherence to the Sunna. On the other, he stated that 'al-Rifāᶜī, al-Jīlānī, al-Badawī, al-Dasūqī, al-Shādhilī, al-Suhrawardī, nay all God's friends in the company of the noble, are brothers on one prayer-carpet.'[47] There are no serious differences in their genuine teachings, but corruptions have crept in and caused deviations, such as those resulting from acceptance of certain false ecstatic utterances (*shaṭḥiyyāt*). The true way is shared by all the great masters and Abū'l-Hudā expresses a readiness to accept the followers of non-Rifāᶜī shaykhs, provided that their views correspond with his own, as he believes will be the case if they keep strictly to the original, uncorrupted teachings of their ṭarīqa.

Shaykh Abū'l-Hudā was the defender of a conservative Sufi vision, working to hold together a crumbling social fabric. However, he was not ready like Aḥmad Rizā Khān of the Indian Barēlwīs to champion every popular belief that critics might label superstitious innovation. Instead he admitted the dangers of straying from the true Sufism, but upheld genuine Sufis as the real Sunnis, on whom the survival of the Ottoman Islamic state depended. Whatever his personal faults, he possessed not inconsiderable skills in communicating with the Muslim populations of Syria and Iraq in terms that were for them religiously meaningful. His work in support of his ṭarīqa and mystical interpretations of Islam helped to strengthen organized Sufism in the Arab East and oversee a successful expansion over some thirty years from the late 1870s, until the revolution of 1908 forced the restoration of the Ottoman constitution and the influence of Shaykh Abū'l-Hudā and his Sufi associates fell into decline.

Syrian Sufis and the Question of Progress Before World War I

Followers of Shaykh Abū'l-Hudā might be presumed to fit al-Afghānī's descriptions of traditionalists who showed no interest in scientific and technological advances and did not seek to know 'the causes of electricity, the steamboat and railroads.' Certainly Abū'l-Hudā's conservative Syrian supporters seem mainly concerned with the defence of Sufism, especially its folk manifestations in the form of visits to shrines and praying for the intercession of *awliyā'*.[48] Their faith is generally buttressed with tales of these saints' miracles rather than by resort to rational proofs. They steadily oppose all calls for *ijtihād* and see dangers in the type of individual reasoning that could be introduced by its use, fearing that it will open the door to the

Westernization of Islamic thought. Would-be reformers are regarded as enemies, aiming at the destruction of Islam and the spread of atheism. This traditionalist stance appears so embattled that it is hard to visualize a more unfavourable soil for the implantation of Western ideas. And yet there are some indications that even such avowed critics of the West were not totally impervious to the penetration of European thought, not wholly uninterested in modern science and technology.

The conservatives found themselves under increasing pressure to compete for popular support with those who advocated the adoption of all means to achieve Western-style progress. Towards the end of April of 1909, Sultan Abdülhamid was forcibly deposed, resulting in a weakening of the traditionalists' position in Damascus. In 1910, in a climate of intense rivalry with their reformist critics, conservative Sufis launched a monthly journal entitled *al-Ḥaqā'iq* (Realities), denoting the Sufi perspective of the editors. What might appear surprising is that they used the publication to call on Muslims 'to achieve progress by borrowing European inventions.'[49] There seems to be no clear realization on their part of the way in which a European-derived concept of progress, alien to Sufi thought, had crept into their consciousness and moulded the outlook of even these arch-traditionalist Sufis. Over two years, until the journal ceased publication in 1912, contributors declared their concern to build factories in order to boost local manufacturers and thus counter the flooding of the market with imports from Europe. They wrote of the need to modernize agriculture by the use of the latest machinery and to improve public health by support for a new water system for Damascus.

The traditionalists, nevertheless, expressed their concerns about the danger to Islamic society from the penetration of Western values and proposed to respond by reviving true Islamic learning. They spoke of the importance of offering better training to a new generation of ᶜulamā', encouraging close adherence to Qur'ān and Sunna, cleaving to the Sunni law schools by strict observance of *taqlīd* (relying on the teachings of their past masters without fresh investigation through ijtihād). The pages of this short-lived journal offer a glimpse of how even the most conservative of Sufis were caught in the pressure to think of material as well as spiritual progress in the years before World War I and, in the process, were led perilously close to effecting a compromise between timeless Sufi ideals and worldly demands.

Notes

1 On Flaubert's journey in Egypt see Francis Steegmuller trans. and ed., *Flaubert in Egypt: A Sensibility on Tour* (Boston: Little, Brown and Co., 1973).

2 My translation from French text of Ernest Renan, *L'avenir de la science* (Paris, 1890), quoted in Albert Hourani, *Arabic Thought in the Liberal Age, 1798–1939* (London: Oxford University Press, 1962), 121. *L'avenir* was written in 1848, but only published in 1890. On Renan and his relationship to the Orient see Edward Said, *Orientalism* (London: Routledge and Kegan Paul Ltd, 1978), 130–48.

3 On popular veneration of the Prophet see Annemarie Schimmel, *And Muḥammad is His Messenger* (Chapel Hill: University of North Carolina Press, 1985).

4 Herbert Spencer was making use of the theory of French biologist Jean Lamarck (1744–1829), according to which an organism's traits acquired during its lifetime were inheritable, a theory which was challenged by Darwin.

5 On Sayyid Aḥmad Khān's early religious writings see Christian W. Troll, *Sayyid Aḥmad Khān: A Reinterpretation of Muslim Theology* (New Delhi: Vikas, 1978), 28–57.

6 Sayyid Aḥmad wrote three political pamphlets relating to the Mutiny: a history of the revolt in Bijnor (1858); *Asbāb-i Baghāwat-i Hind* (Causes of the Indian Revolt) (1858); and *On The Loyal Muhammadans of India* (1860), intended to be published as a journal in Urdu and English, but which closed down after only three issues due to lack of funds.

7 On the Muhammadan Anglo-Oriental College and Sayyid Aḥmad's work in relation to it see David Lelyveld, *Aligarh's First Generation: Muslim Solidarity in British India* (Princeton N.J.: Princeton University Press, 1978).

8 Bashir Aḥmad Dar, *Religious Thought of Sayyid Ahmad Khan*, 2d ed. (Lahore: Institute of Islamic Culture, 1971), remarks (134) on Sayyid Aḥmad's move from 'unbounded admiration' of the jihādists to a rejection of their position owing to their failure. Dar notes that a chapter devoted to them in his early book *Āthār al-ṣanādīd* (1847) was cut out by him from a later edition.

9 *Aligarh Institute Gazette*, 15 October 1869, quoted in Lelyveld, *Aligarh's First Generation*, 106.

10 Quoted in Dar, *Religious Thought*, 11.

11 Sayyid Aḥmad Khān, 'Lecture on Islam' in *Islam in Transition: Muslim Perspectives*, eds. John J. Donohue and John L. Esposito (New York and Oxford: Oxford University Press, 1982), 42. For the full text of the lecture see Troll, *Sayyid Ahmad Khan*, 307–32.

12 *Islam in Transition*, 43.

13 Sayyid Aḥmad had on occasion described himself as 'Wahhābī', alluding to his opposition to certain aspects of Sufism seen by him as accretions covering the pure Islam. The Sufi critic noted is Khayr al-dīn, father of the conservative reformer Abū'l-Kalām Āzād (1888–1958).

14 On Jamāl al-dīn al-Afghānī's treatise, see below (p. 70 and n. 28); for further details, Nikki R. Keddie, *Sayyid Jamal al-din "al-Afghani": A Political Biography* (Berkeley, Los Angeles and London: University of California Press, 1972), 156–81.

15 Dar, *Religious Thought*, 179–80. On Sayyid Aḥmad Khān's understanding of prophethood and the miraculous in general, see Troll, *Sayyid Ahmad Khan*, 171–93.

16 The most extensive attempt to reconstruct al-Afghānī's career is that of Nikki R. Keddie in her biography, *Sayyid Jamal al-Din "al-Afghani"*, noted above.

17 See Albert Hourani, *Arabic Thought*, 107–8. Shaykh Abū'l-Hudā was a Syrian Arab of the Rifāᶜiyya and highly influential at the Ottoman court of Sultan Abdülhamid II. His views on al-Afghānī's Iranian identity were shared (at least in the 1890s in Istanbul) by the Iranian Ambassador, the Ottoman police and perhaps generally by Ottoman officialdom; see Roderic H. Davison, 'Jamal al-Din Afghani: a note on his nationality and on his burial,' *MES* 24 (1988): 110–12.

18 The works of Shihāb al-dīn al-Suhrawardī and Mullā Ṣadrā had also continued to be taught in Indian Sunni mystical circles.

19 Keddie, *Sayyid Jamal al-Din* remarks (38) on his possessing the two treatises, one being a copy in his own handwriting of a twelve-page work of a Neoplatonic theosophical type by Ḥājjī M. Khān Kirmānī, the third Shaykhī leader, dated in al-Afghānī's notebook as copied at Qandahar, Afghanistan in April 1867.

20 On al-Afghānī's association with Azalīs see Mangol Bayat, *Iran's First Revolution: Shi'ism and the Constitutional Revolution of 1905–1909* (New York and Oxford: Oxford University Press, 1991), 22–3, 54–8.

21 Quoted in *Sayyid Jamal al-Din*, 54.

22 Ibid., 38.

23 Ibid., 63. From a speech given at the Darülfünun, Istanbul in February 1870.

24 A. Albert Kudsi-Zadeh provides details of the circle and al-Afghānī's teaching in 'Islamic Reform in Egypt: Some Observations on the Role of Afghani,' *MW* 61 (1971): 1–12.

25 Jamāl al-dīn al-Afghānī, 'Lecture on Teaching and Learning' delivered in Albert Hall, Calcutta, 8 November 1882. Trans. and ed. Nikki R. Keddie, *An Islamic Response to Imperialism: Political and Religious Writings of Sayyid Jamal al-din al-Afghani* 2d ed. (Berkeley: University of California Press, 1983), 101.

26 al-Afghānī, 'Commentary on the Commentator,' in *Islamic Response*, 128. The article was first published (in Persian) in a collection entitled *Maqālāt-i Jamāliyya* in Calcutta in 1884.

27 Ibid., 129.

28 The original Persian version has been translated by Keddie in *Islamic Response*, 130–74. The Arabic translation by Muḥammad ᶜAbduh and Abū Turāb appeared as *al-Radd ᶜalā 'l-dahriyyīn* in Beirut in 1886.

29 Ibid., 156–8.

30 'Lecture on Teaching and Learning' in *Islamic Response*,105.

31 Ibid., 106.

32 On *al-ᶜUrwa* see *Sayyid Jamal al-Din,* Chapter 8. Several articles printed in the journal between 13 March and 16 October 1884 have been translated into French by Marcel Colombe in *Orient* 6–7 (1958–9): see also *Islamic Response.*

33 The assassin, Mirzā Rizā Kirmānī, had been a servant of al-Afghānī and had visited him in Istanbul shortly before travelling to Iran, where he shot Shāh Nāṣir al-dīn at a shrine outside Tehran on 1 May 1896.

34 Keddie, *Sayyid Jamal al-Din,* 398–9 records these stories on the authority of ᶜAbd al-Qādir al-Maghribī, whom she considers generally reliable, although writing many years later (388).

35 Menahem Milson, 'The Elusive Jamāl al-dīn al-Afghānī,' *MW* 58 (1968): 301–4, supports an interpretation of al-Afghānī's actions consistent with a traditional ascetic view on the merits of celibacy, mingled perhaps with a more pragmatic element of caution concerning the Sultan's gifts. He takes issue with Elie Kedourie's more sceptical portrait of al-Afghānī in *Afghani and ᶜAbduh: an essay on religious unbelief and political activism in modern Islam* (London: Frank Cass and Co., 1966).

36 Keddie, *Sayyid Jamal al-Din,* 397–8.

37 Albert Hourani, *Arabic Thought,* 106.

38 While the Rifāᶜiyya, deriving from Aḥmad al-Rifāᶜī (1106–82) in southern Iraq, was one of the earliest to develop a popular following, the Madaniyya arose as a separate ṭarīqa from the Shādhilī tradition in the nineteenth century in Ḥijāz and Libya, spreading to Egypt. In Syria it gave rise to the sub-order of the Yashruṭiyya with its centre at Acre, Palestine. The ᶜAlawiyya, founded in the thirteenth century, was different again in being a family-led ṭarīqa that effectively excluded others from its area of dominance in Haḍramawt.

39 The Ottoman constitution promulgated towards the end of 1876 had provided for an appointed Senate and elected Chamber of Deputies, but was suspended by the new Sultan Abdülhamid shortly after its creation in favour of his personal rule supported by conservative advisers, among whom these Arab Sufi shaykhs were of central importance.

40 Hourani, *Arabic Thought,* 267–8.

41 The outline of Abū'l-Hudā's life and career is based on his own writings and on B. Abu-Manneh, 'Sultan Abdulhamid II and Shaikh Abulhuda al-Sayyadi,' *MES* 15 (1979): 131–53. For his date of birth see Abu-Manneh, 131 and 149 n.2.

42 Muḥammad Abū'l-Hudā al-Ṣayyādī, *Tanwīr al-abṣār fī ṭabaqāt al-sādat al-Rifāᶜiyya al-Akhyār* (Cairo, 1306/1888–9).

43 Abu-Manneh, 132–3 notes Shaykh Bahā' al-dīn's role in certifying Abū'l-Hudā's status as a sayyid and a Rifāᶜī genealogy designed to assist in gaining control over a desirable local shrine endowment (*waqf*) of a Rifāᶜī 'saint', Aḥmad al-Ṣayyād, and to acquire subsequent positions as *naqīb al-ashrāf* of a small township and later of Aleppo.

44 *Tanwīr,* 122–32 on al-Rawwās and 132 on ᶜAlī b. Khayr Allāh.

45 Ibid., 122.

46 Abu-Manneh, 148.

47 M. Abū'l-Hudā al-Ṣayyādī, *al-Ḥaqq al-mubīn fī ibhāt al-ḥāsidīn* (Cairo, 1310/1892–3), 12. The founders of several popular ṭarīqas are named here to stress the essential truth of all.

48 See David Dean Commins, *Islamic Reform: Politics and Social Change in Late Ottoman Syria* (New York and Oxford: Oxford University Press, 1990), Chapter 9, for the views of these conservative Damascus Sufis pre-World War I. A prominent figure under the patronage of Abū'l-Hudā was the Palestinian Shaykh Yūsuf al-Nabahānī (1849–1932), an active writer in defence of the conservative Sufi position.

49 Ibid., 119.

4

The Sufism and Anti-Sufism of the Salafis

Muḥammad ᶜAbduh (1849–1905), Sufi and Anti-Sufi

Muḥammad ᶜAbduh, by far the most renowned of al-Afghānī's Egyptian disciples, was an almost exact contemporary of Abū'l-Hudā al-Ṣayyādī and there are certain similarities in their background and early experience, which might normally pass unnoticed due to the very great differences in their later development. Both were allegedly born in the Islamic year 1266 (1849–50), although there are some mentions of slightly earlier dates. Both were of Arab peasant origins, their fathers illiterate and undergoing some problems in their villages, leading rather unsettled lives themselves, but anxious to secure some improvement for their sons through a religious education. Both arranged for their sons to study the Qur'ān under local shaykhs and advance further through contacts with regional centres of learning and spirituality, Abū'l-Hudā al-Ṣayyādī in Aleppo, Muḥammad ᶜAbduh in Ṭanṭā in the Egyptian delta. But the two boys responded very differently to the traditional systems of religious studies, Abū'l-Hudā adapting readily, the young Muḥammad running away from studies that he found unbearably tedious, as they demanded the rote learning of commentaries on classic texts without any attempt at effective explanation. However, it was through this rebellious escape from formal studies that he was able to discover Sufism.

ᶜAbduh as Sufi

When he ran from his studies in the Aḥmadī Mosque at Ṭanṭā, ᶜAbduh eventually returned home and was married at the age of sixteen. According to a brief sample of autobiography, it was forty days later (surely a spiritually significant timing) that his father made the fateful decision that his son should return to Ṭanṭā. On the way

Muḥammad once again escaped at a village where his father's maternal relatives were living and there he encountered a man who was to have a critical influence on his growth in religious understanding and aspiration, his father's maternal uncle, Shaykh Darwīsh Khaḍir.[1] At this time Abū'l-Hudā had already been initiated into the Rifāᶜiyya by his paternal cousin and was to travel in the following year to Baghdad to his own encounter with destiny in the form of Shaykh al-Rawwās. In both cases critical influences on their spiritual development were relatives and people of humble rural background, but who had travelled in search of knowledge and spiritual guidance. Beyond that there are significant differences in the natures and outlook of these mentors.

As has been noted, Abū'l-Hudā's shaykhs and teachers were tied into the traditional structure of an antique popular ṭarīqa and their careers were closely linked to their progress in the Rifāᶜiyya. They retained an outlook little different, on the whole, from that of their medieval predecessors. There was little opportunity to break free of the old patterns and little incentive to seek advancement by other means for men of their social background in the Eastern Arab provinces of the mid-nineteenth century Ottoman Empire.

While ᶜAbduh's teachers in Ṭanṭā and many of his later masters at al-Azhar were bound in the same traditional world, his two most influential guides were noticeably outside this formal network of ancient scholarship and organized spirituality. With regard to Sufism, they did not accept its actually existing state as all that it should be, although they had been deeply touched by visions of what the mystical life could offer. They were also more open to reflecting on alternative answers to the important questions of existence, even when these answers were proposed by Western non-Muslims. In Egypt in the 1860s and 70s ᶜAbduh was to be exposed through Shaykh Darwīsh and Jamāl al-dīn al-Afghānī to currents of thought denied to his Syrian contemporary.

According to his own account, ᶜAbduh was not immediately receptive to guidance on his first arrival in his great uncle's village. When Shaykh Darwīsh asked him to read aloud from a book of Sufi letters because of his own poor sight, the young Muḥammad cursed reading and anyone connected with it and ran off. However, the shaykh was gently persistent and soon weaned him off his natural preference for amusing himself with the boys of the village, horse-riding and swimming in a nearby river. Within three days, (unless this is a symbolic number), he became totally absorbed in his new-found studies and Sufism began to take over his life, as the shaykh expounded to him textual meanings in a way that he had never previously encountered. Of the book that so enthralled him and won him over, with his great-uncle's persuasion, to the mystical life, he records:

> These letters contained sufistic knowledge (*ma*ᶜ*ārif*), and spoke much of the discipline of the self (*al-nafs*) and training it in noble conduct, purifying it of the filth of vices and arousing in it a dislike of the falseness of the outward appearances of this worldly life.[2]

The letters, in their fine Maghribī script, were the work of Shaykh Darwīsh's own master, Sayyid Muḥammad al-Madanī (d. 1846).[3] ᶜAbduh, looking back on this experience in later life, is anxious to show his uncle as something more perhaps than a peasant who has had contacts only with the more pedestrian aspects of folk Sufism, replete with superstition. He thus narrates his seeking of knowledge beyond the confines of the Egyptian countryside:

> One of my father's uncles, Shaykh Darwīsh, had previously travelled to the Libyan desert and journeyed as far as Tripoli, where he sat at the feet of Sayyid Muḥammad al-Madanī, father of the famous Shaykh Ẓāfir, who used to live in Istanbul and died there. He studied under him and was initiated by him into the Shādhilī *ṭarīqa*. He learned by heart *al-Muwaṭṭa'* (of Mālik b. Anas) and some books of Ḥadīth. He excelled in learning the Qur'ān by heart and understanding it. Then he returned from his travels to his home village and worked in the ordinary way in farming and earning a livelihood by agriculture.[4]

The implication is that Shaykh Darwīsh, despite his peasant status, was no ignorant ecstatic, but his mysticism was underpinned with knowledge of Qur'ān and Ḥadīth and of classical Mālikī jurisprudence. Furthermore, he had gained this knowledge through one of the most highly esteemed shaykhs of the Arab lands, head of the highly successful Shādhiliyya-Madaniyya. Shaykh Ẓāfir has already been noted in the circle of Sultan Abdülhamid II in Istanbul, playing a role within this North African order very similar to that of Abū'l-Hudā al-Ṣayyādī in Syria and Iraq. He was closely associated with Muḥammad Nedim Pasha, when he was governor of Tripoli from 1860–67, and was invited to Istanbul in the 1870s after Nedim rose to the Grand Vizierate. Shaykh Ẓāfir enjoyed the confidence and favour of the

Sultan, who provided him with a *zāwiya* close to the Yildiz Palace. He stayed in Istanbul until his death.[5]

However, Shaykh Darwīsh is not presented by ᶜAbduh as stressing allegiance to the Shādhiliyya-Madaniyya or that this is the path of true Sufism. According to ᶜAbduh:

> On the seventh day I asked the shaykh, 'What is your ṭarīqa?' He said, 'Our ṭarīqa is Islam.' So I said, 'Aren't all these people Muslims?' He said, 'If they were Muslims, I wouldn't have seen them disputing over trivialities and I wouldn't have heard them allying liars with God with or without any reason. These words were like a fire that burned all my old baggage – the baggage of those vain pretensions and false conjectures, the baggage of the delusion that we were all Muslims assured of salvation, even if we were really negligent. I asked him, 'What is your *wird* (litany) that is chanted in retreats or after prayers?' He said, 'We have no *wird* but the Qur'ān, that we recite after every prayer with understanding and meditation.[6]

The nature of the Sufism into which Muḥammad ᶜAbduh claimed to have been inducted by his great-uncle seems at least as important as the fact that it was Sufism that won his enthusiasm at this critical stage in his development. It is characterized by a moral earnestness and a concern with interiorization of the faith that would have satisfied al-Ghazālī. There is a stress on spirituality firmly grounded in the Qur'ān and a belief in the essential bonding between all Muslims who live out their lives in accordance with sound Islamic principles. There is also criticism of those who do not associate Islam with activism and commitment and, it seems, of Sufis who rely on their membership of a particular ṭarīqa, however corrupted, for salvation.

Following the stay with Shaykh Darwīsh, ᶜAbduh returned to Ṭanṭā and was able to complete his studies and proceed to higher training in Cairo at al-Azhar from 1869–77. We hear of his being drawn ever more deeply into mysticism, including the practice of an extreme asceticism, from whose dangers he was rescued by the counsels of Shaykh Darwīsh and subsequently of Jamāl al-dīn al-Afghānī. He tells us that each year his great-uncle would ask after his studies at al-Azhar:

> 'Haven't you studied logic? Haven't you studied arithmetic? Haven't you studied any principles of engineering?' Then I would say to him, 'Some of these branches of knowledge are unknown at al-Azhar.'[7]

Shaykh Darwīsh appears a remarkable man from ᶜAbduh's memories of him. He is shown to be a pivotal figure in leading the young ᶜAbduh to a truer understanding of Islam as a progressive and reasonable religion compatible with modern science and technological advances. He is the guide to Sufism as it ideally should be, offering a system of training by which the human may reach a higher level of being without false and divisive doctrines and superstitious innovations (*bidaᶜ*). How reliable is the portrait of the shaykh? This remains hard to establish. Shaykh Darwīsh probably was instrumental in nourishing the ideals of the young ᶜAbduh and directing him on the path that led to his later work of reform. This being so, he should perhaps be given some of the credit that has usually been assigned to al-Afghānī. However, there are certain problems with regard to ᶜAbduh's account. The fragmentary autobiography was written near the end of his life at a time when he had achieved an international reputation as a reformer. Therefore, the possibility is increased that the details of the narrative may not be exact, but may reflect the views of the older ᶜAbduh that he has projected back onto his young life to demonstrate for public consumption how it was, from the very beginning, the 'right' kind of Sufism that he espoused and to which his great-uncle adhered. The account also fits neatly, perhaps too neatly, into the framework of a stylized spiritual autobiography that has established antecedents in the Islamic tradition, with which ᶜAbduh would have been well-acquainted. His resolution of a spiritual crisis by the discovery of Sufism has been compared to that of al-Ghazālī's famous *al-Munqidh min al-ḍalāl* (The Deliverer from Error).[8] But it also seems quite possible that ᶜAbduh would have been aware of al-Afghānī's own experience recorded by him as a young man in Afghanistan and also compared with that of the great medieval master. He may have consciously wished to relate how he too had emerged from profitless studies with ineffective teachers to achieve the true enlightenment of authentic mystical experience.

ᶜAbduh was first drawn to al-Afghānī through their common interest in mysticism. On their first encounter over supper at the house of Sayyid Jamāl al-dīn, ᶜAbduh is said to have been overwhelmed with wonder and love at the way in which the sayyid expounded the comments of Sufis on Qur'ānic verses.[9] In 1874 he published his one work wholly within the tradition of medieval Sufi theosophy, *Risālat al-wāridāt* (Mystical Inspirations). In the introduction he stresses that it was al-Afghānī who led him to true understanding after his initial interest in Sufism had already been kindled and he had broken free from the bondage of strict subservience to any particular school of thought.

> I came across the traces of true knowledge and developed a passionate love for it, but I did not discover its innermost nature, so I became disturbed and my thoughts began wandering. Whenever I asked a question, they would answer me that it was forbidden (*ḥarām*) for me to concern myself with it and that the scholastic theologians had banned discussion of it. I was truly amazed and the indifference of those who transmitted others' opinions amazed me even more. I meditated on the reason for this and I perceived that one who is ignorant of something hates it and one who keeps far from the sublime rejects it. I found them to be like one who has tasted vine leaves, so that he does not know the bitterness of colocynth or the sweetness of honey. While I was in this state, there arose the sun of truths, who clarified for us their subtle intricacies. (So it came to pass) with the arrival of the perfect sage, truth personified, our master Sayyid Jamāl al-dīn al-Afghānī.[10]

The extreme absorption in mysticism and philosophy weakened under the pressures of political and social realities in Egypt of the 1870s, as well as under Sayyid Jamāl al-dīn's influence towards active participation in the country's affairs. As Egypt slid deeper into debt under the autocratic mismanagement of Khedive Ismā^cīl, British and French bankers demanded greater financial control, which swiftly gave way to direct political intervention. Europeans were included among Egypt's government ministers from 1878. In the atmosphere of heightening tension, ^cAbduh became involved in the national opposition through his contributions to Cairo's periodical press. When al-Afghānī was deported from Egypt in 1879, ^cAbduh was forced to return to his village. However, from 1880–82 he was recalled to Cairo by the Prime Minister to serve as an editor, before becoming chief editor of the Egyptian official gazette, *al-Waqā'i^c al-Miṣriyya* (Egyptian Events). From this time he would play a more significant role in alerting the public to what he perceived as the problems of political and social decay in Egypt, problems that needed to be addressed in order to restore national strength and resist the gathering threat from Britain and France. It was a critical period for the country and for ^cAbduh, culminating in the occupation of Egypt in 1882 and ^cAbduh's arrest, imprisonment and subsequent exile in Paris and Beirut.

ʿAbduh as Anti-Sufi

To the end of his life ʿAbduh retained his deep love for the true Sufism, but he became strongly opposed to what he saw as corrupt manifestations of it in late nineteenth-century Egypt. He believed much of the actually existing Sufism of his own day to have departed from the original authentic faith of Islam. In the pages of *al-Waqā'iʿ al-Miṣriyya* he launched an open attack on certain Sufi orders as guilty of introducing unacceptable innovations (*bidaʿ*) into the mosques and contributing to the social malaise.

A typical expression of ʿAbduh's concern is contained in an article dated 30 November 1880, supporting efforts to outlaw some of the more extravagant Sufi practices at the Imām al-Ḥusayn and Sayyida Zaynab mosques in Cairo.[11] The Ministry of Public Endowments had received complaints from the management of the Ḥusayn mosque about the *dhikr* of the Saʿdiyya, a sub-order of the Rifāʿiyya and one regarded by reformers as dangerously antinomian.[12] ʿAbduh relates the nature of the complaints against the Saʿdīs:

> In the *dhikr* gathering of the Saʿdiyya which is held in that mosque every Tuesday the name of God is mentioned only to the accompaniment of the beating of the kettledrum (*al-bāz*). . . . Visitors to the grave of Imām Ḥusayn and students have censured and opposed this custom, saying it is forbidden by Sharīʿa and the ruler ought to prevent it by issuing an order for its suppression.[13]

The ministry sought a *fatwā* from the Shaykh al-Azhar, Muftī of Egypt, Muḥammad al-Mahdī al-ʿAbbāsī, who ruled that not only was the beating of drums in mosques unlawful, but so were all other noisy disturbances to worshippers, including raising the voice in *dhikr*. He also condemned gatherings which allowed the free mingling of young men and women in the mosque.

ʿAbduh expressed his approval of measures to end all such violations of the Sharīʿa, whether by Saʿdīs or other Sufis, notably Maghribīs celebrating the *mawlid* of Sayyid Ḥusayn by stripping off their clothes and walking on fire in an ecstatic state before a crowd of onlookers. He concludes in the hope that this prevention of reprehensible *bidʿa* will spread from Cairo to the countryside. The climate of public opinion seems to have been receptive to the reformers and, in this instance, their aims appear to have coincided with those of the European consular authorities, who added to the pressure on the government to take action.

Early in 1881 the khedive acted to ban the Sa^{c}dī custom of the *dawsa* (trampling), in which the shaykh rode a horse over the prostrate bodies of the *murīds*. The occasion was colourfully described by E.W. Lane earlier in the century:

> The Sheykh entered the Birket El-Ezbekeeyeh preceded by a very numerous procession of the darweeshes of whom he is the chief. In the way through this place, the procession stopped at a short distance before the house of the Sheykh El-Bekree. Here a considerable number of the darweeshes and others (I am sure that there were more than sixty, but I could not count their number), laid themselves down upon the ground, side by side, as close as possible to each other, having their backs upwards, their legs extended, and their arms placed together beneath their foreheads. They incessantly muttered the word 'Allah!' About twelve or more darweeshes, most without their shoes, then ran over the backs of their prostrate companions; some, beating 'bázes', or little drums, of a hemispherical form, held in the left hand, and exclaiming 'Allah!' and then the Sheykh approached; his horse hesitated, for several minutes, to tread upon the back of the first of the prostrate men; but being pulled, and urged on behind, he at length stepped upon him, and then, without apparent fear, ambled, with a high pace, over them all, led by two persons, who ran over the prostrate men; one sometimes treading on the feet, and the other on the heads. The spectators immediately raised a long cry of 'Allah lá lá lá lá láh!' Not one of the men thus trampled upon by the horse seemed to be hurt; but each, the moment that the animal had passed over him jumped up, and followed the Sheykh. Each of them received two treads from the horse; one from one of his forelegs, and a second from a hind-leg. It is said that these persons, as well as the Sheykh, make use of certain words (that is, repeat prayers and invocations,) on the day preceding this performance, to enable them to endure, without injury, the tread of the horse; and that some, not thus prepared, having ventured to lie down to be ridden over, have, on more than one occasion, been either killed or severely injured. The performance is considered as a miracle effected through supernatural power which has been granted to every successive Sheykh of the Saadeeyeh.[14]

Such was the unacceptable face of Sufism as far as ^{c}Abduh was concerned in this period before his exile. But his opposition to it at this stage was essentially traditional and, in effect, followed in the broad pattern of earlier eighteenth and nineteenth century reformers. Greater exposure to European thought during the years working with al-Afghānī in Paris would bring alterations to the rationale of his critical approaches to the problems of Sufi decadence and excesses.

After al-Afghānī's journal ceased publication, ᶜAbduh travelled East to Beirut where he taught at a school established by a Muslim benevolent society. Here he delivered a series of lectures that were to be developed into his best-known book, *Risālat al-tawḥīd* (The Treatise of Unity).[15] In this exposition of Islamic theology with a modernist bent, ᶜAbduh gives systematic support to a vision of Islam as a religion of reason and progress well-suited to the modern world, compatible with science and technology. There is no room in such a faith for the irrational and the world of saints and their miracles is consequently rejected. The traces of al-Afghānī's thought are evident, although the tone is calmer and more reasonable, the firebrand giving way to the systematic theologian. At the same time ᶜAbduh stops well short of Sayyid Aḥmad Khān and his attempts to rationalize the miraculous. Miracles that contravene the laws of Nature are not totally denied by ᶜAbduh, but he is cautious with regard to those charismatic gifts (*karāmāt*) attributed to saintly Sufis, believing that the ignorant masses have come to hold wrong beliefs concerning them. They have reached the point where they treat *karāmāt* as tools of a saint's profession, in which he competes with others. ᶜAbduh does not commit himself clearly regarding the possibility of such miracles, but admits that most Ashᶜarite theologians acknowledge that they may occur, while most Muᶜtazilites and one major Ashᶜarite reject them. However, he does conclude:

> Sunnis and others are agreed that it is not necessary to believe in the occurrence of any particular miracle (*karāma*) at the hand of any particular saint after the emergence of Islam. So, according to the consensus (*ijmāᶜ*) of the community, any Muslim may deny the occurrence of any miracle at all and, by denying it, he will not be acting contrary to any principles of the faith or deviating from a sound sunna or departing from the straight path.[16]

ᶜAbduh as Salafī Muftī of Egypt

By 1888 ᶜAbduh was permitted by the British occupation authorities to return to Egypt and reconciled to the pursuit of reform by peaceful co-operation. In 1899 he reached the pinnacle of his official career, being appointed as Muftī of Egypt, a position he was to hold until his death in 1905. His considerable energies were then devoted to an overhaul of the legal system and the improvement of Egyptian education, including the reform of al-Azhar.

After attaining high public office in his later life, ᶜAbduh appears to present rather different faces depending on the target of his attentions. The modernist stance is perhaps most familiar from his famous confrontations with the French historian Gabriel Hanotaux in 1900 and the Christian Syrian secularist Faraḥ Anṭūn in 1902.[17] In ᶜAbduh's refutation of Anṭūn's claims that Islam had destroyed the spirit of philosophy, he wrote in defence of the faith as rational and tolerant, contrasting Islam with a picture of Christianity as an irrational religion of miracles, itself far more hostile than Islam to scientific inquiry. Yet the Islam of reason and tolerance was the true and original religion of *al-salaf al-ṣāliḥ* (the righteous ancestors) and not of the later generations of modern Muslims who no longer were familiar with all the great authorities in their heritage. In this context the *salaf* are broadly understood to include the major figures of the 3rd and 4th centuries of Islam/the 9th and 10th centuries C.E., such as the theologians al-Ashᶜari (d. 324/935) and al-Māturīdī (d. 333/945). He also speaks with respect of the Qur'ān commentaries (*tafāsīr*) up to the twelfth century C.E. and these are noted as indispensable for the student of religion due to the wisdom that they contain from an earlier age.[18] Elsewhere *salaf*, sometimes described as *al-salaf al-awwalūn* (the first ancestors), designate more strictly the earliest generation of Muslims, especially the Rightly-Guided Caliphs. Generally, the message to European and Arab secularist critics of Islam is that they should not judge Islam by the state of knowledge and practice among their Muslim contemporaries, but by the standards of the true, original Islam. This true faith will be found to contain everything that modern Europe has only recently come to esteem as essential for enlightened progress.

Another face of ᶜAbduh in later life is that presented to an Egyptian Muslim audience, still speaking of the ideal faith of the *salaf*, but in a wholly traditional framework of Islamic discourse. There is an evident desire to return to the true ways of this early faith without any sense of a need to compare its concepts with those of nineteenth-century European thought. As Muftī of Egypt he would naturally be consulted as to the truth or falsity of much popular belief, in which Sufism occupied a central position. He can thus be seen to be engaged in the search for an authentic *salafī* Sufism. Reference here will be made to two texts from the summer of 1904. The first is a report of a conversation that took place at the house of a village *ᶜumda* in July 1904, during the course of which ᶜAbduh responded to the questions of a Shādhilī shaykh and Muḥammad Rashīd Riḍā, his close associate.[19] The second is a *fatwā* delivered by ᶜAbduh in September 1904 in reply to a question about seeking the intercession of prophets and saints.[20]

Both the conversation and the *fatwā* reveal a concern with the dangers of exposing ignorant people to matters beyond their comprehension and are aimed at correcting popular misunderstandings, especially those that can lead to *bidᶜa*. According to ᶜAbduh, many people have developed an essentially wrong attitude towards Prophet Muḥammad and the dead Sufi saints, *awliyā' Allāh*. This is manifested in the widespread practice of asking the holy dead to intercede with God. In his fatwā ᶜAbduh states that there is no evidence from the Sunna of intercession (*tawassul*) in the first three centuries of Islam, although he does note a rare and controversial case in a ḥadīth reported by al-Tirmidhī. He concludes that it is indeed *bidᶜa* and of the very worst kind that can lead to the sin of *shirk*, associating others with God. The supplicant is guilty of wrong thought about God, presumably in over-exalting the powers of human beings, a view already familiar from the Wahhābīs. Those who call upon the Prophet and saints for such favours are misled in supposing that they delight in praises and panegyrics, in emphatic pronunciation in the *dhikr*,

> and the invention of things which have no basis in the Book of God or Sunna of His messenger and no approval from the righteous ancestors (*al-salaf al-ṣāliḥ*).... This view of the prophets and saints is the worst because they have likened them in that to the tyrants of the people of this world, whose sight is covered by the darkness of ignorance before they meet death.[21]

He argues that the greatest respect they could accord the prophets would be by adhering to the revelations that they brought from God. Similarly with the saints, they would respect them best by choosing in their lives what the *awliyā'* chose for themselves. The necessity is for sound personal morality.

The same problem is addressed in ᶜAbduh's conversation with the Sufi Shaykh Muḥammad al-Dalāṣī. ᶜAbduh remarks to him not only that the practice of intercession is at variance with the guidance of the salaf, but that people ask the saints for this-worldly favours, such as money, a good harvest, healing of illness and revenge on their enemies. It would be more reasonable if they were to ask them about matters relating to the Afterlife, but in truth the mysteries that God has made known to them are only accessible to those who are able to 'taste' them, to experience them directly for themselves.[22]

ᶜAbduh sees considerable dangers arising from misconceptions about the teachings of Sufism. Even those who are well-trained in the exoteric aspects of the faith may not appreciate the real significance of Sufi speech because it is clothed in symbolism and technicalities. Therefore, he maintains that Muslims who read only the exoteric meaning of a text may go astray. Books of Ibn al-ᶜArabī appear on the surface to contradict the principles of the faith, as does *al-Insān al-Kāmil* (The Perfect Man) of ᶜAbd al-Karīm al-Jīlī (d. c. 1410). The latter seems outwardly closer to Christianity than to Islam

> but this exterior meaning is not what is intended and the speech alludes to meanings known only to one who knows their key. . . . When I was in charge of the printing presses, I ordered a ban on printing *al-Futūḥāt al-Makkiyya* (Meccan Revelations) and their like because books of this kind should only be looked at by their own people (i.e. Sufis).[23]

ᶜAbduh's explanation of his reasons for halting the publication of the *Futūḥāt* reveals not a serious disapproval of Ibn al-ᶜArabī's major work but a fear of its corrupting effects on those unable to discover its hidden meanings. His personal respect for Ibn al-ᶜArabī is visible from the fatwā where ᶜAbduh cites comments from the *Futūḥāt* on Sūrat al-Baqara v. 186, counselling against the need for any intercession since God is always near.[24]

Illustrative of the difficulties associated with the allegorical speech of Sufis is a sample of the July 1904 conversation, when Rashīd Riḍā questioned ᶜAbduh about the supposed existence of a council of living and dead saints regulating world affairs. Riḍā expressed his doubts, seeing that the strength of the Muslims was in the past, so how could they be weak now with the agreement of all these saints? ᶜAbduh first mentions the suggestion that 'God's friends' have observed that the Muslims have departed far from the original faith and are hoping to drive them back to Islam through these misfortunes. But he discounts this explanation. The council of saints, he claims, is to be understood as a symbolic reference 'to the situation in the time of the salaf, when this community was alive and well.'[25] However, it was not the Sufis who were to blame for its decline, but the jurists and judges who opposed them and so forced the Sufis to resort to secrecy and the use of technical and symbolic language. ᶜAbduh's explanation is expressed in Sufi terms and makes it plain, as on other occasions, that his sympathies were with the Sufis against their legalist critics. However, he genuinely regretted the move to esotericism for the damage that it had done and was continuing to do to the community, since the majority of Muslims could be misled by it. There is also a point at which ᶜAbduh seems to cross over from unveiling hidden meanings in Sufi style to seeking a rational explanation for an embarrassing superstition.

In addition to the problems arising from misunderstanding of Sufi mysteries, ᶜAbduh locates a further difficulty in the existence, as he maintains, of forged works attributed to famous Sufi masters of the past, such as the sixteenth-century Egyptian Sufi ᶜAbd al-Wahhāb al-Shaᶜrānī (1492–1565). According to ᶜAbduh, these forgeries contain material contrary to the Qur'ān and Sunna. In this context he asserts his own continuing allegiance to the Shādhiliyya, but warns that even some of the prayers of al-Shādhilī are suspect:

> I respect Abū'l-Ḥasan al-Shādhilī and I belong to his ṭarīqa and have not followed any other. But not everything attributed to him is correctly ascribed.[26]

There is, therefore, a serious risk of people being led astray, if they accept such works at face value and follow them even when they are not in conformity with the Qur'ān and Sunna and the views of the salaf.

At the end of his life ᶜAbduh retained a personal commitment to what may be described as salafī Sufism, benefiting from the spiritual training he had received since his early encounters with Shaykh Darwīsh and al-Afghānī, but rejecting any Sufi teachings that might contradict those of al-salaf al-ṣāliḥ. It was an openly élitist view of Islam that he espoused. Sufism was for the spiritual elect, not for the ignorant mass who failed to interpret its messages correctly and fell prey all too easily to charges of bidᶜa. However, his desire to rid popular Sufism of unacceptable accretions was remembered chiefly in terms of anti-Sufism and seen as contributing to the decay of the Sufi orders.

Muḥammad Rashīd Riḍā, Anti-Sufi (1865–1935)

Where Muḥammad ᶜAbduh developed the intellectual foundations for a modern salafī rethinking of Sufism, Muḥammad Rashīd Riḍā built on those foundations and made them known to a wide audience across the Islamic world from Morocco to Indonesia. In the process he also moved and moved others in the direction of a more rigorous anti-Sufism.

Rashīd Riḍā was born in 1865 in a village near the town of Tripoli on the Syrian coast (present day northern Lebanon). It was a town with a strong tradition of Sunni piety, in which Sufi orders played an active role. Riḍā's family background was not dissimilar to that of ᶜAbduh, but he was able to benefit from a more modern education provided by the National Islamic School in Tripoli, which taught Arabic, Turkish and religious studies alongside French, mathematics and natural sciences. Like ᶜAbduh, he was attracted to Sufism at an early age and, also like him and al-Afghānī, recorded his experiences in the form of spiritual autobiography.[27] Riḍā was deeply impressed by al-Ghazālī's *Iḥyā' ᶜulūm al-dīn* (Revival of the Religious Sciences) and it helped to mould his conviction that the Muslim should consciously interiorize the faith and go beyond the mere externals of observance, being constantly aware of the ethical implications of actions. He describes how, for a while, he gave himself up to a régime of severe ascetic practices in order to cultivate the proper spirit of devotion:

> I was striving to follow the Sufi Way by leaving the best food and being satisfied with a little wild thyme with salt and sumac and by sleeping on the ground etc., until it was no longer any trouble deliberately to leave the best food available. But I tried to accustom myself to put up with dirt on my body and clothes, which is not lawful, and I was unable to do so.[28]

He subsequently sought to place himself as a *murīd* under the spiritual guidance of a Naqshabandī shaykh. He records remarkable mystical experiences that he underwent at that time: the sensation of moving outside his body, while reading the *Iḥyā'*; visions of future events; even the claims that his prayers were swiftly answered and that he was enabled to heal the sick in an apparently miraculous way. Another man might have considered such 'gifts' as *karāmāt* and in time accepted the status of a *walī Allāh*. Riḍā seems to have exercised his reason and searched his conscience in a way that eventually led him to reject the validity of much that was accepted in the Sufism of even the most reform-minded and stern of Naqshabandīs, condemning even the silent *dhikr*:

> My daily office in this ṭarīqa was the mention of God's Majesty in my heart, without voicing it, five thousand times, closing my eyes and holding my breath as long as possible, fixing my attention on the bonding of my heart with the heart of the shaykh, and this kind of dhikr is unlawful.[29]

The moment at which he turned off the Way may or may not be encapsulated in his own account of revulsion at bidᶜa, when he attended the dhikr of the Mawlawīs at their well-known *zāwiya* in Tripoli in its idyllic pastoral setting by the River Abū ᶜAlī. He observed the famous dance of the 'Whirling Dervishes' with 'handsome beardless youths among them, dressed in snow-white gowns like brides' dresses, dancing to the moving sound of the reed-pipe, turning swiftly and skilfully so that their robes flew out and formed circles, at harmonious distances and not encroaching on one another.'[30] Riḍā relates that he was overcome with anger at the sight of such 'forbidden acts' and shouted at the assembled company before retiring from the scene. His revulsion at the Mawlawī dhikr seems part of a more vehement and intense reaction against the excesses of 'false' Sufism than anything experienced by ᶜAbduh. Although it might at the time have been in keeping with the outlook of a reformist Naqshabandī, Riḍā would be driven to a more critical questioning of the scope of Sufism than that of Naqshabandīs. While he might come theoretically to acknowledge, with ᶜAbduh, the continuing existence of a 'true' Sufism, for him it would gradually cease to command his personal commitment.

While al-Ghazālī's *Iḥya'* had drawn the youthful Rashīd Riḍā into a concentration on spiritual preparation for the hereafter, his discovery, in 1892, of old copies of *al-ᶜUrwa al-Wuthqā* among his father's papers led him towards a fresh appreciation of Islam as a religion concerned also with this life and the regulation of temporal affairs. He described the effect of the journal on him at that time as like an electric current giving his soul a shock. It was not his earliest encounter with *al-ᶜUrwa*, but it reoriented him at a critical point in his life, helping to harness his energies in new channels of activist reform. He wrote to al-Afghānī in Istanbul, beseeching him to accept him as his *murīd*, showering him with extravagant praises couched in Sufistic terminology, speaking of him as 'the perfect man' (*al-insān al-kāmil*) and the 'beauty of this world and of the faith' (*Jamāl al-dunyā wa'l-dīn*).[31] But the attempt to join al-Afghānī failed and it was not until 1897 (the year of Jamāl al-dīn's death) that Riḍā made his secret journey to join Muḥammad ᶜAbduh in Egypt, secrecy being necessary to avoid attracting the unwelcome attention of the Ottoman authorities.

Once settled in Cairo, Riḍā became almost inseparably associated with ᶜAbduh, acknowledging himself in the role that he had sought with al-Afghānī, that of murīd, but with the proviso that he would not surrender himself totally to his master in the Sufi manner, but would accept only as much as he understood and would retain his independence of judgement. In 1898 he began the publication of the famous periodical *al-Manār*, intended to serve as an organ for the promotion of salafī reform and with the backing of ᶜAbduh. Riḍā was to continue as editor until his death in 1935, proclaiming himself as ᶜAbduh's trusted spiritual heir, although his status as such was questioned in some quarters.[32]

Through the pages of *al-Manār* salafī critiques of contemporary Sufism reached a wide public and generated an extensive correspondence around the *umma*. During ᶜAbduh's lifetime, in early issues from 1898 to 1903, Riḍā's warnings about the dangers of focusing attention on saintly karāmāt clearly reflect his master's concerns. However, in later life Riḍā embraced harsher anti-Sufi views, inspired especially by the teachings of Ibn Taymiyya and Wahhābīs. In the 1920s Wahhābī reassertion was attracting attention on the international scene with Ibn Suᶜūd's expansionist campaigns in Arabia, culminating in his invasion of the Ḥijāz in 1924 and assumption of the title of king of the Ḥijāz in 1926. Riḍā wrote a book at this time in support of Ibn Suᶜūd as a defender of true Sunnism and declared the Wahhābī doctrines to represent the original faith.[33] This was also the stand that he adopted in *al-Manār* and it coincides with forceful attacks on Sufi deviations.

The Tijāniyya was an order that was criticized with a notable degree of zeal.[34] In the issue of 14 March 1926, Riḍā replied to a question from an Algerian correspondent as to the possibility of seeing the Prophet while awake, as Aḥmad al-Tijānī claimed to have done. Riḍā discounted it and somewhat indirectly denounced al-Tijānī as an unbeliever, leading astray millions of people in Africa, and particularly in Algeria. He also published a student's rebuttal of the Tijānī belief that their founder had been taught a special prayer by the Prophet, *al-Ṣalāt al-Fātiḥ*, which was not made known to the Companions in his lifetime. According to the article, this was tantamount to devaluing the Prophet's mission on earth, and even more alarming were the claims of Tijānīs that the prayer was a part of

God's eternal speech, which would only be beneficial to those who acknowledged the truth of such a belief. Riḍā added his own comments to the effect that al-Tijānī was a liar and he condemned all those Sufi shaykhs who exploited their supposed miraculous gifts for their own worldly advancement. The tone of his criticisms would probably have found favour with Ibn Suᶜūd and enemies were ready to accuse him of being a Wahhābī.

Riḍā certainly appears to have gone beyond ᶜAbduh in doubting the acceptability of core aspects of Sufism. He argued against the desirability of pursuing the Path to the point of *fanā'*, maintaining that a Muslim did not need to, and perhaps could not, pass beyond the station of absolute trust in God (*tawakkul*). Nor was there a sound purpose in the spiritual guide-disciple relationship, since it discouraged the development of a personality capable of independent thought and there were risks of being led blindly into erroneous innovations or deceived by unscrupulous shaykhs. Serious psychological damage might even result from certain practices, such as seeking to make contact with dead saints. Generally, there is the sense that Sufism, along with Shīᶜism, has been responsible for bringing into Islam from Zoroastrianism a mass of extraneous matter that has no place in the original Arabian religion. For Riḍā, those who support esoteric interpretations have conspired in the past to undermine Islam from within and to end Arab authority in the state. The latter viewpoint seems tinged with the rising nationalism of the age, as does Riḍā's support for the growing Wahhābī-backed power of Ibn Suᶜūd in the Peninsula.

With the growth of a wider movement of salafī reformism, the appeal was not always for such a severe condemnation of the Sufi approach to Islam, but activists sometimes opted for the moderate face of salafī Sufism favoured by ᶜAbduh and Sufi scholars of a reforming disposition. On other occasions, and with increasing frequency, Riḍā's harsher critique was to feed into the stream of voices of those adopting a more radical anti-Sufi position.

The Salafiyya in the Arab Lands

Syria

In 1901, a friend of Riḍā in Damascus, ᶜAbd al-Ḥamīd al-Zahrāwī (1871–1916), published a long essay in which he launched a fierce attack on the existing state of Islamic legal scholarship and condemned Sufism without reservation.[35] Not only was he extremely critical of current Sufi malpractices, of fraudulent and lazy impostors duping the superstitious to part them from their money rather than seeking any genuine spiritual development, he openly questioned Sufism's Islamic basis, denouncing it as 'a jumble of theosophy, Greek metaphysics, and bits from the Qur'ān and the Sunnah.'[36] The reaction of Sufi ᶜulamā' was so violent that the governor of Damascus had al-Zahrāwī arrested and sent to Istanbul for investigation. Rashīd Riḍā, writing in *al-Manār* shortly after these events, expressed his admiration for al-Zahrāwī's brave stand and the independence that he displayed, but also felt he was somewhat excessive in his assault on Sufism. At a later date he might have been even more openly supportive, but he and other Syrian salafīs were concerned that the essay had unleashed a conservative backlash against them with demands that al-Zahrāwī be put to death as a heretic and unbeliever and that the Sufi ᶜulamā' should determine what did and did not constitute acceptable Islamic doctrine and practice.

A few years later Riḍā witnessed for himself the dangers of offending the traditional Sufi party in Damascus. On a tour through Syria in the autumn of 1908, he paid a visit to the city and on 24 October delivered a public address in the Umayyad Mosque.[37] He attracted a large audience and spoke to them on the now familiar theme of the need for progress through the proper combination of Islam and science. In the course of the lecture Riḍā denounced the practice of seeking the intercession of saints, already prominent in ᶜAbduh's campaign against bidaᶜ, but most familiarly associated in the public mind with Wahhābism. Riḍā was not allowed to complete his speech, as he was interrupted by a Sufi shaykh, who angrily defended the practice, as well as the visitation of tombs and belief in saintly miracles. He cautioned the audience against listening to critics such as the Wahhābīs and Riḍā. Yet another shaykh stirred up the crowd against Wahhābīs, labelling Riḍā as one of them and forcing him to make a hurried retreat from the mosque. In later street disturbances a mob demanded that Riḍā be killed and attacked other Damascus salafīs for holding the same Wahhābī views.

These accusations of Wahhābism occurred long before Riḍā's public appreciation of Ibn Suᶜūd at a time when the third Wahhābī-Suᶜūdī state was still in its infancy in central Arabia. Nevertheless, there was a lingering suspicion in Syria of all manifestations of anti-Sufism as Wahhābī and, therefore, distinctive of elements whose loyalty to the Sultan was doubtful. The conservative Sufis of Damascus backed

Sultan Abdülhamid against the Committee of Union and Progress (CUP), who had taken control of Damascus and replaced the Sultan's men in charge of the city in August 1908, following their successful backing of an army mutiny in Macedonia in July. The Committee had been calling for the restoration of the 1876 Ottoman Constitution. Their backers included the Damascus salafīs, who were consequently regarded with considerable anxiety by the conservatives, who had gained strength in the heyday of Shaykh Abū'l-Hudā al-Ṣayyādī and now found their position weakened. Riḍā thus became embroiled in a dispute which centred on popular Sufism, but was actually as much concerned with politics as with religion. A few months after Riḍā's visit, the conservatives were even more discomforted, when a CUP army division entered Istanbul in April 1909, deposing Sultan Abdülhamid, much to the satisfaction of the salafī faction in Damascus.

Despite all the charges of Wahhābism and the occasional extreme anti-Sufi posturing such as that of al-Zahrāwī, the Damascene salafīs were more typically ᶜAbduh-style moderates, salafī Sufis who condemned excesses and abuses rather than the whole rationale of Sufism. Typical of such figures are those in the circles of the leading reformers Ṭāhir al-Jazā'irī (1852–1920) and Jamāl al-dīn al-Qāsimī (1866–1914).[38] Al-Jazā'irī became prominent in educational reform in the 1880s, when he was also involved in the establishment of the Ẓāhiriyya Library in Damascus, for which he sought out many rare books and manuscripts, showing an especial interest in the works of Ibn Taymiyya and his fellow Ḥanbalī Ibn Qayyim al-Jawziyya.[39] Despite some earlier acquaintance, from 1906 al-Qāsimī became more closely associated with al-Jazā'irī, joining in discussions with him on reform programmes and exchanging manuscripts.

Among Jamāl al-dīn al-Qāsimī's numerous works is one aimed at the removal of innovations in ritual and un-Islamic customs practised in the mosques of Damascus.[40] The attack on popular practices in the visitation of saints' tombs echoes the medieval Ḥanbalī campaigns and those of the Wahhābīs and the Egyptian reformers. The tone is sarcastic towards the conservative Sufis who defend such practices, but there is also a new note of embarrassment at the way in which Sufi processions, with their fire-eaters and rowdy followers, are perceived as attracting the ridicule of Westerners. However, in another short essay al-Qāsimī makes known his generally positive view of the 'true Sufism', very much in the line of ᶜAbduh, taking a position of qualified support for an authentic Islamic philosophy.[41] Real Sufis, in his view, should be humble, sincere ascetics, engaged in constant prayer, unlike the false shaykhs so commonly heading the orders of his own day. Yet the true Sufism has not totally died out, but is still to be found among sober intellectuals, such as some distinguished adherents of the Qādiriyya and Naqshabandiyya. The élitism and paternalism notable in ᶜAbduh's attitude are present also in al-Qāsimī's view of the common people. He considers it better for the ᶜulamā' to limit their contacts with the ignorant, spending time with them only to the extent necessary to teach them to perform their religious duties correctly and improve their morals.

In Syria salafism, whether moderately favourable to Sufism or occasionally more radically anti-Sufi, reached its peak early in the twentieth century before the final collapse of the Ottoman Empire. For a while it would lose ground to the rising force of secular Arab nationalism, for whose advocates questions of religious reform were, for the time being, less urgent.

North West Africa

In the French-occupied lands of North West Africa, salafism reached its peak later than in Syria, being rather more successfully linked to the rising forces of nationalism between the World Wars. The influence of the ideas of Muḥammad ᶜAbduh was strongly felt and notably so in the conflict with the powerful ṭarīqas of the region. Nationalist salafīs were not slow to perceive a connection between the readiness of certain Sufi leaders to collaborate with the French colonialists and corruption in their doctrines, deviating from the true original Sufism.

A small number of Tunisia's ᶜulamā' responded favourably to ᶜAbduh's visits to the country in 1884 and 1903, even though the majority remained staunchly conservative. In 1920 the Destour/ Dustūr (Constitution) Party was formed under the leadership of ᶜAbd al-ᶜAzīz al-Thaᶜālibī, a noted advocate of salafī reforms in the spirit of ᶜAbduh, trained in the traditional style of the Zaytūna Mosque in Tunis, but much criticized by conservatives for his rationalizing approach to the Qur'ān. He saw the French protectorate, established under the al-Marsā Convention ratified by the French Chamber of Deputies in April 1884, as disrupting the natural Islamic development of the country and demanded a radical reversal, rejecting the right of the French to rule in the name of the *bey* and calling for a restoration of the 1860 constitution.[42] The hope of Muslim reformists in the

Destour was initially for independence and the opportunity to press forward with modernization in a manner that would be consistent with salafī rationalist rethinking of Sharīᶜa and the promotion of an Arabic and Islamic ethos purged of the unacceptable innovations of the Sufi orders. However, al-Thaᶜālibī was soon to find himself condemned to fifteen years of exile and, on his return to Tunis in 1937, he and his party were already outmanoeuvred on the nationalist front by the activities of the French-educated Habib Bourguiba and the Neo-Destour.

During his 1903 journey to North Africa, Muḥammad ᶜAbduh had also visited Algeria, calling at Algiers and Constantine. This visit was to sow the seeds of salafī thought in particularly fertile ground, for, among the young Muslims to be impressed by ᶜAbduh, was ᶜAbd al-Ḥamīd b. Badīs (1889–1940), who would become the best-known salafī scholar in North Africa. Ibn Badīs maintained his contacts with the Egyptian reformers, reinforced during the *ḥajj* of 1912. His activities centred on countering the impact of French culture, on the one hand, and, on the other, opposing those Sufi ṭarīqas that failed to defend Islam owing to their co-operation with the colonial authorities and dissemination of false doctrines. In 1931, in conjunction with other scholars of similar views, he founded the Association of Algerian ᶜUlamā' (*Jamᶜiyyat al-ᶜUlamā' al-Muslimīn al-Jazā'iriyyīn*), which worked indefatigably for the preservation and reform of Islam in Algeria up to the war for independence from 1954. Schools and the media were the major organs through which Ibn Badīs and the Association sought to convince a wider sector of the population of their vision for Islamic Algeria. By 1954 they had some 200 schools in operation, running very much the programme originally put forward by ᶜAbduh, with Arabic and reformist Islamic studies taught alongside a modern Western curriculum. They also endeavoured to counter Sufi ṭarīqas, especially the Tijāniyya, through denunciation of them in their periodicals, most prominently in *al-Shihāb* (The Meteor) in the 1930s. The grounds for the assault on the Tijānīs were very similar to those of Rashīd Riḍā a decade earlier: personal criticism of the founder, Aḥmad al-Tijānī, and of his prayer *al-Ṣalāt al-Fātiḥ*, repudiating its being a part of God's eternal speech; condemnation of the Tijānīs as undermining the rites of Islam; charging members of the Tijāniyya with loose morals and explaining this as resulting from their belief that they will not be punished in the hereafter on account of their adherence to the ṭarīqa.[43]

How successful was the Association in convincing the population as a whole to accept their critique of the Sufi orders in Algeria? Although the salafī scholars have been frequently acclaimed for their religio-political role in the modern Algerian Islamic resistance, the extent of their influence is also questioned.[44] They appear as an upwardly mobile urban minority, affecting a rising bourgeoisie in the towns, but making little headway among the poorer classes, particularly in the countryside. Despite their ability to attack, discredit and disrupt the organized bases of Sufism, it is less clear that they managed to oust the faith of the mystics from the hearts of the peasants. However, in the longer term they were to contribute to a deepening of divisions between Sufis and anti-Sufis in the post-colonial Algerian state.

In Morocco, as in Algeria and Tunisia, the rise of salafī thought is closely associated with the growth of nationalist resistance and opposition to Sufis in alliance with colonialist forces.[45] In 1912, when the French assumed a protectorate over most of Morocco and the Spanish over a small northern zone, Sufism predominated in the Islamic outlook of the country, although there had been some salafī attempts to reform teaching in the mosque-university of al-Qarawiyyīn in Fez as a result of contacts with the ᶜAbduh school. The reformers had called for stricter philological, exoteric interpretation of the Qur'ān in the Qarawiyyīn and condemned efforts to interpret through mystical insight and allegorical understandings of the sacred text. It was during the First World War and in the 1920s that Fez would become an increasingly active centre of salafī anti-Sufism.

Meanwhile salafism found militant expression in the Spanish-administered Rif, when Muḥammad b. ᶜAbd al-Karīm, a Berber who had been exposed to this reforming tendency in the Qarawiyyīn from 1904–6, led a *jihād* against the Spanish from 1920 to 1926. His programme included the establishment of a rigorous moral discipline: enforcing prayer, banning *ḥashīsh*-smoking, outlawing un-Islamic customs and appointing *qāḍīs* to judge by the Sharīᶜa. He was sternly opposed to the order of the Darqāwiyya, represented by a number of *zāwiyas* in northern Morocco, seeing them as a dangerous source of corruption and seeking to eliminate their presence in the Rif. His example was, however, not typical of salafī leaders in Morocco, who generally resembled their counterparts in Algeria and Tunisia, working through their associations of like-minded scholars to support nationalist political organizations and found schools. While 1926 saw the suppression of Ibn ᶜAbd al-Karīm's tribal forces by a concerted effort of both Spain and France, it also witnessed the involvement of the salafī scholars of Fez in a wider reform party, Ḥizb al-Iṣlāḥ. They conducted a very similar campaign to that in Algeria against the Tijāniyya and also struggled against the Ṭayyibiyya, allies of the French since the last century, and the Kittāniyya, who joined the ranks of the collaborators from the 1920s. Yet the salafīs themselves are remarked as feigning Sufi devotion, describing their group as the Zāwiya, to provide a cover for their secret meetings in which they organized nationalist activity. Thus they hoped to avert French suspicions of their real purpose.

In December 1943 the Istiqlāl (Independence) Party was formed, led from 1946 by a prominent salafī, ᶜAllāl al-Fāsī. In a book entitled *al-Naqd al-dhātī* (Self-Criticism) he delivered his blueprint for the achievement of an Islamic state and society formed according to the thought of the school of ᶜAbduh; the understanding of Islam to be propagated in the state was that of the religion of reason and progress, in which there would be no place for intermediaries with God in the form of Sufi shaykhs. ᶜAllāl al-Fāsī and the Istiqlāl Party lent their support to the Moroccan Sultan Muḥammad V's efforts to achieve independence and consequently continued their opposition to those Sufi ṭarīqas working in support of an alternative, French-backed candidate for the sultanate. The sultan was deposed in 1953, but restored to office in 1955, eventually witnessing an independent Morocco in March 1956.

Notes

1 For this autobiographical fragment see Muḥammad ᶜAbduh, *Sīratī*, in *al-Aᶜmāl al-kāmila li'l-Imām Muḥammad ᶜAbduh*, ed. Muḥammad ᶜAmāra, 2d ed. (Beirut: al-Mu'assasa al-ᶜArabiyya li'l-dirāsāt wa'l-nashr, 1980), 2: 315–37, and on ᶜAbduh and Shaykh Darwīsh, 329–32.

2 Ibid., 330.

3 Muḥammad Ḥasan b. Ḥamza Ẓāfir al-Madanī (d. 1846) was a disciple of Mawlay al-ᶜArabī al-Darqāwī (d. 1823), founder of the Darqāwiyya in Morocco. On the propagation of the Shādhiliyya-Madaniyya in Egypt see F. de Jong, *Ṭuruq and Ṭuruq-Linked Institutions in Nineteenth Century Egypt* (Leiden: E. J. Brill, 1978), 109–10.

4 ᶜAbduh, *Sīratī*, in *al-Aᶜmāl al-kāmila*, 2: 330.

5 See Abu-Manneh, 'Sultan Abdülhamid II and Shaikh Abu'l-Huda al-Sayyadi,' 139.

6 ᶜAbduh, 2: 331.

7 Ibid., 332.

8 See Charles C. Adams, *Islam and Modernism in Egypt* (London: Oxford University Press, 1933), 25–6, n. 2.

9 Muḥammad Rashīd Riḍā, *Ta'rīkh al-Ustādh al-Imām al-Shaykh Muḥammad ʿAbduh*, 1st ed. (Cairo, 1931), 1: 23; quoted in Hourani, *Arabic Thought*, 131–2.

10 Muḥammad ʿAbduh, *Risālat al-wāridāt*, introduction in *al-Aʿmāl al-kāmila*, 2:413. The full text, originally published in Cairo in 1874, was reprinted in Riḍā, *Ta'rīkh*, 1st ed. (Cairo, 1908), 2: 1–25, but excluded by Riḍā from the 2d ed. in 1925–6, apparently because of Riḍā's own opposition to this type of mystical theology and his reluctance to have ʿAbduh's name linked with it.

11 See Muḥammad ʿAbduh, 'Ibṭāl al-bidaʿ min niẓārat al-awqāf al-ʿumūmiyya,' in *al-Aʿmāl al-kāmila*, 2: 23–6, originally published in *al-Waqā'iʿ al-Miṣriyya*, No. 958, 27 Dhū'l-Ḥijja 1297/30 November 1880.

12 The Saʿdiyya was founded by a Syrian shaykh, Saʿd al-dīn al-Jibāwī (d. 1335) from Jibā near Damascus. This branch of the Rifāʿiyya spread from Syria into Turkey and Egypt.

13 ʿAbduh, 'Ibṭāl,' in *al-Aʿmāl al-kāmila*, 2: 23.

14 E. W. Lane, *An Account of the Manners and Customs of the Modern Egyptians* (London, 1836; reprint, London: J. M. Dent and Sons Ltd., 1936), 458–9 (page citations are to the reprint edition). ʿAbduh, writing in *al-Ahrām*, welcomed the ban. On the measures of 1881 to control the Egyptian ṭarīqas and suppress certain of their practices, including the *dawsa*, see de Jong, *Ṭuruq*, 96–101. De Jong (96, n. 4) notes that, following the khedive's decree, Saʿdīs asked for permission to continue performing the *dawsa* at the *mawlid* of Sīdī Yūnis, their main saint in Egypt, and that their tradition recorded its original performance over bottles and only later over human bodies. After its banning in Egypt, the *dawsa* continued in Syria and was reported in Ḥimṣ as late as the 1940s. See art. D. B. Macdonald, 'Dawsa (Dosa),' in *EI* 2, ii, 181.

15 ʿAbduh, *Risālat al-tawḥīd*, in *al-Aʿmāl al-kāmila*, 3: 353–475.

16 Ibid., 473–4.

17 Gabriel Hanotaux (1853–1944), French Minister of Foreign Affairs and historian. ʿAbduh's response to Hanotaux's critical comments on Islam was first published in a series of newspaper articles in *al-Mu'ayyad* and *al-Ahrām* in 1900. See ʿAbduh, *al-Radd ʿalā Hanotaux (al-Islām wa'l-Muslimūn wa'l-Istiʿmār)*, in *al-Aʿmāl al-kāmila*, 3: 201–40. Faraḥ Anṭūn (1874–1923) published his provocative article on the twelfth century Muslim philosopher Ibn Rushd (Averroes) in his magazine al-*Jāmiʿah* in the spring of 1902. Rashīd Riḍā first brought ʿAbduh's attention to it as a dangerous attack on Islam asserting (following Renan) that the religion was hostile to philosophy. ʿAbduh's public refutation also appeared first in periodical form in *al-Manār* and was later published in book form. For the Arabic text see ʿAbduh, *al-Radd ʿalā Faraḥ Anṭūn (al-Iḍṭihād fi'l-Naṣrāniyya wa'l-Islām)* in *al-Aʿmāl al-kāmila*, 3: 243–350. On the debate see Hourani, *Arabic Thought*, 148–9 and Donald M. Reid, *The Odyssey of Faraḥ Anṭūn* (Minneapolis and Chicago: Bibliotheca Islamica Inc., 1975), ix–x, 80–90.

18 ᶜAbduh, *al-Radd ᶜalā Faraḥ Anṭūn*, in *al-Aᶜmāl al-kāmila*, 3: 341–2.
19 ᶜAbduh, 'Ḥiwār fi'l-taṣawwuf wa'l-walāya,' in *al-Aᶜmāl al-kāmila*, 3: 517–24. Rashīd Riḍā and the *ᶜumda's* father also contributed to the discussion.
20 *Fatwā* published in *al-Manār*, Pt. 13, 7 September 1904; reprinted in *al-Aᶜmāl al-kāmila*, 3: 511–16.
21 Ibid., 514.
22 ᶜAbduh, 'Ḥiwār,' in *al-Aᶜmāl al-kāmila*, 3: 520–1.
23 Ibid., 3: 523.
24 ᶜAbduh, *Fatwā*, in *al-Aᶜmāl al-kāmila*, 3: 513.
25 'Ḥiwār,' in *al-Aᶜmāl*, 3: 517.
26 Ibid., 521.
27 In Muḥammad Rashīd Riḍā, *al-Manār wa'l-Azhar* (Cairo, 1934–5),146–72. See Albert Hourani, 'Sufism and Modern Islam: Rashīd Riḍā,' in *The Emergence of the Modern Middle East*, 90–102 for further discussion of Riḍā's views on Sufism and personal experiences.
28 Riḍā, *al-Manār wa'l-Azhar*, 147.
29 Ibid., 148. Further on Riḍā's adherence to the Naqshabandiyya critically recollected, 148–9.
30 Ibid., 171; translated in Hourani, *Arabic Thought*, 225 and *Emergence*, 90.
31 See Assad Nimer Busool, 'Shaykh Muḥammad Rashīd Riḍā's relations with Jamāl al-dīn al-Afghānī and Muḥammad ᶜAbduh,' *MW* 66 (1976): 272–7 on the impact of *al-ᶜUrwa* on Riḍā and his attempt to join al-Afghānī.
32 Ibid., 278–86.
33 M. Rashīd Riḍā, *al-Wahhābiyyūn wa'l-Ḥijāz* (Cairo, 1926).
34 Abun-Nasr, *Tijāniyya*, 163–85, devotes a chapter to critics of the order, including Riḍā (177–8).
35 ᶜAbd al-Ḥamīd al-Zahrāwī, *al-Fiqh wa'l-taṣawwuf* (Cairo, 1901).
36 Commins, *Islamic Reform*, 58 and for further discussion of the case, 55–9. Commins investigates the origins of Salafism in Damascus from the late nineteenth century to 1914.
37 On Riḍā's visit to Damascus see David Commins, 'Religious Reformers and Arabists in Damascus, 1885–1914,' *IJMES* 18 (1986): 405–25.
38 On Ṭāhir al-Jazā'irī see Joseph H. Escovitz, '"He was the Muḥammad ᶜAbduh of Syria": a study of Ṭāhir al-Jazā'irī and his influence,' *IJMES* 18 (1986): 293–310 and Commins, *Islamic Reform*, 41–2, 89–96; 42–6, 59–63, 65–88 on al-Qāsimī.
39 On Ḥanbalīs, including Ibn Taymiyya (d. 1328) and Ibn Qayyim al-Jawziyya (d. 1350), and the question of their reformist approach to Sufism, see George Makdisi, 'The Ḥanbalī School and Sufism,' *Boletin de la Asociacion Espanola de Orientalistas XV. Madrid* (1979): 115–26; reprinted in idem, *Religion, Law and Learning*.
40 Jamāl al-dīn al-Qāsimī, *Iṣlāḥ al-masājid min al-bidaᶜ wa'l-ᶜawā'id* (Cairo, 1923).
41 See Commins, *Islamic Reform*, 80–1.
42 The Tunisian constitution of 1860 had aimed to reduce the powers of the *bey* through assigning legislative and executive powers to a supreme council, to which ministers were responsible. However, as the council members were appointed by the *bey*, it was no experiment in democracy

and ended in failure, the constitution being suspended after only four years. See Abun-Nasr, *History of the Maghrib*, 272–97 on the events leading to the establishment of the French protectorate and Hourani, *Arabic Thought*, 84–94 on the role of Khayr al-dīn Pasha in the faltering reform efforts of the 1860s and 70s.

43 See Abun-Nasr, *Tijaniyya*, 178–80.

44 Ludmila Hanisch, 'The denunciation of mysticism as a bulwark against reason – a contribution to the expansion of Algerian reformism 1925–1939,' *The Maghreb Review* vol. 11, 5–6 (1986): 102–6, regards the Association's role as overvalued by historians in post-colonial Algeria.

45 On the salafīs in Morocco see Jamil M. Abun-Nasr, 'The Salafiyya movement in Morocco: the religious bases of the Moroccan nationalist movement,' in St. Antony's Papers 16, ed. Albert Hourani *Middle Eastern Affairs* 3 (1963): 90–105; also Abun-Nasr, *History of the Maghrib*, 369–93.

5

Strengthening the Soul of the Nation

In 1876, the year of Abdülhamid II's accession to the Ottoman sultanate, were born two future Muslim intellectuals whose radical rethinking of their faith would be far removed from the conservative religious thought world of the sultan's circle. It would indeed lead them in directions more dramatically removed from traditional Islamic thought than the salafī followers of ᶜAbduh and Riḍā would be ready to envision. Both men were to be poets whose religious and nationalist poetry would lend inspiration to their peoples. Both also were, to varying degrees, acquainted with the Islamic philosophical and spiritual heritage and with Western philosophy. One of them was Ziya Gökalp, born a subject of the sultan at Diyarbekir in eastern Anatolia, destined to be the most eminent ideologue of emergent Turkish nationalism and pioneer of sociology in Turkey. The other was Muḥammad Iqbāl, born far beyond the sultan's borders at Sialkot in the North West Punjab,[1] to become a father figure of nascent Muslim hopes for statehood in the Indian subcontinent.

With reference to Sufism, both Gökalp and Iqbāl would reconsider its social usefulness in their societies in the twentieth century and, in so doing, would seek to graft aspects of Western philosophical and sociological thought onto a world of ideas long dominated by Ibn al-ᶜArabī, Rūmī and kindred spirits. Such attempts at synthesis were bold and highly unconventional in their time, opening up new possibilities for self-strengthening of Muslim nations in an age of vibrant nationalism. But even the audacious Sayyid Jamāl al-dīn al-Afghānī might have been shocked.

Ziya Gökalp (1876–1924)

Enemies of Ziya Gökalp would seek to undermine his ardent Turkism by proclaiming that he was not a Turk at all, but of Kurdish descent.[2]

Whether or not there was any substance to the claims is debatable. He came from a frontier district near the borders of Iran, Iraq and Syria, long open to Arab and Persian influences and where Turks might well develop a frontier mentality, outnumbered on their own territory by a considerable population of Kurds and Armenians. If he had Kurdish ancestry, Gökalp did not allow it to affect his allegiance, since he felt himself to be a Turk. However, growing up in an area of such divided loyalties may have compelled him to think more carefully about his national identity than if he had been reared in a Turkish majority area in central Anatolia. In any case, for him national origin was to become less important in the determination of nationality than feelings of identification with a people.

Early Education and Spiritual Crisis

Despite the budding of Turkish consciousness in the young Ziya Gökalp, nurtured by his father's patriotism, he was exposed during his education to a blend of cultural influences from the Arab-Persian-Turkish Islamic heritage and from Western civilization. His father had hoped that he would be able to complete his studies in Europe, although his hopes were mixed with concern about the dangers to a Muslim youth of being cut off from his own religious and national learning.[3] However, his father's premature death prevented Ziya from travelling abroad. He, therefore, went on to attend the Diyarbekir secondary school where he studied French and received the elements of a Western-style education. Outside the school Ziya's uncle attended further to his Islamic studies, teaching him Arabic and Persian and reading with him classic works of philosophy such as those of Ibn Sīnā (Avicenna), al-Farābī and Ibn Rushd (Averroes) and of Sufism as contained in the writings of Ibn al-ᶜArabī and Rūmī. The attempt to combine Western and Islamic education apparently imposed great strains on the young Gökalp, especially as they were exacerbated by contacts with a small group of revolutionary intellectuals, including a young atheistic Kurdish doctor, Abdullah Cevdet. In addition, his uncle seems to have been less broad-minded than his father and unsympathetic to his state of mental confusion. Ziya's hopes of proceeding to further education in Istanbul were dashed by family pressure on him to remain in Diyarbekir and marry his uncle's daughter.[4] At the age of seventeen, or thereabouts, he attempted suicide.

Near the end of his life, like ᶜAbduh, Gökalp wrote an autobiographical fragment relating to this early crisis, but it presents some similar problems of interpretation.[5] Being written so long after the event, it is unlikely, in any case, to offer an exact record of the author's thoughts and feelings at the time and the probable complexity of the situation that drove him to such despair. Moreover, the account, published early in 1923 as a magazine article by a prominent personality, appears to have had aims other than that of personal reminiscence. The theme of suicide was an important one for the adult Gökalp, who was deeply impressed by the sociology of Emile Durkheim (1858–1917), accepting his view of the causes of suicide as owing to a loss of ideals.[6] Therefore, the topic may have appealed to Gökalp as supplying a useful framework for a lesson to Turkish youth, encouraging them to cherish particular ideals as a means of nourishing in them a devotion to the Turkish nation. It may also be possible to detect the influence yet again of that most famous of Islamic spiritual autobiographies, al-Ghazālī's *Munqidh*, a work to which he was particularly attracted in his youth, but which could not rescue him from his dilemma, unable, so he claimed, to reconcile the study of natural sciences with that of theology.

To return then to Ziya Gökalp's own narrative. He identified his own situation as no different from that of his people and humanity as a whole, impossibly trapped in modern life, from which Sufi illumination could not deliver them, as it had delivered al-Ghazālī in the eleventh century or al-Afghānī and ᶜAbduh somewhat earlier in the nineteenth century. He wrote of this painful experience:

> My heart could not remain content while seeing Man – virtuous and heroic, the only source of my inspirations – turned into a Machine, devoid of will and freedom, and made only of Matter, low, base, servile – sterile.
>
> My greatest desire was to know whether my people – threatened by a thousand dangers and yet unaware of them because of the narcotics of Tyranny – would be able to save themselves by some miraculous effort. What I needed was a philosophy of hope, a theory of salvation. If Man was nothing but a Machine, if he lacked the miraculous power to raise himself above Nature, then my people would not be able to survive. And Humanity too would be destined always to flounder in the wilderness.[7]

According to Gökalp, in his mental anguish he found that neither the medieval Islamic theology nor Sufi mysticism could offer him this 'philosophy of hope' and 'theory of salvation' because their ideals were not those of modern life. As living machines, base matter with no soul to be chastened and rise upwards, the Turkish people appeared to be condemned with the rest of the human race. The age of miracles was past. Nor could reason save him or anyone else.[8] Mathematics, at which he had always excelled, provided no solutions, for its proofs were irrelevant to his case. The old clash between mysticism and rationalism admitted no resolution. He recorded: 'I used to believe that if I were able to reach what I then called the Great Truth, I would be relieved from all pain.'[9] But the longing for that final arrival was driven by disenchantment and hopelessness, not by the high aspiration of the mystic for *fanā'*, nullifying all the base qualities of the self after a long and rigorous spiritual ascent.

Gökalp recalled a sudden, and remarkably neat, answer to his *angst*.

> When I was writing a revolutionary poem, another line flowed suddenly from my pen pointing out where I should seek:
> 'The honour of the nation is today entrusted to us.'
> The Great Truth then was nothing but ideals. And the highest ideals were those of nationality and liberty.[10]

Thus in a few lines the crisis is resolved in harmony with Durkheimian theory and demonstrating Gökalp's revolutionary patriotic idealism. At the same time Gökalp provides an example for Turkish youth to follow in the new Turkey, which had just witnessed the dismemberment of the Ottoman Empire and survived the Greco-Turkish War of 1920–22, in which the Turkish Nationalists under the leadership of Mustafa Kemal had driven the Greeks out of Anatolia and secured their withdrawal from eastern Thrace. As a backer of Kemal in the run-up to the first elections of the new state, Gökalp's version of the discovery of the Great Truth in the ideals of nationalism bears the obvious imprint of the political propagandist. It is too neat, convenient and shallow; and it seems unlikely that it corresponds closely to the facts. However, despite the limitations of the text, it may still offer a glimpse into the mind of the young Ziya, confused by a mingling of traditional Sufism and modern nationalism and approaching perilously close to heresy in his efforts to seek a new spiritually rewarding way forward to substitute for the time-honoured Way to 'the Great Truth'.

Ottoman Islamic Patriotism and Ibn al-ᶜArabī

By 1896 Ziya had recovered sufficiently from his crisis to set out for higher education at the Veterinary College in Istanbul, but he was never to complete his studies there. Nationalist hopes drew him into political activities when he joined Sultan Abdülhamid's opponents in the secret society of Union and Progress. His revolutionary involvement soon brought him under surveillance by the sultan's secret police, whose investigations led to his spending nearly a year in prison. He was subsequently released to an enforced return to Diyarbekir and nine years in which strict government censorship prevented him from publishing as he would have wished. However, it was during these years of solitude that he had the opportunity to read Western, mainly French, philosophy, psychology and sociology.

The dramatic change that brought Gökalp to national attention came with the sultan's abdication in April 1909 and the subsequent increasingly public role for Union and Progress. From being a local activist, Gökalp rose to prominence following the movement's Salonika Congress in the autumn of 1909. He was elected onto the Central Council and remained a member until its dissolution after the armistice of 1918. He soon assumed special responsibilities for the Youth Department and emerged as a popular speaker, attracting large audiences from the younger generation. In 1911–12 he took up a post as a teacher of philosophy and sociology in the Union and Progress secondary school at Salonika. This was the first time that sociology had been taught in a Turkish school and for Gökalp the study of the sociology and psychology of the Turkish people was beginning to assume great importance in his hopes for their national revival. This was also a period when he was experiencing the stimulation of more Westernized intellectual circles and compensating for the years of suppression in Diyarbekir by publishing both journal articles and poetry, including his essential views on Turkism in the poem *Turan* published in 1911.

From 1911 there also dates a boldly innovatory article concerning Ibn al-ᶜArabī and the relationship of his theosophy, and of Sufi doctrine in general, to modern Western philosophy.[11] Gökalp declared Muḥyī'l-dīn b. al-ᶜArabī to be the closest of all Muslim thinkers to the Western philosophy of his own day, but giving 'rational expression to the intuitive states which the Sufis reached through *dhawk* (direct experience).'[12] He then set out to demonstrate the way in which different stages in Sufism had anticipated developments in Western thought. Central to his argument was his attempt to equate Sufism with idealism rather than mysticism and to identify the Sufi as 'a seeker after perfection'. Sufism, he stated, passed through three stages: the first in which the Sufi rejected the existence of the sensory world; the second in which he advanced to the realization that 'The colour of the water is the colour of its container' (*lawn al-mā'i lawn inā'ihi*), 'that the objects which we perceive have an external source and become coloured by the sensibility of our consciousness'; the third, and highest, stage in which the will, 'the most real part of the being . . . not content with existing perfections, strives to perceive and construct those perfections which ought to exist.'[13] Gökalp noted that these perfections were what Ibn al-ᶜArabī had designated the 'eternal essences' (*al-aᶜyān al-thābita*). Turning next to Western philosophy, he discovered the equivalent of the Sufis' first stage in the phenomenalism of Berkeley, of the second stage in Kant's view that we do not perceive objective forms. The third stage he regarded as being identical with that attained by Alfred Fouillée, Guyau, Nietzsche and William James with the understanding 'that ideals are nothing but *idées-forces*, or that hope, will, belief are forces leading to highest and purest happiness by creating new values.'[14] After going to some pains to establish a correspondence between Ibn al-ᶜArabī's 'eternal essences' and the term 'ideal', Gökalp concluded that, long before Fouillée, Ibn al-ᶜArabī had shown the creative role of ideals in evolution.

Gökalp's somewhat eccentric interpretation is surely not a dispassionate enquiry into comparative philosophy, but makes more sense if read as a manifestation of ardent Islamic patriotism. During this period of his career, Turkish nationalism had not completely displaced the desire to nourish pride in a broader Islamic heritage. Hence it suits his purpose to recall the achievements of Ibn al-ᶜArabī as a great Muslim thinker, despite his being an Arab, and to seek to encourage his present-day compatriots to develop their values, their ideals, by exploring the treasures of Sufism. If they return to these sources of strength, they can be inspired to achieve the highest goals without the need to be dependent on European thinkers who have only recently reached a stage attained by Muslims in the thirteenth century.

Towards a Durkheimian Social Sufism

Gökalp's faith in the possibilities of Ottoman Islamic patriotism combining with Turkism were to be shattered very shortly after this by the Balkan Wars of 1912–13. They ended with the Ottoman loss of all their remaining European territories with the exception of eastern Thrace, including the city of Edirne. Salonika had been lost, the Union and Progress Party headquarters moved to Istanbul, where Gökalp was also to make his new home during the years of increasing upheaval of the First World War. In 1915 he was appointed the first professor of sociology at the University of Istanbul.

By this time he had turned his back on thoughts of 'creating new values' under the inspiration of Ibn al-ᶜArabī. Increasingly it was Durkheim, the French sociologist, who inspired his social vision for the Turkish people rather than the Arab mystic. Under his influence Gökalp became convinced that there was no need to move upwards along an evolutionary path towards an ideal perfection, reached through the creative force of an individual's ideas, opinions and beliefs. Rather the national ideals were already existent deep in the collective soul and were waiting to be discovered and brought forth as Durkheim's 'collective representations' (*representations collectives*). This remained his cherished view to the end of his life. In a late essay he explained Durkheim's term by examples drawn from the Turkish context:

> There were workers in Turkey even before the 1908 Revolution, but their common consciousness held no such thought as 'we constitute the working class.' Since that thought did not exist neither did a working class. There were also many Turks in our country; but since there was, in their collective consciousness, no concept of 'we are the Turkish nation,' no Turkish nation then existed. In other words, a group is not a social group unless there is a conscious realization of that status in the common consciousness of its individual members....
>
> From these statements, it is evident that social phenomena must be found as conscious realizations in the collective consciousness of the group to which they pertain. Such conscious realizations are termed 'collective representations'.[15]

However, while Durkheim was substituted for the high intellectual Sufi tradition of Ibn al-ᶜArabī, Sufi influences coloured the way in which Gökalp endeavoured to apply Durkheimian ideas to Turkish society.[16] This becomes evident in his writings during the war years in Istanbul.

Gökalp accepted Durkheim's classifications of social groups into primitive, 'segmentary' societies, composed of the segments of family, clan, phratry and tribe and complex, 'organic' societies where the economic life is based on a division of labour, giving rise to varied occupational and professional groupings. In an article dating from 1915, he discusses the social functions of religion in these two types of societies.[17] He notes that in primitive societies religious authority is the only form of authority, whereas in organic societies political and cultural authorities exist in addition to the religious. However, his concern is essentially with organic society and the function of religion within it. This could be valuable when confined to spiritual matters and fostering the 'collective conscience of society', but dangerous if religion were applied to political institutions outside its proper sphere.

Durkheim's concerns with social cohesion, developed with the aid of this collective conscience, are translated by Gökalp into an intense anti-individualism that also accords with Sufi training in the elimination of undesirable individual characteristics. He speaks of the need for 'negative ritual', those associated with the conscientious performance of the Pillars of Islam, in order to isolate the individual from his individuality, to elevate him to the status which is 'the negation of individuality', that is 'forsaking the world'.[18] Rituals such as ablution serve to wash away the moral filth, to weaken the human's love for his ego, a necessary step to the socialization of the individual. Where the individual Sufi self is negated to prepare for the immersion in the Divine oneness, the individual nationalist self is to be negated to prepare for its immersion in a society composed of those mystically united to create the nation. The extremely ascetic Sufi has a role to set an example of self-discipline, but is not a beneficial model for the majority.

Negative rituals performed by the individual are the preliminary to the 'positive rituals' performed collectively. The positive rituals are primarily those of Friday and holy-day prayers, and *ḥajj*, although Gökalp does also admit the desirability of daily worship in the mosque. He attaches a high value to the collective experience of emotion and even ecstasy in such communal participation in ritual, drawing into existence the 'collective soul'. There is a strongly mystical element contained in this positive ritual.

> The worshipper seeks to reach an audience with his deity, a sacred communion with it. To do this, it is necessary, above all, to silence the 'bestial ego' which is awake in the soul, and then to arouse 'the sacred self' which lies in a dormant state. To do the first it is necessary to be freed from individuality; to do the

> second it is necessary to come into a state of collectivity. It is only when a person frees himself from profanity and acquires a sacred nature that he can enter into that audience for which he longs so much.[19]

In a volume of poems published at about the same time, he included one entitled 'Tevhid, According to Social Sufism'.[20] It may be going too far to say with Uriel Heyd, 'Gökalp's God is society.'[21] Gökalp's God is God, most intensely experienced in the collective sacred self of society achieved through the mystical bonding of individuals who have overcome the profanity of their individualism.

If such was Gökalp's vision early in the First World War, by 1917 he had become convinced that this new social *fanā'* (annihilation of the individual soul) was only truly achievable in a state of national crisis of the type that now presented itself. Extraordinary events were needed to eliminate harmful individualities and replace them with the purified, mystically united nation.[22]

The Return to Turkish Folk Sufism

Following the Ottoman defeat in 1918 and the Allied occupation of the capital, Gökalp was arrested, briefly imprisoned and deported to Malta. It was 1921 before he was enabled to return to Turkey, but only back to Diyarbekir with no prominent post in prospect. After some time spent again in teaching and journalism, it was not until the end of 1922, after the November abolition of the Ottoman sultanate, that he was given the opportunity to play an official role in Mustafa Kemal's public policy of Turkification as chairman of the Committee for Writing and Translation. In 1923 he campaigned in support of Kemal and subsequently became representative for Diyarbekir in the new Parliament of the Turkish Republic, being especially active through the Parliamentary Education Committee working to develop a modernized school curriculum. At this time he composed his most systematic presentation of his Turkish nationalist ideology, *Türkçülüğün esasları* (The Principles of Turkism). In this final crucial work Gökalp's commitment is to the strengthening of the Turkish soul through identification with the essentially Turkish national culture, to which he ascribes all positive and desirable characteristics conducive to the development of a harmonious society. Islam, including its sufistic aspects, has a part to play, but Gökalp's appreciation is reserved for that understanding of the faith that is natural to the Turkish people, the folk Sufism of the Anatolian village, not that of the scholarly élite. For him simple, sincere piety, free of asceticism and fanaticism, formed a natural part of Turkish culture, and he remarks:

> The importance that Turks attach to hymns and reading of the *mawlūd* in the mosques and to poetry and music in the dervish convents springs from their adherence to the pattern of aesthetic piety.[23]

Gökalp made a clear distinction between culture and civilization.[24] According to his analysis, each ethnic group had its own initial culture, and civilization arose later with the emergence of a powerful state. He was ambivalent regarding the benefits of civilization and its ability to produce a harmonious social system. Already in 1918 he had concluded that civilization did not represent 'the real personality of a society but its acquisitions. Like learning in the life of individuals, civilization is something acquired and learned.'[25] The conscious intellectual adoption of a civilization is often negatively contrasted with the natural development of a culture that expresses an ethnic community's authentic feelings, emotions and ideals and that thus ensures a true communal solidarity.

For Gökalp civilization needed to be grafted onto a national culture, but he saw grave dangers to the nation that borrowed elements from different foreign cultures. Such a fate had befallen the Ottomans, as he observed:

> Ottoman civilization is an amalgam of institutions stemming from Turkish, Persian and Arab cultures, from Islam, and from Eastern and, more recently, Western civilizations. These institutions never merged and blended and, therefore, never produced a harmonious system.[26]

Gökalp was sceptical about a supposedly 'Islamic' civilization composed of Arab, Persian and Turkish elements and argued that the Ottomans had actually borrowed part of their civilization from Muslim Arabs and Persians who had already borrowed from Byzantine civilization. Consequently, the origins of 'Islamic' civilization were to be sought in the Eastern Roman civilization and, looking further back, in the civilizations of ancient Rome and Greece.

In the context of demonstrating the dependence of Muslim Arabs on these older civilizations, Gökalp completely changed his perception of Ibn al-ᶜArabī and the intellectual Sufi tradition. Instead of being an original thinker who anticipated certain aspects of modern Western philosophy, Ibn al-ᶜArabī is presented in *The Principles* as intellectually dependent on Plato. His 'eternal essences' (*aᶜyān thābita*) were nothing but Plato's ideal patterns.[27] No longer could the Arab Sufi intellectual provide a source of inspiration, but must be demonstrated to be the representative of an essentially alien civilization. Progress was no longer to be achieved by searching for ideals in a past that Gökalp was anxious to discredit and jettison, desiring to disassociate the Turks from Ottoman failures. The harsh experience of the collapse of empire had led him far from his early hopes at Salonika. For him the solution was for Turkish Muslims to adopt Western civilization wholeheartedly, while remaining true to their religion and national culture.

The logical outcome of such a proposal was Gökalp's demand for 'religious Turkism', meaning that 'all religious books, sermons and prayers shall be in Turkish.'[28] The simple statement might appear to border on the jingoistic, were it not for the evident depth of Gökalp's concern that his people should participate as fully and meaningfully as possible in Islamic devotion as a sacralized and mystically bonded entity. Grounding himself in the authority of Abū Ḥanīfa, he noted his view 'that it was permissible for the suras to be read in a national language, even in ritual prayers, since the rapture to be received from the devotion was dependent on complete understanding of the prayers read.'[29] Gökalp did not live long enough to witness the full extent of the superficial and insensitive way in which parts of this Turkish ideology were to be implemented.

He had viewed with approval Mustafa Kemal's early attempts to free Islam in Turkey from its Ottoman heritage and a moribund religious hierarchy controlling the lives of the Turkish people. Thus he welcomed the initial separation of the secular authority of the Sultanate from the religious office of the Caliphate and subsequently the abolition of the Sultanate in November 1922. Similarly, he saw carried through his own demands for various reforms in the religious administration, such as the ending of the traditional post of *Şeyhülislam* as the most senior authority on religious matters and of the Ministry of Pious Endowments (*Evkaf*). But Mustafa Kemal's measures to separate religion and state were already proceeding beyond Gökalp's hopes for institutional change, when a few months before his death the Caliphate was abolished on 1 March 1924. Thus ended Gökalp's dream of a new and glorious age for the Islamic *umma* under the leadership of a caliph with purely spiritual authority at the head of a modernized system more representative of the community than that in the hands of reactionary *ᶜulamā'*. Eight months later, on 25 October 1924 at the age of forty-eight, Ziya Gökalp succombed to his final fatal illness after years of poor health.

As regards Gökalp's proposals for an active contribution by Turkish folk Sufism to the life of the nation, these were to be summarily dismissed, when the *ṭarīqas* were seen to present a serious challenge to Mustafa Kemal. Despite promises made in 1919 to the Kurds of eastern Anatolia that they would have the same rights as Turks in the new nation, the reality was a concerted state effort to suppress every vestige of Kurdish identity. Dissatisfaction was increased by the government confiscation of much Kurdish-owned land and its redistribution among Turks, especially those who had been displaced from Europe. In February 1925 a major rebellion erupted, led by Shaykh Saᶜid of the Naqshabandiyya and described by him in terms of *jihād*. Allegiance to Shaykh Saᶜid and allied Sufi leaders was based on a combination of ṭarīqa and tribal loyalties, centring on the smaller hill tribes and especially that of the Zaza. Ironically, Gökalp's home town of Diyarbekir lay at the heart of the disturbances and it was there that the captured Shaykh Saᶜid and forty-seven other leading rebels were condemned to death by one of the recently constituted Independence Tribunals on 29 June 1925. All were hanged. All the Kurdish Sufi convents were ordered to be closed.

In August Mustafa Kemal toured the Anatolian countryside, castigating the Sufi leadership for standing in the way of enlightened progress. In one such speech he expressed his disbelief that 'there exist, in the civilized community of Turkey, men so primitive as to seek their material and moral well-being from the guidance of one or another *shaikh*. Gentlemen, you and the whole nation must know, and know well, that the Republic of Turkey cannot be the land of *shaikhs*, dervishes, disciples and lay brothers.'[30] All Sufi orders in Turkey were to be dissolved, their assets sequestrated, convents permanently shut down, gatherings for *dhikr* and visitation (*ziyāra*) to shrines and tombs forbidden. In 1930 at Menemen near Izmir in the South-West of Turkey, a further Naqshabandī move to revolt was quickly suppressed. State anti-Sufism was to be harshly enforced throughout the Kemalist period and for many years beyond. There was to be no distinction between a healthy Sufism of the Turkish folk nourishing their collective soul and an alien Arabo-Persian Sufism with no positive social role in the modern Turkish state. Religious Turkism was to be promoted mainly through somewhat crude moves towards the wider use of Turkish language for religious purposes. The introduction in 1932 of the call to prayer in Turkish rather than Arabic proved particularly unpopular. The Turkish 'sacred self' was left unstirred, its potential for mystical absorption in the nation unrealized.

Two years later, in 1934, Mustafa Kemal adopted the surname of Atatürk ('Father of the Turks'). In 1937 Turkey's commitment to secularism was written into its constitution. By this time Atatürk had not softened his attitude towards the Sufi ṭarīqas and seems to have had little concern for Islam in any form. On 10 November 1938 he died and was mourned by huge crowds of worshippers gathering in the mosques.

Muḥammad Iqbāl (1876?–1938)

Like Ziya Gökalp, Muḥammad Iqbāl traced his origins to a frontier region and one deeply divided in its political aspirations: Kashmir, for which he retained a sincere affection throughout his life and in whose problematic affairs he would become involved.[31] Despite his Kashmiri ancestry, he was born, as noted earlier, at Sialkot in the North-West Punjab at an uncertain date. While it is most commonly mentioned as 22 February 1873, he himself writes in the introduction to his doctoral thesis that he was born on 3 Dhū'l-Qaᶜda 1294/1876.[32] Unfortunately, this does not settle the issue, as the *hijrī* year 1294 began only on 16 January 1877, but a birthdate in 1876 or 1877 seems most probable in view of his own testimony and the subsequent dates of his career.

Education and Early Views of Sufism

Iqbāl's father appears to have been illiterate, but with pious Sufi inclinations, and his mother, to whom he was devoted, was similarly religious. Following a traditional early schooling, Iqbāl entered a Scottish mission college in Sialkot in 1893. Two years later he went on for higher education at Lahore Government College and there first came into contact with Western scholarship, as mediated by the British Orientalist Sir Thomas Arnold, perhaps most familiar as the author of *The Preaching of Islam*, in which he sought to demonstrate that, contrary to widespread popular belief among non-Muslims, Islam had been spread largely through *da^cwa* efforts, notably by Sufis rather than through armed *jihād*. The young Muḥammad Iqbāl developed a high regard for Arnold. By 1899 Iqbāl had completed his M.A. and was appointed McLeod Arabic Reader in the Punjab University Oriental College, lecturing in History and Political Economy for approximately three years. He then returned to Lahore Government College where he taught Philosophy. In 1904 he was saddened by Arnold's return to Europe and wrote a poem of complaint at separation. A year later he obtained a study leave and himself travelled to Europe, first to England to pursue further studies in Philosophy at Trinity College, Cambridge under the direction of McTaggart, subsequently to Heidelberg, then Munich in Germany where he presented his doctoral thesis, *The Development of Metaphysics in Persia*, drawing on some previously unknown Sufi manuscripts.[33] After a short period in legal training in London, he returned late in 1908 to Lahore, to teach briefly at his old college before setting up in practice as a barrister.

Well before his studies in Europe, Iqbāl had shown an interest in applying modern philosophy in his intellectual exploration of Sufism. In an early article published in the *Indian Antiquary* at Bombay in 1900, he seeks to show the originality of certain Sufi thought.[34] He aims to rescue it from being 'generally condemned under the contemptuous name of mysticism' and to demonstrate that it is 'essentially a system of verification – a spiritual method by which the ego realizes as fact what intellect has understood as theory.'[35] The object of his particular attention here is the conception of the 'perfect man' (*al-insān al-kāmil*) according to the fourteenth century Sufi ᶜAbd al-Karīm al-Jīlī. He remarks of the ultimate spiritual experience of the Divine being achieved through the instrument of the heart (*qalb*), describing it as the eye which sees eventually the Absolute Reality. 'It owes its existence to a mysterious combination of soul and mind (*Nafs wa Rūḥ*) and becomes by its very nature the organ for the recognition of the ultimate realities of existence.'[36] In that recognition the human rises to a temporary realization of himself as 'god-man', fathoming the deepest mysteries of his own being; 'but when that particular spiritual realization is over, man is man and God is God. Had the experience been permanent, a great moral force would have been lost and society overturned.'[37] The perfect man, 'god-man' in al-Jīlī's understanding, is noted as the 'joining link' between the human and the Divine, sharing in the attributes of both. Iqbāl observes that, among the

Divine attributes described by al-Jīlī, the first four are Independent Life, Knowledge, Will and Power. Will is displayed in love, which has nine manifestations, the last being that in which lover and beloved merge into one identity. Such love is the Absolute Essence. Power gives expression to itself in self-creation. Thus the universe, according to al-Jīlī, existed in God's self before its existence as an idea.

In evaluating al-Jīlī's philosophical contribution, Iqbāl is anxious to accord the Muslim thinker credit for having anticipated many doctrines of modern German philosophy. At the same time he is ready to concede that the medieval Sufi's weakness is in the unsystematic nature of his thought:

> He perceives the truth, but being unequipped with the instrumentality of a sound philosophical method, he cannot advance positive proofs for his position, or rather cannot present his views in a systematic unity. He is keenly alive to the necessity of philosophical precision yet his mysticism constantly leads him to drop vague, obscure remarks savouring of Platonic poetry rather than philosophy. His book is a confused jumble of metaphysics, mysticism and ethics, very often excluding all likelihood of analysis.[38]

Iqbāl appears almost embarrassed by the mystical content of his own heritage, affected perhaps by European Orientalist attitudes and feeling not quite able to save al-Jīlī from the contempt of Western philosophers. Yet his fascination with him was to continue, his early study being included in his doctoral thesis and stimulating him to rethink the conception of the perfect man and the potentialities for human spiritual development.

Self-Assertion and God's Vicegerents

The necessity of establishing himself in the legal profession made considerable demands on Iqbāl, but he nevertheless managed to devote time to literary production. Although far removed physically from the scene of action, he was both saddened and angered by the Ottoman loss of Muslim territory in Europe through the First Balkan War in 1912. His distress moved him to pour forth his despair in an impassioned Urdu poem, *Shikwā* (Complaint), in which he expresses the pervading sense of Muslim shock at their loss of authority and fortune in the world. He asks God why the faithful have been so neglected and unbelievers given the pleasures of Paradise on Earth. About a year later there followed a second major poem, *Javāb-i Shikwā* (Answer to the Complaint), a harsh indictment of the Muslims of his own day, whose current weakness is due to their failure to live and act as true Muslims. No longer do they follow the Sunna of the Messenger, but are neglectful of the core duties of religion, morally decadent and corrupted by the attraction of non-Muslim ways. They have abandoned Islamic religious unity for worldly nationalism, but are reminded that nations are born through that very faith that they lack. At this point on the eve of the First World War, Iqbāl was moving towards a growing conviction that nothing but a spiritual rebirth *en masse* could save his correligionists. He began to devote his efforts towards stimulating such a revival.

In 1915, when Gökalp was expounding his doctrine of social Sufism, Iqbāl published his own radical rethinking of Sufi spirituality and its social functions in a long philosophical poem written in Persian, *Asrār-i Khudī* (Secrets of the Self). Apologising for any deficiencies in his language, he admits that it is not his own, but that only Persian is suited to such lofty thoughts. In choosing Persian Iqbāl is setting himself within the high poetic Sufi tradition and acknowledging his link to Jalāl al-dīn Rūmī, who, he claims, appeared to him in a dream in the role of his spiritual guide urging him:

> Thou art fire: fill the world with thy glow!
> Make others burn with thy burning!
> Proclaim the secrets of the old wine-seller;
> Be thou a surge of wine, and the crystal cup thy robe!
> Shatter the mirror of fear,
> Break the bottles in the bazaar!
> Like the reed-flute, bring a message from the reed-bed.[39]

The imagery at this point must have seemed comfortingly familiar to readers accustomed to the old 'master of Rūm', but already there are hints that the poet is imbued with a new spirit and that his message from the 'reed-bed' will be different from that of his distinguished guide. In view of the startling nature of the new message, Iqbāl's choice of Persian also appears judicious in that it targets an élite educated readership, hopefully more receptive to its deep meanings. It seems that he also hoped to make his work accessible to educated Afghans and Persians, and apparently also to Orientalists such as the Cambridge scholar Reynold Nicholson who translated the *Secrets* into English and thus aided its wider recognition.

Despite the French sociological influence, especially that of Durkheim, Ziya Gökalp still appears somewhat closer than Iqbāl to traditional Sufi views of the individual. Gökalp continued to speak negatively of the 'bestial ego' and the need to suppress individualistic desires. For Iqbāl there is no longer a concern to discipline the *khudī* (Arabic *nafs*), the self or ego with its undesirable human attributes. The desire of the individual is not to be suppressed. Desire is essential for the preservation and enrichment of life.

From the flame of desire the heart takes life,
And when it takes life, all dies that is not true.
When it refrains from forming desires,
Its pinion breaks and it cannot soar.
. . . .
Negation of desire is death to the living,
Even as absence of heat extinguishes the flame.[40]

Contrary to the Sufi concern to weaken the self to enable its final dissolution in *fanā'*, Iqbāl presents a plea for the strengthening of the human personality, declaring

When the Self is made strong by Love
Its power rules the whole world.[41]

The ideal strengthened individual self is portrayed in the person of Prophet Muḥammad, the model of his community, 'the soul of this society'. Such is the perfect man whom all Muslims should seek to emulate 'by the might of Love' and so become, in their turn, God's vicegerents.

The origins of Iqbāl's interpretation of God's vicegerent are to be sought both in the medieval Sufi heritage, especially al-Jīlī's understanding of 'perfect man' and in the philosophical irrationalism of nineteenth century Europe, as contained in the work of Schopenhauer, Nietzsche and Bergson.[42] Iqbāl's poetic exhortation may be regarded as an attempt to overcome negative characteristics in his sources and provide a viable model that can reinspire Muslims in his own day. European irrationalism, with its revolt against purely rational and scientific explanations of life and its acknowledgement of mysterious forces unfathomable by the mere application of intelligence, had a strong appeal for one steeped in Sufi tradition. A mystical spirit informed the outlook of both. The major barrier to Iqbāl's ready acceptance of certain irrationalist views of the human being lay in an incompatibility between his own Islamic moral values and those of the philosophers. In Schopenhauer's pessimistic interpretation of life, the Will is a terrible driving force causing the human to strive endlessly without purpose, to desire without achieving satisfaction, to create and destroy. For Nietzsche, the Will of his *Übermensch*, or Superman, is trained to develop him into the superior being of the hero, but it is a totally ruthless, pitiless Will to power that sets its possessor beyond moral restraint. There is a considerable gap between such expressions of Will and the Will of al-Jīlī's 'god-man', that manifests itself in love.

In the *Asrār* (Secrets), Iqbāl appears to be seeking a middle path that will bring some more idealistic purpose to his human vicegerent, whose self will be strengthened, but by the force of love. Even if its power may rule the world, it will not be to oppress, but to arbitrate in all the quarrels of the world. In certain passages Iqbāl seems to reflect the view of Henri Bergson on the *élan vital*, the mysterious cosmic force of creation that is beyond reason and makes intelligence its servant.

> What is the essence of the mind that strives after new discoveries and scales the heavens?
> Knowest thou what works this miracle?
> 'Tis desire that enriches Life,
> And the mind is a child of its womb.
>
> . . . .
>
> Thought, imagination, feeling, memory, and understanding –
> All these are weapons devised by Life for self-preservation
> In its ceaseless struggle.
> The object of science and art is not knowledge,
> The object of the garden is not the bud and the flower.
> Science is an instrument for the preservation of Life,
> Science is a means of invigorating the Self.
> Science and art are servants of Life,
> Slaves born and bred in its house.[43]

The message here looks thoroughly Bergsonian. There is a wonder at the creative process of life that is beyond the reach of rational thought and science alone, but more fully comprehended with the aid of 'intuition' that is a higher type of intellect and, for Bergson, the key to grasping the inner nature of life. Life is engaged in 'ceaseless struggle', but in Iqbāl's vision

> Life is preserved by purpose.[44]

It is not the purposeless striving of Schopenhauer and does not culminate in the Nietzschean *Übermensch* of monstrous dimensions. Rather the life that reaches perfection in Iqbāl's vicegerent of God appears to follow the lines of development described by Bergson in terms of 'creative evolution':

> Everywhere but in man consciousness had to come to a stand; in man alone it has kept on its way. Man, then, continues the vital movement indefinitely, although he does not draw along with him all that life carries in itself.... It is as if a vague and formless being, whom we may call, as we will, man or superman, had sought to realize himself, and had succeeded only by abandoning of himself on the way.[45]

The vicegerent of the *Asrār* is very much the man or superman whose consciousness is of the highest order and 'continues the vital movement indefinitely', but the dynamic life-force in him is kept vibrant through the formation of ideals. It is such idealism that enables him to achieve a supreme degree of self-realization and to burn all that is other than God in the fire of

> An ideal higher than Heaven.[46]

However, it is the centrality of the creative manifestation of Love that provides the essential link with al-Jīlī's Perfect Man without the entanglements of sufistic metaphysics.

Yet there are also darker Nietzschean echoes in the poem, as it proceeds to describe how self-negation is a doctrine of subject races who scheme to undermine the power of their conquerors. In seeking to discredit the traditional Sufi path to *fanā'*, Iqbāl utilizes an allegorical tale in which the 'fierce tigers' (the Arabs) are victorious over the sheep (the Persians), whose slave mentality aims to sap the vitality of their rulers. The tigers are successful while they act in accordance with their nature, slaughtering the sheep and depriving them of their freedom, manifesting their strength in conquest and dominion. Danger awaits, when they listen to an old sheep, 'cunning as a weather-beaten wolf', who

> Made complaint of the course of Destiny
> And sought by craft to restore the fortunes of his race.
> The weak, in order to preserve themselves,
> Seek devices from skilled intelligence.[47]

The sheep's crafty use of intelligence is contrasted negatively with the natural violence of the tigers. The sheep counsels the tigers that they should repent of their evil deeds, renounce violence and strength and seek the Paradise that is reserved only for the weak.

> O thou that delightest in the slaughter of sheep,
> Slay thy self, and thou wilt have honour!
> Life is rendered unstable
> By violence, oppression, revenge and exercise of power.[48]

When the tigers accept the advice of the sheep, they are perceived by the poet as succombing in stupidity. The message to the Muslims is that they have been weakened by the importation of Sufi quietism and self-abnegation, which is not natural and original to them, but adopted from the conquered peoples. Disconcertingly, Iqbāl's fascination with Nietzsche appears at this point to have overwhelmed his sense of Islamic morality, for the merciless tigers are not the followers of the Prophet's Sunna, but the embodiment of Nietzschean Übermensch with their hard, proud and inhumane assertion and will to power.

The publication of the *Asrār* received a stormy reception from many who were horrified by its assault on traditional Sufi conceptions and the apparently immoral egotism of Iqbāl's approach. Even at the end of his life Iqbāl found it necessary to defend himself against such criticisms of *Asrār*, as is demonstrated by a note dictated by him in the summer of 1937.[49] On that occasion he sought to distance himself from Nietzsche and maintain that his poem is diametrically opposed to Nietzschean ideas, that his higher man is inspired by the moral and spiritual values of the Islamic Perfect Man and is not the immoral product of Nietzschean materialism, which turns the human ego into a monster. His intention is to envisage a human ego which will be self-assertive in a positive ethical manner in the cause of truth, justice and duty. It will be strengthened to resist the forces of disintegration and destruction and achieve personal immortality. Iqbāl is anxious to place this conception of the ego within the framework of true Islamic mysticism and to overthrow the inheritance of false mysticism:

> In condemning self-negation I am condemning those forms of conduct which lead to the extinction of the "I" as a metaphysical force, for its extinction would mean its dissolution, its incapacity for personal immortality. The ideal of Islamic Mysticism according to my understanding is not the extinction of the "I". The *fanā'* in the Islamic mysticism means not extinction but complete surrender of the human ego to the Divine Ego.

> The ideal of Islamic mysticism is a stage beyond the stage of *fanā'* i.e. *baqā'* which from my point of view is the highest stage of self-affirmation.[50]

Such an interpretation of his ideas of selfhood places Iqbāl safely within defensible Islamic norms of ethics, but it seems to be inconsistent with at least parts of the *Asrār.* Probably it represents a later stage of disenchantment with European irrationalism and an attempt to draw back from the brink of heresy into more peaceful Islamic intellectual territory.

'Into the brilliant desert-sunshine of Arabia'

In the aftermath of *Asrār-i Khudī,* Iqbāl passed into a stage of marked antagonism towards certain eminent Sufis of the past and also towards what he saw around him of actually existing Sufism. By 1916 he had become acquainted with Louis Massignon's edition of *Kitāb al-ṭawāsīn,* published two years previously. In a letter of 17 May 1916 he wrote that he had found Massignon's notes very useful and now understood the essential ideas of al-Ḥallāj. He had become convinced that the jurists who condemned him to death were absolutely correct.[51] Similarly in the case of Ibn al-ᶜArabī, Iqbāl evinced open hostility towards his thought in a letter of 19 July 1916, condemning his *Fuṣūṣ al-Ḥikam* (Bezels of Wisdom) as anti-Islamic and blasphemous.[52]

A year later he was writing in harshly anti-Sufi tones of the dangers to Islam from 'a false Mysticism born of the heart and brain of Persia!', attacking it as symptomatic of current Muslim decadence.[53]

> The present-day Muslim prefers to roam about aimlessly in the dusky valleys of Hellenic-Persian Mysticism which teaches us to shut our eyes to the hard Reality around, and to fix our gaze on what it describes as "Illuminations" – blue, red and yellow Reality springing up from the cells of an overworked brain.[54]

His frustration with his contemporaries is evident, as he lashes out against obscurantism and declares that there is nothing esoteric in the teaching of the 'great democratic Prophet'. He associates the greatness of early Islam with its democracy and readiness to observe a God-given system of law. But, while democracy and law were the twin pillars of Muslim strength, they were undermined and in time displaced by the creeping decadence of 'Persianism' and its 'gloomy, pessimistic mysticism', its secret doctrines accessible only to the initiated. Thus the majority of Muslims were enslaved and supposedly cut off from enlightenment, forming a lower class and the Sufi shaykhs constituting a spiritual aristocracy, the whole system being quite alien to original Islam. Addressing Muslim youth, Iqbāl calls on them to return to the beginnings and cast off the Sufi noose from their necks:

> The regeneration of the Muslim world lies in the strong uncompromising, ethical Monotheism which was preached to the Arabs thirteen hundred years ago. Come, then, out of the fogs of Persianism and walk into the brilliant desert-sunshine of Arabia.[55]

The stirring, direct language of this assault on Sufism for the guidance of Muslim youth contrasts markedly with Iqbāl's philosophical writing, whether in poetry or prose, and its much more complex approach to the merits and demerits of Sufism.

That Iqbāl did not totally reject all Sufism is evidenced in his personal lifelong adherence to the Qādiriyya and in a continuing appreciation of a certain type of mystical experience. However, the task of examining his evolving attitude towards Sufism, as expressed in his later work of the 1920s and 30s, is complicated by apparent inconsistencies in his views. On the one hand, he is ready to admire such an uncompromising anti-Sufi as Muḥammad b. ᶜAbd al-Wahhāb, on the other he comes to appreciate al-Ḥallāj as a model of the struggling mystical hero, despite his previous denigration of him. While condemning Persian mysticism, he nevertheless maintains his close spiritual relationship with Rūmī, inspirer of the *Asrār*, who becomes his guide on the heavenly journey in his *Jāvīdnāme*, his major Persian poem composed in 1932 and dedicated to his son Jāvīd.[56] How are such inconsistencies to be interpreted and can they be reconciled? It is proposed here to look at the problem with reference both to Iqbāl's famous lectures of 1928–29, *The Reconstruction of Religious Thought in Islam*, and to an essay of 1934 in response to questions raised by Pandit Jawahar Lal Nehru and seeking to explain 'the present spiritual unrest in the world of Islam'.[57]

Towards the end of 1928 and in the first few weeks of 1929 Iqbāl delivered a series of lectures, at the request of the Madras Muslim Association, in the Universities of Madras, Hyderabad and Aligarh. First entitled *Six Lectures on the Reconstruction of Religious Thought in*

Islam, the study appears to be a conscious echo of al-Ghazālī's *Iḥyā' ʿulūm al-dīn* (Revivification of the Religious Sciences). The author declares in the Preface that he is aiming 'to reconstruct Muslim religious philosophy with due regard to the philosophical traditions of Islam and the more recent developments in the various domains of human knowledge.'[58] With regard to Sufism, he states:

> The more genuine schools of Sufism have, no doubt, done good work in shaping and directing the evolution of religious experience in Islam; but their latter-day representatives, owing to their ignorance of the modern mind, have become absolutely incapable of receiving any inspiration from modern thought and experience. They are perpetuating methods which were created for generations possessing a cultural outlook differing, in important respects, from our own.[59]

This summarizes his overall view, that Sufism had its genuine exponents in the early period, but Sufis of his own time are hopelessly out of touch with modern ideas to the point that they can be of no assistance to the new generations. Such a view enables him to select facets of certain past Sufis for admiration, while castigating Sufi developments which do not provide suitable role models for modern humanity.

On what grounds does he make his selection of those who have made positive contributions to Islamic religious experience? If there is any single quality shared by these respected individuals, it is **dynamism**. Despite other significant differences, they all partake fully in a dynamic engagement with life that allows them to embody the heroic approach that can be sharply contrasted with the fatalism that Iqbāl abhors and holds responsible for the ills of the Muslim world of his day. In Lecture V of *The Reconstruction*, 'The Spirit of Muslim Culture,' Iqbāl writes of the differences between the prophetic type of mystical consciousness and the type more frequently found among Sufi saints. The prophet is marked as the one in whom the 'unitary experience' leads him to return to an active role in society, seeking 'opportunities of redirecting or refashioning the forces of collective life'. In his personality the finite centre of life sinks into his own infinite depths only to spring up again, with fresh vigour, to destroy the old, and to disclose the new directions of life.[60] In Prophet Muḥammad the process reaches finality, for, according to Iqbāl, the spirit of his revelation is to bring an end to the primacy of knowledge acquired through non-rational modes of consciousness. With the birth of Islam the way forward is for humans to become masters of their environment through the use of inductive reason. Iqbāl does not wish to deny all value to continuing mystical experience which he declares to be perfectly natural and a source of knowledge of God's signs alongside the rational. However, he does not seem to appreciate the type of Sufi mystic consciousness that has no wish to return from the 'unitary experience' to give benefit to society, but to remain forever in the spiritual repose of other-worldliness. For Iqbāl it is the retreat into this totally other-worldly Sufism that caused the most brilliant minds of the Muslim world to withdraw from the guidance of the Islamic state, leaving this important task to the intellectually mediocre.[61]

In Lecture IV, 'The Human Ego – His Freedom and Immortality,' Iqbāl shows that he has completely revised his opinion of al-Ḥallāj, the nature of whose mysticism is now positively perceived. His words '*Anā al-Ḥaqq*' ('I am the Creative Truth') are no longer interpreted pantheistically, but as the culmination of a true religious experience that did not deny the transcendence of God. Al-Ḥallāj comes to represent 'not the drop slipping into the sea' as in the traditional concept of *fanā*', 'but the realization and bold affirmation in an undying phrase of the reality and permanence of the human ego in a profounder personality.'[62] Such an explanation transforms the martyr-saint into the vicegerent of the *Asrār* whose 'Self is made strong by Love,' the epitome of the dynamic Muslim hero who struggles with noble purpose. The same positive vision of al-Ḥallāj is carried over three years later into the *Jāvīdnāme*, in addition to his continuing fascination with Rūmī, also a dynamic exemplar of the devoted lover of God.

But what of Iqbāl's praise for those who are extremely critical of traditional Sufism or even totally anti-Sufi? Both in *The Reconstruction* and in his essay of 1934 addressed to Pandit Nehru Iqbāl expresses approval of those who have made valuable contributions to developing Islamic society and strengthening whatever he sees as the true spirit of Islam. A certain type of other-worldly Sufism has no place here. Iqbāl decries the kind of mysticism that 'has already robbed Muslims of their healthy instincts and given them only obscure thinking in return.'[63] Reforming activists, men of healthy instincts, are prominent role models: Ibn Taymiyya and Shāh Walī Allāh, Ibn ᶜAbd al-Wahhāb and al-Afghānī. In his own time the list includes the autocratic modernizing figures of Mustafa Kemal Atatürk of Turkey and Reza Shah Pahlavi of Iran, 'men who, relying on their healthy instincts, had the courage to rush into sun-lit space and do, even by force, what the new conditions of life demanded.'[64]

If it is at all possible to understand Iqbāl's choice of heroes, the key may lie in his search for a Muslim nationalist ideology. All the personalities, whether Sufi or anti-Sufi, can be harnessed to the cause of building up the assertive human ego necessary in the process of spiritual self-strengthening in Muslim nations. At the end of his life Iqbāl even endeavours to apply al-Ḥallāj's exclamation *'Anā al-Ḥaqq'* to a nationalist purpose in a posthumously published poem:

> If the individual says *anā al-ḥaqq*, punishment is better –
> If a nation says it, it is not illicit.[65]

In stressing this ideal of the nation's struggle to be a living witness to God's Creative Truth, Iqbāl appears to be close to the nationalist social Sufism of Gökalp.

Like Gökalp, Iqbāl was actively involved in efforts to influence Muslim political opinion during the last years of his life. In late 1930 he presided over the annual session of the Muslim League, held in Allahabad. It was to be the occasion for the delivery of a famous speech, which is commonly regarded as sowing the seeds that would later give rise to Pakistan as a separate state for India's Muslims. The passage in which Iqbāl stated his aims is frequently quoted: 'I would like to see the Punjab, North-West Frontier Province, Sind and Baluchistan amalgamated into a single state. Self-government within the British Empire or without the British Empire, the formation of a consolidated North-West Indian Muslim state appears to me to be the final destiny of the Muslims at least of North-West India.'[66] The North-East area that would become East Pakistan from 1947–71, and subsequently Bangladesh, is noticeably excluded. However, Iqbāl's expressed wish at this time was not yet for an independent sovereign state, but for something less, an autonomous Muslim state within an Indian Federation. Furthermore, there appears to have been no popular eagerness to act on his suggestions until the last year of his life, by which time he had become sadly disillusioned with nationalism of any variety.

Financial difficulties clouded the last years of his life, exacerbated by the expenses of illness, as in the case of Ziya Gökalp. In a New Year's message of 1 January 1938, broadcast on Radio Lahore, Iqbāl spoke of his sorrow at the political problems of the 1930s, in Spain, Abyssinia, Palestine and Germany. He called for unity of the brotherhood of man and the need to overcome divisions of race, nationality, colour and language. In March 1938 he wrote an article defending the internationalism of Islam. By this time he was seriously ill. He died on 21 April 1938.

Iqbāl left behind him a reputation as the spiritual inspirer of the Muslim state of Pakistan created in 1947, the poet-philosopher of the new nation, whose verse had so strengthened the souls of India's Muslims to aspire to nationhood. Whether he would have been entirely happy with the result is far from certain.

Notes

1 Iqbāl's date of birth is not known exactly, but 1876 is the year he mentions himself in the introduction to his doctoral thesis. See following discussion on Iqbāl.
2 See Uriel Heyd, *Foundations of Turkish Nationalism: The Life and Teachings of Ziya Gökalp* (London: Luzac, 1950), 19–40 and 20–21 on his possible Kurdish ancestry.
3 Gökalp recorded his father's views in 'Babamın Vasiyeti,' *Küçük Mecmua* 17 (1923), a journal that he published in Diyarbekir from June 1922-March 1923; translated as 'My Father's Testament' in Niyazi Berkes, *Turkish Nationalism and Western Civilization: Selected Essays of Ziya Gökalp* (London: George Allen and Unwin Ltd, 1959), 35–7.
4 See Heyd, *Foundations*, 26 for these views on the background to Gökalp's suicide attempt.
5 Ziya Gökalp published this brief account as an article, 'Hocamın Vasiyeti,' *Küçük Mecmua* 18 (1923); translated as 'My Teacher's Testament' in Berkes, Turkish Nationalism, 37–9.
6 Emile Durkheim, *Le Suicide* (Paris, 1897).
7 Berkes, *Turkish Nationalism*, 37.
8 Ibid.
9 Ibid., 38.
10 Ibid., 38–9.
11 Ibid., 50–5; originally published as 'Muhiddin-i Arabi,' *Genç Kalemler* 8 (1911) under a pseudonym, Tevfik Sedat.
12 Ibid., 50.
13 Ibid., 51.
14 Ibid.
15 Ziya Gökalp, *The Principles of Turkism*, translated from the Turkish by Robert Devereux (Leiden: E.J. Brill, 1968), 51; originally published as an article, 'Tarihi Maddecilik ve İçtimai Mefkürecilik,' (Historical Materialism and Sociological Idealism) *Yeni Gün* (Ankara, 8 March 1923); reprinted in *Türkçülüğün Esasları* (The Principles of Turkism) (Ankara, 1923).
16 See Elton L. Daniel, 'Theology and Mysticism in the Writings of Ziya Gökalp,' *MW* 67 (1977): 175–84 for a view that Gökalp, as a deeply

religious and mystically inclined nationalist, found Durkheim's sociology attractive in providing a theoretical framework for Turkish nationalism because of its affinity to mysticism.

17 'Dinin İçtimai Vazifeleri,' *Islam Mecmuası* (III, Nos. 34 and 36, Istanbul, 1915); translated as 'Social Functions of Religion' in Berkes, *Turkish Nationalism*, 184–93.

18 Ibid., 187.

19 Ibid., 191.

20 In *Kizil Elma* (Istanbul, 1914–15). Uriel Heyd, *Foundations*, 56 quotes a verse of the poem
In the bodies there is multiplicity,
In the hearts there is unity,
There are no individuals, there is (only) society.
There is no God but Allah.

21 Ibid.

22 Gökalp's view in 1917 presented in his 'Milli İçtimaiyat,' *İçtimaiyat Mecmuası* (I No. 1, Istanbul, 1917); translated as 'National Sociology' in Berkes, *Turkish Nationalism*,171–83.

23 Ziya Gökalp, *The Principles of Turkism*, 30. The *mawlūd* was a poem recited on the Prophet's birthday, a popular one in Turkey being that of Süleyman Çelebi (d. 1421).

24 Heyd, *Foundations*, 66–8 suggests an indirect borrowing by Gökalp of his theory of culture and civilization from German sociology, probably from Ferdinand Tönnies, *Gemeinschaft und Gesellschaft*, first published in 1887. Heyd assumes that he has been influenced by French sociologists drawing on Tönnies' ideas.

25 Berkes, *Turkish Nationalism*, 142. From a lecture given by Gökalp in 1918, entitled 'Türkiye Asrî Bir Cemiyet Mi?' (Is Turkey a Modern Society?), published in *Doğu* (Nos. 5–6, Zonguldak, 1943).

26 Gökalp, *Principles*, 31.

27 Ibid., 42–3.

28 Ibid., 119.

29 Ibid.

30 Bernard Lewis, *The Emergence of Modern Turkey* (London: Oxford University Press, 1961), 404–5.

31 He was to serve as President of the All India Kashmir Committee.

32 Muḥammad Iqbāl, 'Lebenslauf,' in *Thoughts and Reflections of Iqbāl*, ed. Syed Abdul Vahid (Lahore: Ashraf Press, 1964), 28. 3 Dhu'l-Qa'da 1294 would correspond to 9 November 1877.

33 These included works of Suhrawardī Maqtūl, ʿAbd al-Karīm al-Jīlī and Mullā Ṣadrā. For details on the thesis see Annemarie Schimmel, *Gabriel's Wing: a study into the religious ideas of Sir Muḥammad Iqbal* 2d ed. (Lahore: Iqbāl Academy, 1989), 37–9.

34 Muḥammad Iqbāl, 'The Doctrine of Absolute Unity as expounded by Abdulkarim al-Jilani,' *Indian Antiquary* (September 1900); reprinted in *Thoughts*, ed. Vahid, 3–27. Al-Jīlānī is better known as al-Jīlī.

35 Ibid., 4.

36 Ibid., 21.

37 Ibid., 21–2.

38 Ibid., 26.
39 Muḥammad Iqbāl, *Asrār-i Khudī*, trans. Reynold A. Nicholson, *The Secrets of the Self* (Lahore: Sh. Muḥammad Ashraf, 1955), 11.
40 Ibid., 24.
41 Ibid., 43.
42 Among examinations of the origins of Iqbāl's Perfect Man see Aziz Aḥmad, 'Sources of Iqbāl's Perfect Man' in *Studies in Iqbāl's Thought and Art*, ed. M. Saeed Sheikh (Lahore: Bazm-i Iqbāl, 1972), 107–32. Aḥmad argues that the influence of Henri Bergson is dominant.
43 Iqbāl, *Secrets*, 25–6.
44 Ibid., 23.
45 Henri Bergson, *Creative Evolution* (London: Macmillan, 1954), 280–1; quoted in Ahmad, 'Sources,' 119.
46 Iqbāl, *Secrets*, 27.
47 Ibid., 49–50.
48 Ibid., 52.
49 Muḥammad Iqbāl, 'Note on Nietzsche' in *Thoughts*, 238–44.
50 Ibid., 244. *Baqā'* is the state in which the mystic continues to live in God after proceeding beyond *fanā'*.
51 See Schimmel, *Gabriel's Wing*, 34–52 on the development of Iqbāl's views on al-Ḥallāj.
52 Ahmad, 'Sources of Iqbāl's Perfect Man,' 115.
53 See Muḥammad Iqbāl, 'Islam and Mysticism,' *New Era* 28 July 1917; reprinted in *Thoughts*, 80–3.
54 Ibid., 80.
55 Ibid., 83.
56 See Schimmel, *Gabriel's Wing*, 52–4, 353–61 on *Jāvīdnāme* and on Iqbāl's relationship to Rūmī.
57 Muḥammad Iqbāl, *The Reconstruction of Religious Thought in Islam* (Lahore: Sh. Muhammad Ashraf, 1977), reprint of *Six Lectures on the Reconstruction of Religious Thought in Islam* (Lahore, 1930) and idem, 'Reply to questions raised by Pandit Jawahar Lal Nehru' (1934), reprinted in *Thoughts*, 257–90.
58 Iqbāl, *Reconstruction*, v–vi.
59 Ibid., v.
60 Ibid., 125.
61 See ibid., 150–1.
62 Ibid., 96.
63 Muḥammad Iqbāl, 'Reply,' 275.
64 Ibid., 280.
65 Quoted in Schimmel, *Gabriel's Wing*, 350.
66 Muḥammad Iqbāl, 'A Separate Muslim State in the Subcontinent,' in J. Donohue and J. L. Esposito, *Islam in Transition*, 93.

6

Contemporary Sufism and Anti-Sufism

Sufi Ṭarīqas, 1950s–1960s: Decline and Continuity

By the 1950s it was not uncommon for Western observers to view the *ṭarīqas* as movements that were destined to fade, as Muslim countries followed Western models of development and the educated élites abandoned the traditional forms of religious organization. A. J. Arberry's comments of 1950 are representative of such a viewpoint: 'Though the Sufi Orders continued – and in many countries continue – to hold the interest and allegiance of the ignorant masses, no man of education would care to speak in their favour.'[1] The observation was made with special reference to Egypt and apparently also with the Arab Middle East primarily in mind, but ten years later Clifford Geertz was expressing quite similar opinions with regard to the *ṭarīqas* in Java, perceiving them as the preserve of old men on the social periphery, ready to be forced out of existence with the growing strength of the modernists.[2]

More recent scholarship would be inclined to see such observers as somewhat too eager to sound the death knell of the Sufi orders, when 'on the contrary Sufism is not only surviving but in many areas flourishes.'[3] However, it is arguable that it is easier to remark the vitality of Sufism in various parts of the world in the 1980s and 1990s than it was in the 1950s and 1960s. In some cases there has been considerable revival where there was notable decline at mid-century and the expectation of still further decline, rather than revival, was not confined to Western scholars. Some prominent Muslim intellectuals shared this perception, having been nourished on the ideas of the reform-minded critics of the orders and become convinced that they, and not the traditional Sufi shaykhs, would mould the thinking of the younger generations. These men of education who declined to speak in favour of the orders not infrequently enjoyed a high profile in the secularized circles of certain nationalist leaders emerging with the reassertion of independence in a number of Muslim states following World War II.

Apart from the unpredicted revival in some countries and ṭarīqas, there has also been increased study of organized Sufi activity, embracing a greater range of areas and orders and including those where these bodies have achieved persistent expansion or at least maintained a reasonable level of continuity. A high proportion of the research has been undertaken by sociologists and anthropologists and sometimes also political scientists, but certainly far less by those for whom the classical Sufi tradition is of major concern.

It is proposed here to make a brief examination of cases where either decline or continuity has been studied with reference to organized Sufism in the fifties and sixties. Egypt has been chosen as an area of well-documented decline in that period and Sudan and Senegal as areas of evident vitality in particular ṭarīqas.

The Decline of the Ṭarīqas in Egypt

If the Egyptian ṭarīqas could appear moribund by 1950, the 1952 revolution of the Free Officers did nothing to reinstate their position. The years that witnessed the rise to power of Jamāl ᶜAbd al-Nāṣir and his presidency from 1956–70 oversaw a phase of decline that was widely presumed to be terminal. Viewed from the vantage point of his nationalist and socialist government, the orders represented all that it hoped to leave behind: ignorance, superstition and quietist toleration of foreign intervention in Egyptian affairs. While they might not represent the direct threat of a religious opposition, they were nevertheless looked upon with some misgivings on account of their traditional associations with the old landed classes in the countryside and their potential use as the tools of reactionary political forces.

By the mid-1960s, Michael Gilsenan, conducting anthropological research on a reformed branch of the Shādhiliyya, observed of the Egyptian orders:

> To the encroachments of Western imperialism and scientific knowledge, to the changing political conditions of Egypt after independence, to the revolution of 1952 and all that it has meant in terms of social change, the Orders offered nothing save an image of intellectual irrelevance, superstitious beliefs and practices which degraded Islam.[4]

He saw their survival as owing to their appeal to the conservatively religious and illiterate peasants and urban lower class. They also seemed to present some outlet for those to whom other avenues of religious expression were closed with the government clampdown on the politically activist Muslim Brotherhood. Founded in 1928 by Ḥasan al-Bannā', a salafī Sufi and close associate of Rashīd Riḍā, the Brotherhood had expanded to attract a membership of around half a million by the time of his death in 1949 at the hands of the secret police. It had continued to grow, but had developed increasingly anti-Sufi attitudes, generally highly critical of the decaying ṭarīqas. However, for those who sought the tranquillity, reassurance and comparative security of traditional spiritual guidance and brotherhood, the Sufi orders of the 1960s might at least provide a temporary refuge from the pressures of dramatic changes in the world around them.

On the other hand, for those who actively sought progressive change in their society, the ṭarīqas had little to offer. They lacked intellectual, articulate and dynamic leadership that might have attracted the more educated and appeared too loosely structured to foster a strong sense of corporate identity. Multiple membership of orders was common, so that *murīds* did not owe exclusive allegiance to the group. There was also a pronounced tendency for ṭarīqas to splinter into a number of sub-sections with leadership disputes and rivalries. In 1960 there were twenty-one orders represented in the Supreme Council of Sufi Orders apart from some minor unregistered orders.[5] While such numbers might give the impression of strength, the reality was one of underlying weakness with a proliferation of amorphous bodies. Had the religious climate enabled the emergence of fewer, but more highly organized, orders, Sufism in Egypt might have experienced a much improved potential for empowerment.

At this period the weak and fissionable Egyptian ṭarīqas presented a stark contrast to the apparent strength of the Sanūsiyya in neighbouring Libya, the Sanūsīs providing the political power base for the then independent kingdom ruled over by the head of their order and grandson of its founder. In 1951 Sayyid Idrīs had taken a truly extraordinary step for a prominent Sufi shaykh, assuming the non-Muslim title of king with British backing for his rule and going on to preside over a régime of spiralling corruption, only to be toppled by the coup of Colonel Mu^{c}ammar al-Qadhdhāfī in September 1969. In the fifties and sixties it would have been inconceivable for an Egyptian ṭarīqa head to play a role equivalent to that of the Sanūsī leader, but at the same time the very weakness of the orders could offer a certain protection, since they were unable to constitute a threat serious enough to demand real efforts at containment or suppression. They could simply be left to wither with the possibility that times and their fortunes might change.

Continuity in the Sudan and Senegal

Elsewhere in Africa certain powerful ṭarīqas supply models of greater success in self-preservation and adaptation to new conditions. Writing at the beginning of the 1970s, John Voll observed the situation in the Sudan to be somewhat unusual on account of the continuing vitality of Sufi religous leadership, notably represented by the Mīrghanī family of the Khatmiyya from the reformist Idrīsī tradition, still facing their Mahdist rivals.[6] Unlike their counterparts further North, they seemed to have managed far more effectively to cross the divide between the traditional religious outlook and that of those who had received a Westernized style of education, whom Voll classes as 'new men'. During the years between the World Wars, the Khatmiyya leader, Sayyid ᶜAli al-Mīrghanī, and Sayyid ᶜAbd al-Raḥmān al-Mahdī of the Mahdiyya had assiduously developed links with the new men. Following World War II, both parties had skilfully retained credibility and local backing. The Khatmiyya, despite an earlier history of connections with the British, emerged in support of a pro-Egyptian radical nationalism. The Mahdists favoured a more gradualist path to independence, cooperating with British plans for Sudanese self-government, but winning over Sudanese who remained suspicious of Egyptian intentions towards the Sudan. Thus after gaining independence in 1956, these traditional religious organizations still enjoyed large-scale membership and influence among the new nationalist politicians.

The same was to hold true of the Sufi orders in Senegal, after its achievement of independence from France in 1960. A United States Army handbook estimated that, in 1960–61, three major ṭarīqas accounted for over 97% of all Muslims in the country, the remainder numbering only 60,000 out of the total of 2,500,000 Muslims.[7] Muslims constituted 78.5% of the population with adherents of traditional religions making up a further 18% and Roman Catholics (including Europeans and Lebanese) 3.5%.

The strongest of the ṭarīqas in numerical terms was the Tijāniyya, whose 1,400,000 affiliates comprised well over half of the total

Senegalese population, divided into three branches: the ᶜUmarian Tijānīs following the holy lineage of al-Ḥājj ᶜUmar Tal who first propagated the ṭarīqa in nineteenth century Senegal, the Niass Tijānīs who emerged as a new section in the 1920s under the leadership of Shaykh Ibrāhīm Niass and, finally, those attached to the Sy lineage of Tivouane. These divisions would tend, to some extent, to reduce the otherwise considerable strength of the organization. The Qādiriyya was the smallest, most loosely structured and least influential of the orders with members owing their prime allegiance to their local shaykhs, but still counting over 400,000 members, 17% of the population. The third order, exclusively Senegalese, and the most tightly organized with the clearest sense of group identity, was that of the Murīds (Mourides), second to the Tijāniyya in numbers with 575,000 members, over 23% of the population. Founded by Amadu Bamba Mbacké (c. 1850–1927) as an offshoot of the Qādiriyya, the order, after initial French persecution, managed to negotiate an important role for itself in the political economy of Senegal, opening up previously uncultivated land for peanut production by its devoted murīds in a process of steady expansion from the 1920s to the 1960s.[8] The extraordinary economic success story of this period has been variously interpreted as exploitation of poor peasant farmers to the benefit of a wealthy spiritual leadership or a fair deal by which these 'wretched of the earth' were given economic and religious security in exchange for their services.[9]

Despite the dominance of these ṭarīqas in Senegalese society, the 1950s presented them with some challenges in the run-up to independence. Opposition arose from two principal quarters: from urban leftist nationalists and salafī anti-Sufis. The leftists charged the shaykhs of the orders with being the tools of the French colonialists, feudalist exploiters and religious frauds. The salafīs organized themselves around the Union Culturelle Musulmane, founded in 1953 by a graduate of the Ben Badīs Institute of Algiers, Shaykh Touré. The accusations levelled by the Union against the Sufis were of a broadly similar nature, the criticisms focusing on the record of the ṭarīqas as unpatriotic collaborators and in more detail on their corruptions of the faith, essentially in the style of the North African salafīs.

However, with the advent of the newly independent state under President Léopold Senghor from 1960–80, the ṭarīqas found their position generally unimpaired and their leaders courted for support by all political parties. When Senghor faced disturbances among city workers and students in 1968–9, he turned to the rural Sufi shaykhs and saw his salvation in their backing for his régime.[10]

The continuing strength of Sufi organizations in both Sudan and Senegal in the 1950s and 60s bears witness to the advantages of a few powerful orders, able to deliver services to their members and influence political developments, without being so closely tied to a particular régime that its demise inevitably leads to their own eclipse, the situation experienced by the Sanūsīs in Libya.

The Ṭarīqas and the Contemporary Islamic Revival

In the climate of Islamic revivalism that has expanded worldwide since the 1970s, especially following the Iranian revolution of 1979, previous predictions about the future of the ṭarīqas have proved all too often seriously flawed. Much attention has been paid to the politically active Islamist elements in the revival, who are frequently anti-Sufi with their demands for an Islamic order with its basis in exoteric legalism. It might be assumed that the prominence of such trends would have a largely negative effect on Sufism in posing even stronger challenges to the ṭarīqas. While such an assumption has often been valid, there have also been positive aspects to the revival as far as organized Sufism is concerned.

Politically Resurgent Sufism

Sufis could find encouragement in seeing that not all proponents of the political resurgence of Islam have been anti-Sufi in outlook. Perhaps the most outstanding example to be noted is that of Āyat Allāh Khumaynī himself, for whom Sufi spirituality was central to his vision of an Islamic system to regenerate Iran and the wider *umma*.[11] Despite much populist talk about oppressed and oppressors, his concern in post-revolutionary Iran was not solely to improve the material lot of the poor, but to restore a sense of spiritual equilibrium to a people whom he perceived to be sick with the Western diseases of materialism and self-love. Therefore, a solution which addressed only material needs would be inadequate, since his own country initially required purification from un-Islamic and anti-Islamic thinking. Such a view is reflected in a series of lectures delivered before an audience of religious students in Najaf towards the end of

1972, several years before the revolution. Entitled *Mubāraza bā Nafs yā jihād-i akbar* (The Struggle against the Self or the Greater Jihād), it is concerned with admonishing the students to beware of this world and its attractions and warns of the dangers of diseases of the spirit, which are painless and may even be pleasurable, but which lead to hellfire. They are urged to reject love of this world and its goods:

> If you have any tie or link binding you to this world in love, try to sever it. This world, despite all its apparent splendour and charm, is too worthless to be loved, particularly if one is deprived of what it has to offer.... What value does this transient and seemingly sweet life (supposing that it is indeed spent pleasantly) have when compared to infinite torment? For the torment suffered by those attached to this world is indeed sometimes infinite.
>
> Those attached to this world are mistaken when they imagine that they are in possession of it and its various benefits and advantages. Everyone looks upon the world through the aperture of his own environment and place of residence, imagines that the world consists of what he possesses. But this corporeal world is vaster than man can even imagine, let alone traverse or possess. Despite all the adornments with which He equipped it, God has never looked upon this world with mercy, according to a certain tradition. We must see, then, what the other world is upon which God, Almighty and Exalted, did look in mercy and what the 'fountainhead of magnificence' is to which He is summoning man.[12]

Khumaynī's tone appears little different from that set by the early ascetics and seems quite reminiscent of that of al-Ḥasan al-Baṣri (d. 728), addressing the Umayyad Caliph ᶜUmar b. ᶜAbd al-ᶜAzīz and likening this world to a serpent, smooth to the touch, but whose venom may prove fatal.

Khumaynī had even hoped to include non-Muslims in this call to purification, writing in a letter to President Gorbachev of the U.S.S.R. of his conviction that the Soviets could benefit from studying the Islam of Ibn al-ᶜArabī and Ibn Sīnā.[13] However, if this appeal was of little avail in such quarters, it met with a warmer reception among some Muslim supporters of the Āyat Allāh's revolution. For example, in West Africa certain Sufi leaders showed eagerness to foster links with Iran. In Nigeria Iranian Shīᶜī literature began to circulate in the 1980s, being published in English, Arabic and Hausa and adding a further sectarian dimension to local controversies over the Islamic credentials of the Sufi orders, when Nigerian Sufis expressed their approval of Khumaynī's ideas. In 1987 a senior Tijānī, Shaykh Dahira Usman Bauchi, was invited to Iran to attend the eighth anniversary celebrations of the revolution.[14] Pro-Khumaynī activity also led to splits in the Muslim Students Society in this period and the emergence of a new group, known locally as the Yan Shia, although this did not literally mean that they were Shī^{c}īs.[15] In Ghana, Tijānīs have also looked to Iran for support and it has been remarked that some of the Tijāniyya in Tamale and Accra have become Shī^{c}īs with an 'Iranian-sponsored school of Shi^{c}ite piety' being founded in Accra, apparently with the intention of serving as a training centre for the region.[16] However, once again, it is by no means clear what becoming Shī^{c}ī really involves beyond a radicalization of ṭarīqa activity in the area.

Looked at more generally, the wider climate of revivalism may be seen as having stimulated a variety of forms of Islamic religious expression, including Sufism. As it has given confidence to Muslims of different perspectives to assert their faith, many have turned to ṭarīqas for spiritual satisfaction, leading to the sudden expansion of some old orders, such as the Burhāniyya in the Sudan and Egypt under the influence of the Sudanese Shaykh Muḥammad ^{c}Uthmān ^{c}Abduh al-Burhānī (d. 1983), who claimed followers in the millions, including three million in Egypt.[17] The revival has also led to the creation of pan-Sufi umbrella organizations, such as the Aḥbāsh in Lebanon, which owes its support especially to the Qādiriyya, Rifā^{c}iyya and Naqshabandiyya.[18]

In some cases, Sufi movements have become more consciously politicized in reaction against the assault on them by anti-Sufi organizations, as has happened in the Nigerian and Ghanaian situations just noted and with the Lebanese Aḥbāsh, who, like their West African counterparts, have been influenced to some extent by Shī^{c}ī spirituality. The Aḥbāsh take their name from the organization's founder, Shaykh ^{c}Abd Allāh al-Ḥabashī, of Ethiopian origin, but settled in Beirut since 1950.[19] The movement developed from 1983 as a successor to the Society of Philanthropic Projects, first founded in 1930.

Viewing themselves as salafī Sufis, the Aḥbāsh defended themselves against criticisms by arguing that they accepted only 'good' *bida^{c}*, innovations that were consistent with Qur'ān and Sunna, such as 'giving *bay^{c}a* (allegiance) to the pious ancestors (*al-salaf al-*

ṣāliḥ); upholding the name of Allah by prayer and singing (*taḥlīl)* celebrating the Prophet's birthday; visiting the shrines of saintly ancestors for their blessing; praying loudly after mosque services; and keeping meditation boxes (*miḥrāb*) in the mosques.'[20] However, they were anxious to distance themselves from those ṭarīqas that they considered guilty of practising 'bad' innovations, condemning the Shādhiliyya, Mawlawiyya and Khalwatiyya, although the last two have been in marked decline in Lebanon, as they have been elsewhere in the Middle East.

The Aḥbāsh managed to appeal to a cross-section of the Lebanese Muslim population during the years of the civil war and its aftermath, presenting a moderate blend of Sunni and Shīᶜī theology and a message of tolerance and determination to preserve Lebanon's religiously pluralistic society against any attempts to impose an Islamic order. While they infiltrated and recruited from the militias, they maintained a strict opposition to violence which ensured good relations for their followers with Arab governments, helping their peaceful spread to Syria and Jordan and as far afield as Tajikistan and Australia.

However, their denunciation of Sunni anti-Sufi views from Ibn Taymiyya to Sayyid Quṭb and of organizations from the Muslim Brotherhood to more radical groups, such as al-Takfīr wa'l-Hijra, al-Jihād and the local al-Jamāᶜa al-Islāmiyya, led to increasing tensions. By 1992 they came into open conflict with the Lebanese al-Jamāᶜa, whom they condemned as unbelievers (*kuffār*), clashing with them in the coastal cities of Sidon and Tripoli. At this time the Aḥbāsh were becoming less distinctively apolitical, as they put forward candidates in the 1992 parliamentary elections, rather surprisingly allying themselves with the Shīᶜī movement of Ḥizb Allāh, despite their criticisms of Ḥizb Allāh's demands for an Iranian-inspired Islamic order.

Apolitical Resurgent Sufism

In other cases the representatives of organized Sufism have remained consistently apolitical, while profiting from the heightening of Islamic consciousness with the wider revival. Returning to Egypt, where weakness and decline had been characteristic of the orders in the 1950s and 60s, a remarkable resurgence of a generally apolitical nature could be witnessed. A clear indication of increasing ṭarīqa activity has been provided by the rising numbers of Sufis attending the annual ceremonies in honour of the Prophet's birthday, an occasion on which they would traditionally gather for several days in the vicinity of the Imām al-Ḥusayn mosque in Cairo's Old City prior to the grand parade. In order to take part in the parade, ṭarīqas have been required to register with the Supreme Council of Sufi Orders. A tripling of the number of participants was observed in the period from 1970 to 1985. According to an Egyptian sociologist, Saad Eddin Ibrāhīm:

> In the mid-1960s the parade march took no more than two hours following the afternoon prayer (*al-asr*) and ending well before the sunset prayer (*al-maghreb*). In the mid-1980s, the parade begins after the noon prayer (*al-zuhr*) and may continue long after sunset.[21]

Yet despite the huge upsurge in Egyptian Sufi activity since the 1970s, deep and damaging divisions have continued to plague its organized expression. Such a state of affairs may be seen as a visible long-term effect of the salafīs' reform efforts, part of the heritage of Muḥammad ᶜAbduh and associates. It is also a significant reflection of state policies designed to support the supposedly respectable face of Sufism approved by the Supreme Council, who stress its conformity with Sharīᶜa and place in mainstream Sunnism. However, such officially-backed reformism has led to a widening gulf between the registered and sanitized orders and those persisting in the traditional forms of popular Sufism.

Awareness of the dangers of officially-approved Sufism degenerating into an empty shell without the substance of true Sufism is already evident in the 1961 novel, *al-Liṣṣ wa'l-Kilāb* (The Thief and the Dogs) of Najīb Maḥfūẓ.[22] A Sufi shaykh, ᶜAlī al-Junaydī plays a pivotal role as the model of the sober Sufi master sanctioned by the authorities (hence the association of the name with al-Junayd). In a dream of the novel's severely alienated hero, the thief and murderer Saᶜīd Mahrān, the shaykh actually appears to demand an identity card from Saᶜīd:

> Said was surprised and objected that a Sufi disciple didn't need an identity card, that in the eyes of the mystical order the righteous and the sinner were alike. When the Sheikh replied that he did not like the righteous and wanted to make sure that Said was really a sinner, Said handed him the revolver, explaining that every missing bullet meant a murder, but the

> sheikh insisted on seeing his card; the government instructions, he said, were stringent on this point.[23]

The shaykh had all the outward appearance of a true guide, the austere ascetic who sees the other world more clearly than this world, his language cloaked in symbolism and inaccessible to the uninitiated ears of the ordinary man. However, Shaykh ᶜAlī al-Junaydī is not to be taken at face value, for his behaviour and, it is implied, his inner state is not that of the true Sufi. Real spirituality, through which the human might actually journey towards God, is to be found beyond the confines of state-registered piety.

With the end of the Nasserist period in 1970 and the advent to power of President Anwar Sādāt, the state became concerned with more than the mere control and limitation of religious groups, including the ṭarīqas. 'Safe' versions of Sufism were actively encouraged as a bulwark against leftist political activity, initially, and somewhat ironically, alongside the largely anti-Sufi Muslim Brothers, who were being offered respectable reinstatement in Egyptian public life. But state encouragement was also backed by even more controls with the powers of the Supreme Council to regulate Sufi affairs being further strengthened in 1976 and 1978.

A prominent example of the type of order to receive such state backing is the Ḥāmidiyya Shādhiliyya, a sub-order founded by a civil servant, Shaykh Salāma Ḥasan al-Rāḍī (1867–1939). This was the Shādhilī branch studied by Michael Gilsenan in 1964–6 and visited by him once again in the late 1970s, when he discovered striking changes.[24] The organization whose original appeal had been to the poor of Cairo and the Nile Delta had gathered a growing number of middle-class members, who had gained influence within the ṭarīqa and moved it in an ever more reformist direction. They stressed the intellectual abilities of the founding shaykh rather than his miraculous gifts, his skill in outwitting the *ᶜulamā'* in knowledge of Sharīᶜa, not his power to intervene in his followers' lives by communication with them from beyond the grave, by saving them from death by drowning or bringing them some unexpected good fortune. Finally, the increasing social divisions led to a split in the leadership, with the bourgeois élite breaking away completely and developing their own well-equipped and costly mosque and associated teaching centre, library and other facilities in the fashionable Cairo district of Zamalek. Such was the desired, government-approved model of a Sufi order, far removed from the working-class followers massing at the tomb of Shaykh Salāma in the port quarter of Bulaq.

The dilemmas of the middle-class seeker had also already been highlighted in the 1960s in the novels of Maḥfūẓ, notably in *al-Summān wa'l-Kharīf* (The Quail and Autumn, 1962) and *al-Shaḥḥādh* (The Beggar, 1965).[25] Shut out from the spiritual reassurance of traditional ṭarīqa membership, characters turn to book knowledge of Sufism or embark on their own lone struggle towards mystical enlightenment. The former course seems relatively harmless and at least provides some comfort and sense of purpose for Samīr ᶜAbd al-Bāqī in *al-Summān*, a civil servant who has lost his government post and taken a job with an uncle as accounts director and junior partner in his furniture business. Armed with a copy of the eleventh century popular summary of Sufi teaching and practice, al-Qushayrī's *Risāla*, he endeavours to persuade a disenchanted ex-colleague of the benefits of Sufism.

Far more problematic is the search of the successful, but spiritually sick, lawyer, ᶜUmar al-Ḥamzāwī, chief protagonist and spiritual beggar of *al-Shaḥḥādh*. Bound to a base everyday life dominated by materialistic concerns, his loneliness is 'the loneliness of the wave absorbed by the sand, which never returns to the sea,' his soul lost in the sand of worldliness and never able to return to the ocean of God.[26] The turning point comes for him one night when he drives out to the Pyramids and experiences an ecstatic state, as the sunrise eliminates the utter darkness of his human sin, replacing it with a marvellous light. Nothing worldly matters any longer and he gives up his work and family to retreat in the countryside. There he immerses himself in book knowledge of Sufism in a far more dangerous way than that of Samīr ᶜAbd al-Bāqī, hoping once again to taste ecstasy. The result, without the proper guidance or support of ṭarīqa brotherhood, is a severe psychotic illness with al-Ḥamzāwī overwhelmed by hallucinations and delusions.

With the Sufi revival in Egypt such seekers from a more secularized educational background have sometimes found their niche within the new ranks of the Ḥāmidiyya Shādhiliyya or comparable reformed ṭarīqa sections. Sometimes they have carved out a place for themselves in smaller intellectual Sufi circles open to the exploration of medieval theosophy and far removed from what they perceive as the debased street religion of the traditional popular orders.

While the ṭarīqas were criticized by such circles, they were also open to criticism from the Rector of al-Azhar from 1973 to 1978, ᶜAbd al-Ḥalīm Maḥmūd, himself a scholarly Shādhilī pressing the case for reform.[27] For Maḥmūd the current state of the Egyptian ṭarīqas was one of decay and he supported a return to the classical sources to rediscover an authentic and austere style of Sufism that would stress social responsibility and a life in obedience to the Sharīᶜa, attempting to achieve its inner meanings. This, he believed, could be accomplished through a renewal of the Shādhilī path, setting out his blueprint for this project in his major contribution to Sufi theory, *al-Madrasa al-Shādhiliyya al-Ḥadītha* (The New Shādhilī School). His vision was essentially of an intellectual and spiritual elect

> to reflect on the true Islamic tradition in a secular environment which is progressively hostile to religion and where Sufism is perceived as a complicated system of superstition and innovation in religion. In explaining the concept of the elect, Maḥmūd says that, "it is in the nature of things that there should be an aristocracy; it is the concept of the elect – those people who are divinely gifted by an acute sense, a sharp intelligence, and by a spiritual instinct."[28]

By contrast with the reformist Sufism of varying degrees able to win government approval, the revival has also borne witness to a vibrant undercurrent of traditional, popular Sufi activity in those orders that could not expect establishment approbation.[29] Valerie Hoffman-Ladd, researching these popular understandings of Sufism in Egypt in the late 1980s, noted of her interviews with Sufis:

> I would often begin my interviews by asking members and affiliates of Sufi orders what Sufism (*taṣawwuf*) was. Sometimes, particularly among illiterate Sufis, the term *taṣawwuf* was not understood, or was understood to mean "fanaticism". But most respondents defined Sufism as purification of the heart, sincerity of worship, and renunciation of fleshly passions. These ends were largely met through practices of devotion to the Prophet, his family, and one's own sheikh.[30]

One Rifāᶜī *wakīl* whom she met defined Sufism as 'love for the family of the Prophet,' and the Rifāᶜiyya, formerly a prime target of attacks by Muḥammad ᶜAbduh and the salafīs, is notable among the major orders participating in devotional activities of *dhikr* and the celebration of *mawlids* at the many shrines throughout the country. Apart from the occasion of the Prophet's birthday celebrated in locations all over Egypt, other *mawlids* are remembered at the tombs and shrines of members of his family (*ahl al-bayt*), such as Imām al-Ḥusayn and

Sayyida Zaynab with mosques in Cairo, already noted as the scenes of reprehensible innovations in the eyes of nineteenth century reformers.

In the mid-1970s the Burhāniyya attracted unwelcome attention from the Ministry of Awqāf, when one of its publications was denounced as containing unorthodox doctrines concerning the Prophet and *ahl al-bayt* and a media campaign was initiated against the order's alleged extremist and Shīᶜī-inspired views.[31] Effectively this was an attack on major figures of the medieval Sufi tradition, since the book was largely a compilation of extracts from their writings long absorbed in the teachings of Egyptian ṭarīqas and by no means exclusive to the Burhāniyya. These would include Ibn al-ᶜArabī and ᶜAbd al-Karīm al-Jīlī.

Thus remaining apolitical has not necessarily enabled ṭarīqas to escape condemnation by the state, although it may enable considerable numbers of Sufis to continue in traditional expressions of their faith without systematic efforts to suppress their organizations.

State Anti-Sufism

States continued to function as major actors among the forces of anti-Sufism in the post-World War II period. Both Muslim states and non-Muslim states with substantial Muslim populations were among those concerned about the dangers of politically activist Sufis, although the threat of Sufi-led armed *jihād* had passed in most parts of the Islamic world. The confrontation between Sufism's proponents and governments hostile to its purposes was rooted not only in practical power politics, but also contained varying forms of ideological conflict. In Communist lands state opposition to Sufism normally constituted part of a wider anti-religious programme, in which Sufis were targeted as representative of reactionary Muslim elements and as potential or actual subversives.

Soviet Anti-Sufism: Return to the North Caucasus

In the Soviet Union the Sufi orders were viewed as primary enemies of the Communist state and people, whether in Central Asia or the Caucasian region. It is proposed here to look once again at the North Caucasus, examining it as an example of an area where anti-Sufi policies were resolutely pursued, hardly surprisingly, since the ṭarīqas had refused to abandon their old commitment to *jihād*, directing their energies against the atheistic régime, as they had against its Christian Tsarist predecessor in a series of uprisings from 1917 to 1943.[32] In February 1944 Stalin ordered the mass deportation of the entire population of Chechnya-Ingushetia, some 800,000 people, to be sent to prison camps in Siberia and Kazakhstan. The alleged reason for this drastic action was that the people of the Chechen-Ingush Republic had collaborated with the Germans against the Red Army, despite a complete absence of any German presence in or anywhere near the territory. In fact, the local Sufi leadership had been quite sufficiently able to instigate anti-Soviet resistance without any external incitement to unrest. Some Sufis even managed to avoid deportation and, under a shaykh of the Batal Haji branch of the Qādiriyya, continued to fight a guerrilla war from the high mountains. The Batal Haji were noted for their puritanical strictness and exclusivism, refusing to eat with the uninitiated and marrying only among themselves. A Soviet observer remarked of the Sufis of the Caucasus in 1947:

> They are distinguished by their blind, unlimited and unreasoning faith in God: they actively propagate their religious beliefs and cannot endure those who do not share them. They endeavour to force their religion upon their relatives, their friends and their children and isolate themselves from the social and cultural collective life.[33]

The experience of exile only served to build a closer association between Sufism and nationalism, as they clung to both, while also promoting Sufism among the Kazakhs, Uzbeks and Karakalpaks of Central Asia. Following mass repatriation to their homeland in the late 1950s during Khrushchev's programme of de-Stalinization, the Soviet physical and verbal assault on the ṭarīqas persisted. They were branded as reactionaries, fanatics and criminals, as the Soviet press reported a number of trials of Sufi shaykhs and their murīds, particularly Naqshabandīs and Batal Hajīs. Major trials took place in 1958 and 1963–4.

The Soviet authorities identified the Sufi orders with ensuring the survival of the traditional religious order and the refusal to integrate into the Soviet way of life. They were seen to reject the learning of Russian, to avoid association with the Communist Party and military service. From the Soviet perspective, one of the most dangerous aspects of their influence lay in their efforts to attract the young by illegal religious education, allowing them to observe dhikr, distributing Sufi literature and taking children and young people to visit shrines. These included a number of tombs of Naqshabandīs and Qādirīs killed in anti-Russian and later anti-Soviet guerrilla fighting.[34] As part of their campaign to discourage such pilgrimage visits (*ziyārāt*), official establishment ᶜulamā' were co-opted to denounce the practice through the publication of *fatwās*. A *fatwā* issued by Haji Kurbanov, muftī of the North Caucasus and Daghestan in the 1960s, condemns the seeking of intercession at a grave:

> Question: Does Shariᶜyat law permit meeting at a *mazār* to pray?
>
> Answer: No, it does not. Our Prophet said that those people (who meet at a *mazār*) are sinners. He also said that during the pre-Islamic era of ignorance, when a man died, great honours were bestowed on him, a temple was built and people would pray at his image. This is paganism and those who practice it will have to answer on the Day of Judgment. The Prophet also said: "When I die, do not meet at my grave."
>
> Question: Is it allowed to ask a dead one for healing?
>
> Answer: No, this would be a sin, and moreover a useless one. The dead don't listen. . . .[35]

The fatwā seems oddly reminiscent of ᶜAbduh's fatwā of 1904 against intercession, but much less subtle and scholarly and not really concerned with the reform of Sufism, but with political control of Sufis.

However, notwithstanding official condemnation, holy places provided important opportunities for uniting Sufi religious activity with nationalist sentiments. Instead of dwindling under the force of Soviet anti-Sufism, the numbers of shrines and pilgrimages actually increased into the 1980s.[36]

By the time of the collapse of the Soviet Union in 1991, the failure of Soviet anti-Sufism was increasingly conspicuous. As Russian specialists had recognized, the vitality of Islam in the region was largely owing to the ṭarīqas. In Daghestan alone the number of working mosques had grown from 27 in 1974 to 600 in 1991. In Chechnya, where there had been no mosques between 1943 and 1978, there had been a huge upsurge in their restoration and construction.[37] But where Soviet anti-Sufism had failed, the Sufis of the North Caucasus would be faced with a new round of participation in resistance to the Russians.

Turkey: Sufis Between Secularists and Islamists

In Muslim lands Sufi concepts of the nature and role of the state were, in various cases, perceived to differ from those of controlling governments. Turkey provides a notable example of this type of conflict where efforts by the Kemalist government of the 1920s and 30s to create the new Turkish nation-state ran counter to the concept of the Islamic state supported by traditional Sufis, but also competed with incipient Kurdish nationalism in eastern Anatolia. In 1945, with the end of the one-party system controlled by the Republican People's Party, political parties were inclined to attempt the accommodation of Islam within the secular state. Hence there were moves away from extreme anti-Sufism, marked in 1949 by the reopening of tombs for pilgrimage visits (*ziyārāt*). Despite being officially banned, the ṭarīqas remained popular and, during the 1950s, began to make their influence felt politically behind the scenes.[38] This was especially so in the East where Sufi shaykhs effectively delivered the votes of their constituencies to allied politicians, the Democratic Party being notably assiduous in cultivating their support. The strength of the Naqshabandiyya in this regard was remarkable.[39] But the new movement of the Nurcus, a modernist spiritual organization originating from the Naqshabandiyya, was also courted.[40] Its founder, Bediüzzaman Said Nursi (1876–1960) hoped to see Turkey restored to the light of faith by a new sufistic interpretation of the Qur'ān for modern conditions, propagated through his treatises known as *Risale-i Nur* (Epistles of Light).

However, while the co-operation of Sufis and their fellow-travellers might be sought by anxious politicians, anti-Sufi measures were not completely suspended in the 1950s. On 3 February 1954, seventeen leading Naqshabandīs were arrested for attending an illegal dhikr. The mainly African order of the Tijāniyya, introduced into Turkey after World War I and forced underground in the general suppression of 1925, re-emerged under the leadership of an Ankara businessman and lawyer, Kemal Pilavoğlu. Its openly violent rejection of the Turkish secular state was expressed in the smashing of statues and busts of Atatürk, regarded by the Tijānīs as idols encouraging the Turks in a new form of *shirk*. The Tijānīs were quickly suppressed, Pilavoğlu sentenced to fifteen years' imprisonment. The government saw no benefit in seeking an accommodation with the Tijānīs. Even if it had been practicable, they had no large body of votes to be delivered.

In the 1960s and 70s, the more powerful Naqshabandīs and Nurcus continued to offer valued support for the Justice Party, successor to the

Democratic Party. However, the Naqshabandīs felt the position of their order further fortified by a widening membership, with other ṭarīqas, in the shanty towns growing up with mass rural-urban migration.[41] They were also to profit from the creation of a succession of religious parties: the National Order Party (1970–72), National Salvation Party (1973–80), and Welfare Party (1983–98), all headed by Dr. Necmettin Erbakan, himself maintaining close links with the Naqshabandīs.[42] Naqshabandīs were seen to be dominant in the grassroots of these parties' organization and of critical importance in ensuring funding through religiously-approved business enterprises. They were also active in journalism, promoting a Sufi spiritual orientation and opposing it to state-supported secularism and the establishment Islam approved by the Directorate of Religious Affairs.[43]

Welfare (Refah) experienced growing success in the 1990s, leading to a substantial share of the poll in the general elections of December 1995. Despite combined secularist party attempts to block Welfare's way to power, Erbakan succeeded in the spring of 1996 in becoming prime minister at the head of a shaky coalition government. However, the secularist position gathered reinforcement from the army and, under such pressure, Erbakan stepped down in June 1997. In January 1998 Welfare was shut down and Erbakan banned from politics for five years.

Secularist anti-Sufi politicians and military in Turkey have found themselves faced not simply by influential traditional ṭarīqas with demands for an Islamic state on the old Ottoman lines. Instead, they have been encountering modern-educated technocrats with sympathies for an activist Sufi agenda to be implemented through a new style of political organization influenced by the thinking of Sufi and non-Sufi Islamists outside Turkey. Links had been forged in the 1980s with Iran, perhaps not so surprising in view of Khumayni's personal spiritual commitment and sympathy for the Naqshabandiyya. More ironically, funding links were also developed with Saudi Arabia, most ideologically dedicated of anti-Sufi states, through the Saudi-sponsored Rābiṭat al-ᶜĀlam al-Islāmī (Islamic World League) interested in replacing the secular state with one based on Sharīᶜa.

Saudi Arabia and New Wahhābī Influences

Much change had occurred in the Suᶜūdī state since the time in the 1920s when Rashīd Riḍā had been so enthusiastic about the revival of

Wahhābism in the Arabian peninsula under the leadership of Ibn Su^cūd. ^cAbd al-^cAzīz b. Su^cūd (1876–1953) had continued to struggle for the extension of his authority in Arabia until the establishment of the kingdom of Saudi Arabia in 1932.[44] In spite of his evident piety and dedication to Wahhābī doctrines, not all Su^cūdīs would be convinced of the adequacy of his religious zeal. Among those matters which aroused their anxiety was his perceived readiness to compromise strict Wahhābī principles by showing a willingness to deal with those who did not accept their interpretation of the faith. This was seen, for example, in his reaching agreement with the British over the new kingdom's boundaries, allowing American engineers into the country to prospect for oil, surrounding himself with non-Wahhābī Syrian and Egyptian advisers and administrators and failing to enforce Wahhābism among the Shī^ca, particularly in the eastern part of the country.[45] Following the death of Ibn Su^cūd in 1953, the lapse from original Wahhābism was felt by critics to have become more marked, especially as oil revenues brought ever increasing luxury into an austere society.

Yet however far Saudi Arabia might deviate from the norms prescribed by Muḥammad b. ^cAbd al-Wahhāb, official support for his anti-Sufi position remained.[46] Among Su^cūdīs themselves, it might appear a matter of marginal contemporary concern but, with increasing wealth available to promote the Wahhābī message abroad, it became one aspect of Wahhābism that could be readily exported to areas where Sufism was still strong. It served to bolster a public image abroad of being true to reformist ideals which included a policy of anti-Sufism, even though the state might in practice be prepared to ease its relations with Sufis where it suited them, as in the Turkish case in which Sufism seemed to be less abhorrent than secularism in the eyes of Su^cūdī policymakers.

The founding of the above-noted Islamic World League in Mecca in 1962 was a key measure in the worldwide struggle to promote Wahhābī-approved understanding of Islam, cleansed of Sufi innovation. The League has devoted considerable funds for the training of those engaged in mission (*da^cwa*) and established regional councils such as the European Council of Mosques and the Islamic Co-ordinating Council of North America.

The European headquarters of the League in Brussels has been responsible for various prestigious projects, including the opening of the Centre Islamique et Culturel de Belgique in 1969, when the Belgian Minister of Justice handed the keys to King Fayṣal of Saudi

Arabia in a high profile public ceremony.[47] In its work among Muslim minorities in Europe, the League has lent its backing to those whom their enemies have often inaccurately labelled 'Wahhābī', notably the originally South Asian Deobandīs, Ahl-i Ḥadīth and the more recent reformist organization of Jamāᶜat-i Islāmī (founded 1941). The Barēlwīs, with their commitment to traditional Sufism, have been heavily criticized, being viewed as a dangerous innovating sect. In their turn, they established the World Islamic Mission in 1973 as a means of countering the Suᶜūdī attacks on their faith.[48] Their resentment of the Wahhābī assault on their position is evident in some resolutions passed at their conference held at the Wembley Conference Centre in May 1985:

> condemning Saudi officials for confiscating and allegedly destroying translations of the Qur'ān by Aḥmad Raza Khān and devotional books; complaining about the draconian measures to which Muslims in Medina and Mecca were exposed when they sought to celebrate the Prophet's birthday; seeking assurances that remaining sites associated with the Prophet, his family and companions would be respected and maintained.[49]

About one third of all the League's missionary *dāᶜīs* are working in Africa where they have been involved in propagating Wahhābī ideas in areas traditionally associated with the dominance of Sufi ṭarīqas. In Nigeria the Sardauna of Sokoto and premier of the Northern Region, Alhaji Sir Aḥmadu Bello (d. 1966), became linked with the League from early on in its establishment, being nominated Vice-President at its third meeting in 1963.[50] He was then heavily financed from Saudi Arabia for the work of *daᶜwa* in Nigeria and for the building of the Central Mosque in Lagos, interestingly despite the fact that he had personal connections with both the Qādiriyya and Tijāniyya and had performed pilgrimage visits to the tombs of their founders. However, the main conduit of Wahhābī ideology into Nigeria at this period was the chief judge (*qāḍī*) of Northern Nigeria, Alhaji Abubakr Gumi (d. 1992), a man more strictly dedicated to the struggle against Sufism than the Sardauna. Perhaps he was more suited to such campaigns through his training in Arabic legalism. In 1978 he founded the Society for the Eradication of Innovation and the Establishment of the Sunna, generally known as Izāla (Eradication).[51]

The 1960s also witnessed an influx of Saudi-backed Wahhābī influence in Ghana, albeit with less high level support than in

Nigeria.[52] The clash in this case was primarily with the Tijāniyya, especially as represented by the new branch associated with the Senegalese Ibrāhīm Niass (d. 1975). Niassi Tijānīs were readily charged by Wahhābīs with corrupting the purity of the faith due to such factors as their excessive reverence for Shaykh Ibrāhīm as the Seal of the Seal of the Saints (*khātim khātim al-awliyā'*), their belief that he would guarantee them salvation in the next world and that any member could achieve the degree of *quṭbāniyya* the highest point of mystical enlightenment.

Among Ghana's neighbours to the West, so-called 'Wahhābism' in Ivory Coast, Burkina Faso, Mali and Guinea has undergone vigorous development since the 1940s, but is only partially due to the direct influence of Saudi Arabia.[53] Anti-Sufism is a powerful element within it, but is owing to a variety of sources: actual Wahhābism imbibed directly by pilgrims during the *ḥajj* since the early period of Ibn Suᶜūd's gaining control of Mecca; the salafī reformism of ᶜAbduh and Riḍā as mediated by students returning from al-Azhar and contacts with the religious associations of Egypt, Jamāᶜat al-Shubbān al-Muslimīn (Society of Muslim Youth) founded in 1927 (hence the local name of the movement – Subbanu), also with the Muslim Brothers; a more recent overlay of Suᶜūdī contacts and funding. Saudi Arabia has undertaken the training of 'Wahhābī' teachers and *dāᶜīs*, who are seen to have the advantage of fluency in Arabic and access to a higher level of Islamic scholarship than most local non-Wahhābīs. Robert Launay, an anthropologist working among a Dyula community in the northern Ivory Coast, noted the impression made on local Muslims by a sermon given by one such returnee in 1985:

> Local Dyula, particularly those educated in French, were impressed. It was pointed out to me that he could pronounce Arabic in the way that Arabs do ... and not with the heavy accent of locally trained scholars. He read texts fluently out loud (rather than reciting them from memory) and could comment readily on the meaning of different words, glossing them in Dyula with greater ease, in the opinion of his audience, than local scholars could.[54]

However, there may also be the risk for trained Wahhābīs of being viewed with scepticism at times as agents of the Suᶜūdīs, which may not necessarily help the cause of anti-Sufism in the region.

Radical Rethinking of the Way

In the rising swell of voices critical of Sufism, many seem content with arguments that go little beyond those of the salafīs, which they reiterate usually in a simplified form. For most anti-Sufis there is little perceived need for the kind of adventurous rethinking attempted by Gökalp and Iqbāl between the Wars, so as to consider a new role for mysticism in contemporary Islamic society. It is sufficient to criticize the corruptions of traditional ṭarīqas and to conclude, with Sayyid Quṭb (1906–66) of the Egyptian Muslim Brothers, that lazy and superstitious Sufi shaykhs and their murīds should be excluded from the government of an Islamic state.[55] Two radical voices that would concur with such a view, but have also attempted a bolder rethinking are those of the Sunni Pakistani Abū'l-Aᶜlā Mawdūdī and the Shīᶜī Iranian ᶜAli Sharīᶜati. Both have been markedly influential in the contemporary Islamic revival, across sectarian lines and among both Sufis and anti-Sufis.

Abū'l-Aᶜlā Mawdūdī (1903–79)

The most prominent of contemporary Muslim revivalists in South Asia, Abū'l-Aᶜlā Mawdūdī would appear to have had all the right connections for the task of reassessing and even finding solutions to the problems facing Sufism in the subcontinent.[56] His own Sufi ancestry was impeccable, since he could claim descent, through a line of Mawdūdī *sayyids*, from distinguished masters of the great order of the Chishtiyya, including his eponymous ancestor Abū'l-Aᶜlā Mawdūdī (d. 1527), said to have introduced the order into India from Afghanistan. His own father, a lawyer by profession, was deeply involved in the ascetic pursuit of Sufism at the time of Abū'l-Aᶜlā's birth in 1903, to the extent that his family suffered privation as a result of his absorption in the mystical life. Regarding his reform credentials, Mawdūdī was a great admirer of Shāh Walī Allāh of Delhi, related through his paternal grandmother to Sayyid Aḥmad Khān and having personal working contacts with Muḥammad Iqbāl in 1937–8, when he was selected to administer Iqbāl's proposed model *dār al-ᶜulūm* at Pathankot in the Punjab, intended to train a new generation of Muslim leaders. Mawdūdī does not seem to have been Iqbāl's first choice for the post, but he and Jamāᶜat-i Islāmī, the revivalist organization which he founded in Lahore in 1941, were to stress the connection with the revered poet as a source of legitimacy for their movement.[57]

Mawdūdī was well-acquainted with aspects of Sufi theosophy and practice, not only through his father, but also through formal studies under Deobandī ᶜulamā' at the seminary of the Fatihpuri mosque in Delhi, where in 1926 he received a certificate (*ijāza*) to the effect that he had completed the study of texts on 'gradations of mystical ecstasy'.[58] He was also exposed to Deobandī reformist ideas critical of expressions of popular Sufism. Although he was working largely in journalism in the 1920s and 30s, Mawdūdī was involved in some more scholarly pursuits, including, in 1931, a translation into Urdu of *al-Asfār al-Arbaᶜa* (The Four Journeys) of Mullā Ṣadrā (1571–1641), a major theosophical text studied in India. Ṣadrā's views on the necessity of Sharīᶜa for the human's spiritual ascension seem to have made a deep impression on him at that time, which is probably reflected in his best-known short book, *Risāla-i dīniyya* (Treatise on Religion), written in fifteen days in 1932 and translated into English under the title *Towards Understanding Islam.*[59] In discussing *taṣawwuf* he remarked of later Sufis:

> They polluted the pure spring of Islamic *Taṣawwuf* with absurdities that could not be justified by any stretch of imagination on the basis of the Qur'ān and the Ḥadīth. Gradually a section of Muslims appeared who thought and proclaimed themselves immune to and above the requirements of the *Sharīᶜah*. These people are totally ignorant of Islam, for Islam cannot admit of Taṣawwuf that loosens itself out of the Sharīᶜah and takes liberties with it. No Sufi has the right to transgress the limits of the Sharīᶜah or treat lightly the primary obligations such as daily prayers, fasting, *zakāt* and the *ḥajj.*[60]

While apparently under Ṣadrāian influence, it is not difficult to see why his comments should have won enthusiastic approval in Saudi Arabia and in other anti-Sufi circles in the Arab world, being extensively promoted by the Muslim Brothers in the 1950s and 60s. This is even more understandable, when he goes on to attempt a redefinition of Sufism as no more than 'an intense love of Allāh and Muḥammad (peace be upon him),' requiring 'a strict obedience to their commands as embodied in the Book of God and the Sunnah of His Prophet.' Such a complete rejection of the entire esoteric tradition of Sufism would lead many members of the Jamāᶜat and admirers of

Mawdūdī to assume the major influences on him to have come from Ibn Taymiyya and Ibn ᶜAbd al-Wahhāb. Thus Maryam Jameelah, influential American convert from Judaism, claimed that 'the Maulana fully shared their unrelenting antagonism against Sufism in its developed form in favour of a rational exposition of the Faith in contemporary idiom to attract modern youth.'[61] However, she also felt dissatisfied with this redefinition of Sufism, labelling it 'limited' and 'superficial'.[62]

Poetry composed by Mawdūdī in the same period suggests that his private thoughts were far less simplistic and clear-cut than the popular message would suggest. They show a much stronger influence from the Sufi poetic heritage and probably also from Iqbāl's positive, life-asserting rethinking of the self. Thus, twisting the old imagery of *fanā'*, the moth burnt in the candle's flame, he wrote of the need for a new religious activism in the world:

> You have a hidden fire within you,
> So you don't need the candle.
> O, the burning desire of the moth become a radiant flame yourself.[63]

But the poetic Mawdūdī was not the one for widespread dissemination to a new generation of revivalist youth. The anti-ascetic message that would be remembered and issued in numerous reprints in the years of his old age, and after his death in 1979, was usually simpler and prosaic. Spiritual development was to be seen not as the exclusive preserve of traditional Sufis, but available to all humans as God's vicegerents, and not only as individuals, but as whole communities and nations.[64] The body was not to be denied and mortified as a prison for the soul, but regarded positively as its workshop, in which the soul could grow and develop through undertaking essential religious duties and responsibilities. There was no room for seclusion and retreat from the world and the new, life-affirming spiritual path led the believers closer to God through faith, obedience and piety until they reached the state in which their human will became identified with the will of God. The highest point would indeed by reached when the path was followed collectively and realized in the virtuous Islamic state. Such an alternative, uncomplicated Way would inspire younger generations far beyond Pakistan's borders, whether in Britain or Central Asia or Malaysia, often to rather crude and reductionist assaults on Sufis as representatives of an anachronistic and irrelevant esotericism.

Yet neither the older Mawdūdī nor all members of the Jamāᶜat totally abandoned traditional Sufism. In the 1970s towards the end of his life, Mawdūdī was ready to return to some of the Sufi devotional practices that he had previously rejected and even acted as a shaykh initiating followers into the Chishtiyya.[65] In the 1980s and 90s the Jamāᶜat was prepared to make concessions to popular Sufism in Pakistan, including shrine visitation. However, further afield the anti-Sufi orientation would usually be more dominant.

ᶜAlī Sharīᶜatī (1933–77)

Thirty years younger than Mawdūdī and brought up near Mashhad in eastern Iran by a father committed to modernist interpretation of the faith, ᶜAli Sharīᶜatī had fewer ties to the Sufi tradition than the Pakistani Sunni revivalist. He shared his father's concern to bring modern-educated youth back to Islam, to free them from Western ideologies irrelevant to Third World needs and at the same time offer them Islamic solutions more suited to life in the modern world than the obscurantist religion of the clerics. Sufism was for him a central element in that obscurantism which represented a retreat from the necessary active struggle to establish an Islamic order. The list of those whom Sharīᶜatī admired as precursors in true Islamic revolutionary reform over the last two centuries contains the names of some of the most notable reformers of Sufism and rethinkers of its social role: ᶜAbd al-Qādir of Algeria, Sayyid Aḥmad Khān, al-Afghānī, ᶜAbduh and the Salafiyya, Ḥasan al-Bannā' and Iqbāl.[66] However, as a Shīᶜi, Sharīᶜatī did not include Ibn ᶜAbd al-Wahhāb among the illustrious champions of reform, but noted the Wahhābīs along with Bābīs and Bahā'īs as guilty of introducing corrupt innovation into Islam. Their anti-Sufi stance did not serve to create a common ground between them.

Among the reformists, al-Afghānī and Iqbāl are singled out for the highest praise by Sharīᶜatī and seem to have the strongest impact on his own thinking. He speaks with respect of al-Afghānī's refusal to become absorbed in 'unraveling mystical intuitions, by conducting mortification of the flesh or by conducting hair-splitting research in jurisprudence, literature, philosophy etc.'[67] Iqbāl is similarly approved for not isolating himself from his society, on completion of his Ph.D., not burying himself in philosophical and mystical studies, spending his time with Socrates, Aristotle, Plato, Ibn Sīnā, Mullā Ṣadrā and Jalāl al-dīn Mawlawī (i.e. Rūmī).

> He realized that he had been sent on a mission to his people. His selfhood (*khudī*) philosophy was not a specialized theory. It was a revolutionary spirit that he wanted to blow into the skeleton of his society.[68]

Sharīᶜatī readily acknowledged the great poet-philosopher as a role model and seems to have felt much in common with him. He also had the experience of studying for a Ph.D. in Europe, in his case from 1960–1964 at the University of Paris. There he presented his doctoral thesis, an edition and translation of *Faḍā'il al-Balkh* (The Merits of Balkh), a medieval Persian text, although his personal studies of sociology were arguably far more influential on him and better known to a wider public. In France he was also politically active in the campaign of opposition to the Shah, founding the Liberation Movement of Iran Abroad soon after his arrival in 1960 and helping in the publication of *Free Iran*, a journal directed at Iranians in Europe. Not surprisingly, he was arrested as soon as he returned to Iran and spent six months in gaol. After his release, he could find employment only in high school, but later worked for a short while on the evening teaching programme at Mashhad University. But he became particularly well-known from the late 1960s, when he was invited to give lectures at the Ḥusayniyya Ershād Institute in Tehran and his dynamic oratory began to attract large audiences.[69] The Institute was far from being a traditional *ḥusayniyya*, a Shīᶜī teaching centre to encourage the emotional remembrance of Imām Ḥusayn's martyrdom at Karbalā in 680 C.E. It was intended instead to function as a teaching and research institute to propagate a modernist Shīᶜism. Sharīᶜatī, emerging as its brightest star, won the increasing enmity both of the Shah whose régime he indirectly attacked for despotism and corruption and of the religious conservatives. Much of his published writing resulted from talks at the Institute, in which Sufism is frequently condemned as part of a more generalized attack on clericalism. Eventually the Shah himself ordered the closing of the Institute in 1972 and Sharīᶜatī was once again imprisoned. Upon his release, he travelled to England, hoping apparently to seek a university teaching post in Algeria, but died in Southampton of a heart attack on 19 June 1977, although suspicions lingered among his sympathizers that SAVAK, the Shah's secret police, might be implicated in his death.

When Sharīᶜatī spoke in negative terms about Sufism, and he did so frequently, it was not that he denied the virtue of mysticism completely, but rather that he associated the way it had developed with reactionary clericalism, 'the degenerate and narcotizing religion' that he saw as opposed to 'the progressive and awakening religion.'[70] While admitting that advanced industrial societies stood in need of spirituality and mysticism to overcome their materialistic environment, he believed that this was far less the case with Third World and Islamic societies and that excessive devotion to such pursuits could distract the best minds from active involvement in their communities' affairs. He regarded it as a tragedy of history that societies were often either worldly or ascetic, when what was needed was a balance between the two. Human beings should be capable of combining responsible activity in the world with the spiritual dimension in order to achieve their true potential as God's vicegerents.[71] Sufis have gone wrong where they have failed to fulfil the first part of the human's duty to act responsibly in the world and have opted for the life of total seclusion.

With regard to particular Sufis, Sharīᶜatī displays mixed feelings. Those in the modern reformist tradition, such as the Algerian jihādist ᶜAbd al-Qādir, are obviously admired, since they do participate in the twin worldly and spiritual dimensions of life. Other earlier figures, such as Jalāl al-dīn Rūmī (d. 1273) or Mullā Ṣadrā (d. 1641), are sometimes referred to with respect and their opinions valued. Thus he expresses agreement with Rūmī in his interpretation of Qur'ān 33: 72 regarding the nature of the trust offered by God to humans as His representatives on earth, i.e. that this is the capacity for exercising free will and choice so as to be able to act contrary to one's nature.[72] As for Mullā Ṣadrā, he is regarded as exemplary of authentic Persian Islamic thought and values.[73] By contrast, the suffering martyr of divine love al-Ḥallāj (d. 922) is negatively depicted as a man aflame with the passionate love of God, but without any sense of social responsibility:

> Ḥallāj was constantly immersed in the burning invocation of God, and this was a source of true exaltation for him. But imagine if Iranian society were to consist of 25 million Ḥallāj's. It would be nothing but a vast lunatic asylum...'[74]

The society that emulated al-Ḥallāj, Sharīᶜatī concluded, would be heading for nothing but 'wretchedness and destruction'.

Yet, while Sharīᶜatī perceives acute dangers for the society obsessed with asceticism and overwhelmed by its pursuit of ecstatic experience, he is still making some moves in the direction of a modernist Islamic mysticism, which he would wish to distinguish from Sufism.[75] Unlike

Mawdūdī, he does indeed see the body as a prison for the soul and speaks of the need to free oneself from this last prison by the force of love, which, he claims, does not mean Sufi or theosophic love:

> By love I mean an Almighty force (which is beyond my rational and discretionary faculty) in the very depth of my being that can blow me apart and help me to rebel against my self. Since the prison is in me, my inside should be set aflame. How? Why fire? Why can't I liberate myself from this prison by utilizing my rational faculties?[76]

But the language in which he speaks of the need to free the 'I' from the dungeon of selfhood seems all too familiarly Sufi, and indeed Ḥallājian. It is reminiscent of al-Ḥallāj in the last days before his martyrdom causing both himself and his prison to disappear from view, as he had surmounted this dungeon of the self. But Sharīᶜatī, rather oddly, cannot bring himself to refer to such a source of inspiration, but looks to a non-Muslim as authority for his views, stating that man, 'in order to free himself from the prison of his self, as Radhakrishnan states, "He needs religion and love."'[77]

Sharīᶜatī's new strain of Islamic mysticism, if it can be so-called, is communal as much as it is individual. In this it has something in common with Mawdūdī's vision, and perhaps more with that of Ziya Gökalp fifty to sixty years earlier. This is possibly most clearly reflected in his book on the Pilgrimage, entitled simply *Ḥajj*.[78] The experience of the ḥajj is related in terms of an uplifting social transformation, in which the pilgrims aspire to free themselves from the forces of evil that keep their souls enslaved. In their struggle to break free of worldly entanglements, symbolized by their sacrifice of whatever they hold most dear (the equivalent of the Prophet Abraham's sacrifice of his son Ishmael), they are collectively purified and brought nearer to God as members of an Islamic society with a heightened sense of social responsibility. Mystical awareness leads them forward to active service in the community, not to isolation from it in the pursuit of personal, unshared and incommunicable ecstasy.

Unlike Mawdūdī, ᶜAli Sharīᶜatī founded no Islamic organization, but his voice would nevertheless be influential not only in progressive religious circles in Iran, especially among the youth, but would also be heard by Sunni as well as Shīᶜī revivalists much further afield, among the radical Sufis of Turkey and Central Asia as well as among Muslim activists disposed to share his critical perspective on Sufism.

Notes

1 A. J. Arberry, *Sufism* (1950), 122.
2 Clifford Geertz, *The Religion of Java* (Glencoe, Illinois: Free Press, 1960).
3 Julian Baldick, *Mystical Islam* (London: I. B. Tauris, 1989), 153.
4 M. D. Gilsenan, 'Some Factors in the Decline of the Sufi Orders in Modern Egypt,' *MW* 57 (1967): 17. Gilsenan was studying the Ḥāmidiyya Shādhiliyya from 1964 to 1966, a modern branch of the Shādhiliyya which had first gained recognition from the Supreme Council of Sufi Orders in 1926. Gilsenan viewed its growth as an exception to the general decline in Egyptian orders and ascribed its expansion to its 'relative newness' and hence energy and its high degree of centralized organization. For further details see Michael Gilsenan, *Saint and Sufi in Modern Egypt: an Essay in the Sociology of Religion* (Oxford: Oxford University Press, 1973).
5 See Saad Eddin Ibrahim, 'Egypt's Islamic Activism in the 1980s,' *TWQ* 10 (1988): 638–9 for figures of ṭarīqa membership from the 1960s to 1980s.
6 John Voll, 'Mahdīs, Walis and New Men in the Sudan,' in *Scholars, Saints and Sufis*, ed. Nikki Keddie (Berkeley, Los Angeles and London: University of California Press, 1972), 367–84.
7 Figures cited in Donal B. Cruise O'Brien, *Saints and Politicians: Essays in the Organization of a Senegalese Peasant Society* (Cambridge: Cambridge University Press, 1975), 157, giving estimates published in United States Army, *Area Handbook for Senegal* (Washington, D.C., 1963), 181.
8 For a re-examination of the emergence of the Murīds and their relationship to the French colonialists see David Robinson, 'Beyond Resistance and Collaboration: Amadu Bamba and the Murids of Senegal,' *JRA* 21 (1991): 149–71.
9 Donal B. Cruise O'Brien, *The Mourides of Senegal* (Oxford: Oxford University Press, 1971) for the first view and idem, *Saints and Politicians* for a revised opinion.
10 On Sufi involvement in Senegalese politics in this period see Donal Cruise O'Brien, 'Sufi Politics in Senegal,' in *Islam in the Political Process*, ed. James P. Piscatori (Cambridge: Cambridge University Press, 1983), 122–37.
11 On Āyat Allāh Khumaynī's mysticism see Mohammad Javad Gohari, 'Ibn al-ᶜArabī and Shīᶜism' (Ph.D. diss., University of Leeds, 1996), 240–306; Alexander Knysh, '*ᶜIrfān* Revisited: Khomeini and the Legacy of Islamic Mysticism,' *MEJ* 46 (1992): 631–53.
12 Imām Khomeini, *Islam and Revolution: Writings and Declarations*, trans. Hamid Algar (London: Kegan Paul International, 1985), 357–8.
13 Gohari, 'Ibn al-ᶜArabī and Shīᶜism,' 3 and 286–8. Text of letter reproduced in *International Ettela'at* No. 263, June 1995.
14 See Muhammad Sani Umar, 'Changing Islamic Identity in Nigeria from the 1960s to the 1980s: From Sufism to Anti-Sufism,' in *Muslim Identity and Social Change in Sub-Saharan Africa*, ed. Louis Brenner (London: Hurst and Co., 1993), 172–3.

15 See John Hunwick, 'Sub-Saharan Africa and the Wider World of Islam: Historical and Contemporary Perspectives' *JRA* 26 (1996): 240–1.

16 Patrick J. Ryan, 'Ariadne auf Naxos: Islam and Politics in a Religiously Pluralistic African Society,' *JRA* 26 (1996): 323.

17 The Burhāniyya was founded in the thirteenth century by Ibrāhīm b. Abī'l-Majd al-Dasūqī (c. 1246–1288), the name being taken from his *laqab* Burhān al-dīn. The order was also known previously as the Ibrāhīmiyya and the Dasūqiyya.

18 On the Aḥbāsh see A. Nizar Hamzeh and R. Hrair Dekmejian, 'A Sufi Response to Political Islamism: Al-Aḥbāsh of Lebanon' *IJMES* 28 (1996): 217–29.

19 Ibid.: 219 where the shaykh's name is given in full as ᶜAbd Allāh b. Muḥammad b. Yūsuf al-Ḥirārī al-Shībī al-ᶜAbdarī, 'also known as al-Ḥabashī,' born in al-Ḥirāra, near Somalia in 1920. He is noted as moving to the Ḥijāz in 1947 after his expulsion from Ethiopia by Emperor Haile Selassie on account of the perceived threat from his teachings. In 1948 he moved to Jerusalem and Damascus, studying with Rifāᶜī and Qādirī Sufis, before settling in Beirut.

20 Ibid.: 221.

21 Saad Eddin Ibrāhīm, 'Egypt's Islamic Activism': 639.

22 Najīb Maḥfūẓ, *al-Liṣṣ wa'l-Kilāb*, 4th ed. (Tunis: Dār al-Tūnisiyya li'l-Nashr, 1990), trans. Trevor Le Gassick and M. M. Badawi, revised by John Rodenbeck, *The Thief and the Dogs* (Cairo: American University in Cairo Press, 1961).

23 Ibid., trans., 52.

24 See Michael Gilsenan, *Saint and Sufi in Modern Egypt* for his earlier study and idem, *Recognizing Islam: Religion and Society in the Modern Middle East* (London and New York: I. B. Tauris and Co. Ltd., 1990), 229–43.

25 Najīb Maḥfūz, *al-Summān wa'l-Kharīf* (Cairo: Maktabat Misr, 1962), trans. Roger Allen, *Autumn Quail* (Cairo: American University in Cairo Press, 1985); idem, *al-Shaḥḥādh* (Cairo: Maktabat Miṣr, 1965), trans. Kristin Walker Henry and Nariman Khales Naili al-Warraki, *The Beggar* (Cairo: American University in Cairo Press, 1988).

26 Maḥfūẓ, *al-Shaḥḥādh*, 56; trans. Henry and Warraki, 39. Maḥfūẓ has here adapted the classical Sufi imagery of the soul being absorbed in God's ocean.

27 On ᶜAbd al-Ḥalīm Maḥmūd's views on Sufism and the Shādhiliyya see Ibrāhīm M. Abu-Rabi', 'Al-Azhar Sufism in Modern Egypt: the Sufi Thought of 'Abd al-Halim Mahmud' *IQ* 32 (1988): 207–35.

28 Ibid.: 221.

29 See further on this contemporary traditional Sufism in Egypt, Valerie Hoffman-Ladd, 'Devotion to the Prophet and His Family in Egyptian Sufism' *IJMES* 24 (1992): 615–39.

30 Ibid.: 618.

31 Ibid.: 618–19 on the controversy surrounding Muḥammad ᶜUthmān al-Burhānī's *Tabri'at al-dhimma fī nuṣḥ al-umma*.

32 On this Sufi-led resistance to the Soviets see Alexandre Bennigsen, 'Muslim Guerrilla Warfare in the Caucasus (1918–1928),' *CAS* 2 (1983): 45–56; Marie Bennigsen Broxup, 'The Last Ghazawat: The 1920–1921

Uprising,' in *The North Caucasus Barrier: The Russian Advance towards the Muslim World* (London: Hurst and Co., 112–45; and Abdurahman Avtorkhanov, 'The Chechens and the Ingush during the Soviet Period and its Antecedents' in ibid., 146–94.

33 V. G. Pivovarov, *Na Etapakh Sotsiologicheskogo Issledovaniia* (Groznyi, 1947),35, quoted in Chantal Lemercier-Quelquejay, 'Sufi Brotherhoods in the USSR: A Historical Survey' *CAS* 2 (1983): 17–18.

34 On Sufi tombs in the Soviet Union, including the North Caucasus, see Maria Eva Subtelny, 'The Cult of Holy Places: Religious Practices among Soviet Muslims' *MEJ* 43 (1989): 594–604. On Soviet attempts to deal with Sufism and nationalism in the North Caucasus in the 1970s and 80s, see Fanny E. B. Bryan, 'Internationalism, Nationalism and Islam' in *The North Caucasus Barrier*, 195–218.

35 Text of *fatwā* in I. A. Makatov, 'Kul't sviatykh v Islame,' *Voprosy Nauchnogo Ateizma* 3 (1967): 173–4, quoted in Alexandre Bennigsen and S. Enders Wimbush, *Mystics and Commissars: Sufism in the Soviet Union* (Berkeley and Los Angeles: University of California Press, 1985), 41.

36 Bryan, 'Internationalism,' 209–10.

37 Numbers of Soviet mosques in the 1970s provided in Alexandre Bennigsen and S. Enders Wimbush, *Muslims of the Soviet Empire: A Guide* (London and Bloomington: C. Hurst and Indiana University Press, 1986), 17–18; numbers in 1991 in Alexei V. Malashenko, 'Islam and Politics in the Southern Zone of the Former USSR,' in *Central Asia and Transcaucasia: Ethnicity and Conflict*, ed. Vitaly V. Naumkin (Westport and London: Greenwood Press, 1994), 111.

38 See Feroz Ahmad, 'Politics and Islam in Modern Turkey' *MES* 27 (1991): 3–21 on relations between Turkish political parties and Sufi orders.

39 On the Naqshabandiyya influence in the state in Turkey see Şerif Mardin, 'The Nakşibendi Order in Turkish History,' in *Islam in Modern Turkey*, ed. Richard Tapper (London and New York: I. B. Tauris, 1991), 121–42.

40 Ibid., 132–3; Ahmad, 'Politics and Islam': 11–12.

41 See Ozay Mehmet, *Islamic Identity and Development* (London and New York: Routledge, 1990), 121–5 on the changing social and political situation of Turkey's Sufi orders in the 1960s–80s.

42 On Erbakan and the National Salvation Party see Binnaz Toprak, 'Politicisation of Islam in a Secular State: The National Salvation Party in Turkey,' in *From Nationalism to Revolutionary Islam*, ed. Said Amir Arjomand (London and Basingstoke: Macmillan, 1984), 119–33.

43 For discussion of some themes in these Sufi journals see Sencer Ayata, 'Traditional Sufi Orders on the Periphery: Kadiri and Nakşibendi Islam in Konya and Trabzon,' in *Islam in Modern Turkey*, 223–53.

44 On the creation of the kingdom of Saudi Arabia see e.g. J. Kostiner, *The Making of Saudi Arabia 1916–1936: From Chieftancy to Monarchical State* (Oxford: Oxford University Press, 1993); L. McLoughlin, *Ibn Saud, Founder of a Kingdom* (Basingstoke: Macmillan, 1993).

45 The Shīᶜa constitute approximately 10% of the population of Saudi Arabia, concentrated mainly in the oil-rich area in the oases of al-Ḥasā and Qatīf in Eastern Province, with a small number in the Ḥijāz and near the Yemeni border.

46 See e.g. William Ochsenwald, 'Saudi Arabia and the Islamic Revival' *IJMES* 13 (1981): 271–86 on some aspects of contemporary Wahhābī thinking in Saudi Arabia. Ochsenwald (283) discusses a defence of Wahhābism by Dr. Muhammad Khalil Harras, Head of the Department of Theology in the College of Holy Law in Mecca, who remarks that 'the monarchy has acted correctly . . . in moving against spiritual enemies such as the mystics (*ṣūfīs*).'

47 On the Centre Islamique et Culturel de Belgique and its Muslim critics see Felice Dassetto, 'The Tabligh Organization in Belgium,' in *The New Islamic Presence in Western Europe*, ed. Tomas Gerholm and Yngve Georg Lithman (London: Mansell, 1988), 165–7 and 172 n. 16.

48 See Philip Lewis, *Islamic Britain, Religion, Politics and Identity among British Muslims: Bradford in the 1990s* (London and New York: I. B. Tauris, 1994), 83–5, 160–1, 164–5 on the Islamic World League and Barēlwī opposition to it in Britain.

49 Ibid., 85.

50 See John Hunwick, 'Sub-Saharan Africa': 238–41 on the links of Saudi Arabia and the Islamic World League with Nigeria, also (241) with Burkina Faso.

51 For further details on Abubakar Gumi and Izāla see Muḥammad Sani Umar, 'Changing Islamic Identity,' 154–78.

52 See Patrick J. Ryan, 'Ariadne auf Naxos': 323.

53 On the Subbanu 'Wahhābīs' see, for example, Lansine Kaba, *The Wahhabiyya: Islamic Reform and Politics in French West Africa* (Evanston: Northwestern University Press, 1974); Jean-Loup Amselle, 'A Case of Fundamentalism in West Africa: Wahabism in Bamako,' in *Studies in Religious Fundamentalism*, ed. Lionel Caplan (Basingstoke: Macmillan, 1987); R. W. Niezen, 'The "Community of Helpers of the Sunna": Islamic Reform among the Songhay of Gao (Mali)' *Africa* 60 (1990): 399–425; Louis Brenner, 'Constructing Muslim Identities in Mali,' in *Muslim Identity*, ed. Brenner, 59–78; René Otayek, 'Muslim Charisma in Burkina Faso,' in *Charisma and Brotherhood in African Islam*, eds. Donal B. Cruise O'Brien and Christian Coulon (Oxford: Clarendon Press, 1988), 91–112.

54 Robert Launay, *Beyond the Stream: Islam and Society in a West African Town* (Berkeley, Los Angeles and Oxford: University of California Press, 1992), 94–5.

55 Youssef M. Choueiri, *Islamic Fundamentalism* (London: Pinter, 1990), 99 on Quṭb's attitude to Sufis, but also (121) his greater concern with the secular state as the greater enemy of Islam than corrupt Sufi orders.

56 Of the numerous writings on Abū'l-Aᶜlā Mawdūdī, many are concerned with the political aspects of his career and thought on Islamic government. For a recent biography which takes into consideration his relationship to Sufism, see Seyyed Vali Reza Nasr, *Mawdudi and the Making of Islamic Revivalism* (New York and Oxford: Oxford University Press, 1996), to which I am indebted for information in this short account.

57 Ibid., 34–9 on relations between Mawdūdī and Iqbāl and the Dār al-Islām project.

58 Ibid., 18–19 and 147–8, n. 78 on these Deobandī studies.

59 Abū'l-Aʿlā Mawdūdī, *Towards Understanding Islam* (London: U.K. Islamic Mission, 1980), 104–5 on *Taṣawwuf*.
60 Ibid., 105.
61 Maryam Jameelah, 'An Appraisal of Some Aspects of Maulana Sayyid Ala Maudoodi's Life and Thought' *IQ* 31 (1987): 118.
62 Ibid., 129.
63 Poem dated 18 July 1932, trans. in Nasr, *Mawdudi*, 141.
64 See the development of this theme of an activist Islamic road to spirituality in Abū'l-Aʿlā Mawdūdī, 'The Spiritual System of Islam,' in *Islamic Way of Life*, trans. Khurshid Aḥmad (Damascus: The Holy Koran Publishing House, 1977), 80–92. This is the text of a talk originally broadcast on Radio Pakistan on 16 March 1948.
65 Nasr, *Mawdudi*, 128.
66 From a list cited in ʿAli Sharīʿatī, *What Is to be Done: The Enlightened Thinkers and an Islamic Renaissance*, ed. Farhang Rajaee (Houston, Texas: The Institute for Research and Islamic Studies, 1986), 148–9.
67 Ibid., 58.
68 Ibid., 59.
69 On the Ḥusayniyya Ershād Institute see e.g. H.E. Chehabi, *Iranian Politics and Religious Modernism: The Liberation Movement of Iran under the Shah and Khomeini* (London: I. B. Tauris, 1990), 202–10.
70 Sharīʿatī, *What Is to be Done*, 63.
71 ʿAli Sharīʿatī, *Man and Islam*, trans. Fatollah Marjani (Houston, Texas: Free Islamic Literatures Inc., 1981), 6–9.
72 Ibid., 5.
73 Ibid., 118.
74 ʿAli Sharīʿatī, *On the Sociology of Islam*, trans. Hamid Algar (Berkeley: Mizan Press, 1979), 68.
75 On this mystical tendency in Sharīʿatī, compare Steven R. Benson, 'Islam and Social Change in the Writings of ʿAli Sharīʿatī: His *Ḥajj* as a Mystical Handbook for Revolutionaries' *MW* 81 (1991): 9–26.
76 Sharīʿatī, *Man and Islam*, 60.
77 Ibid., 62.
78 Idem, *Ḥajj*, trans. ʿAli A. Behzadnia and Najla Denny (Houston: Free Islamic Literatures Inc., 1974).

Conclusion: Many Ways Towards the One

When, in 1731, Shāh Walī Allāh accepted the mantle of the Prophet, the options for the reform of Sufism would have been recognizable to practitioners of the classical Sufi tradition. By 1930, when Muḥammad Iqbāl published his *Reconstruction of Religious Thought in Islam*, this was no longer the case. While there was still a strong sense of continuity, the range of possibilities for reconstructing thought about Islamic mysticism had extended in unfamiliar directions, as had the grounds for varying degrees of rejection of Sufism. The two hundred years from the 1730s to 1930s mark a critical period in which Muslims were moved to reassess their relationship to Sufism as a key area of their religious tradition and to reconsider its role in their societies.

The great Islamic revival of the eighteenth and early nineteenth centuries laid the essential foundations for modern reform, whether by reformist Sufis or devoted anti-Sufi Wahhābīs. Despite differences of opinion on the need for mystical guidance, they have been seen to share a number of concerns: the desire to root out un-Islamic accretions to the faith and to raise the level of religious observance in conformity with Sharīᶜa in the wider community beyond the circles of the ᶜulamā'. This would frequently involve the formation of large-scale movements with centralized organization, sometimes leading to the birth of Islamic states. The reformers' efforts were to remain a point of reference for successive generations. For Sufis there were many charismatic models, with whom connections would be traced through networks of initiation. Thus in Africa members of the Tijāniyya could look back to Aḥmad al-Tijānī, Nigerian Qādirīs to Usuman dan Fodio, Libyan Sanūsīs and Sudanese Sufis of the Khatmiyya, Rashīdiyya and its offshoots to Aḥmad b. Idrīs, who would also inspire the reformist thought of the Sudanese Mahdī. The Naqshabandiyya would link the great Sufi jihādists ᶜAbd al-Qādir of Algeria and Shamīl of the Caucasus to the Walī Allāhī reforming chain, connecting them with the order in India. But the line of Shāh Walī Allāh would also lend inspiration to all shades of critical and uncritical opinion with regard to Sufism in late nineteenth century India and its spiritual heritage be claimed by all competing visions of reform to the present day. For the total rejecters of Sufism the paradigm was supplied by the distinctly uncharismatic model of Muḥammad b. ᶜAbd al-Wahhāb and the first Wahhābī-Suᶜūdī state in Arabia, for whom an excessive respect for Sufi charisma was anathema.

Throughout the nineteenth century Sufis of all complexions, along with the smaller numbers of anti-Sufi Muslims, would be challenged by the forces of European modernity on both a physical and intellectual level. The Sufi activists who countered the physical European assault generally mark a continuation of the revivalist patterns, but failure, quietism or collaboration could damage their credibility for the future. Alternatively, successful jihād and implementation of moral reform, or at times European colonialist support for a ṭarīqa, might lead to expansion. When, as in India, defenders of traditional and reformist Sufism and anti-Sufis all sought ways to preserve their idea of an Islamic order alongside the realities of British rule, their thought remained mainly within an identifiable Islamic and Sufi framework.

Real change occurred from the late nineteenth century with increasing interaction of Sufi and modern Western thought, as early Muslim modernists followed the lead of Sayyid Aḥmad Khān and Jamāl al-dīn al-Afghānī in attempting to envisage a rational and progressive religion wrested from the inadequate safekeeping of Sufi shaykhs. For these same Sufi shaykhs, the modernists represented the real enemies of the faith who threatened to spread atheism among the people. To the prominent Rifāᶜī Shaykh Abū'l-Hudā al-Ṣayyādī the acute need was for a united front of ṭarīqas and their organized expansion in the Ottoman Empire to resist the contamination of authentic Sufi faith by un-Islamic accretions from the ideas of the West. The voices of Westernizing and modernizing critics have been more often heard than those of the Sufi defenders of the spiritual *status quo*, but perhaps the Sufis should be given rather more credit for identifying the essential incompatibility between their theosophy and the new rationalism.

However, questions lingered about the nature of the true Sufism, which the Egyptian Shādhilī Sufi and scholar, Muḥammad ᶜAbduh, identified as part of the original pure religion of Islam, the faith of the pious ancestors, fully able to adjust to the modern world in an enlightened and reasonable manner. All that was needed was to strip away the corrupt manifestations of Sufism that had encrusted it over the centuries. In his attacks on the familiar corruptions, ᶜAbduh made use of quite traditional Islamic argumentation, in spite of the lip service paid to adaptation to the new conditions of the late nineteenth to early twentieth centuries. His most famous disciple, Rashīd Riḍā, and activists in the Salafiyya movement also displayed a rather conservative attachment to older ways, even when these showed a closer relationship to anti-Sufi Wahhābism than would be approved by ᶜAbduh.

The more radical pioneering thought about a new style of Islamic mysticism is that associated with Ziya Gökalp in Turkey and with Muḥammad Iqbāl in India. This indicates much more of a break with mainstream Islamic reforming ideas about Sufism and attempts to employ both Sufi theosophy and modern European philosophy and sociology in the effort to make mysticism relevant to the construction of new Muslim nations. However, they seem to have had few successors. While both could and did inspire generations of nationalist youth, their thinking may be seen as too adventurous and lacking the sense of Islamic authenticity conferred by remaining more fully attached to indigenous models of reform. Consequently, they emerge as somewhat isolated exemplars of the possibilities of rethinking a mystical Islam rather than builders of mass movements. One of their few genuine and successfully influential heirs was ᶜAlī Sharīᶜatī.

For the most part, it is the more traditional and largely indigenous thought for and against Sufism that has proved most durable, ṭarīqas, whether traditional or reformed to any extent, facing anti-Sufi organizations modelled on ideologies owing much to the Wahhābīs and Salafīs. Both Sufis and anti-Sufis have flourished in the contemporary Islamic revival and frequently continue to be embattled, although at times they may also show awareness of the need to overcome differences in order to withstand the threat to both from the creeping dangers of secularism and the attractions of the material world.

Bibliography

ᶜAbduh, Muḥammad. *Al-Aᶜmāl al-Kāmila li'l-Imām Muḥammad ᶜAbduh.* Edited by Muḥammad ᶜAmāra. 2d ed. Vols. 2 and 3. Beirut: al-Mu'assasa al-ᶜArabiyya li'l-dirāsāt wa'l-nashr 1980.

Abu-Manneh, Butrus. 'Sultan Abdulhamid II and Shaikh Abulhuda al-Ṣayyādī.' *Middle Eastern Studies* 15 (1979): 131–53.

——. 'The Naqshabandiyya-Mujaddidiyya in the Ottoman Lands in the Early 19th Century.' *Die Welt des Islams* 12 (1982): 1–36.

Abun-Nasr, Jamil M. *A History of the Maghrib in the Islamic Period.* Cambridge: Cambridge University Press, 1987.

——. 'The Salafiyya Movement in Morocco: the religious bases of the Moroccan nationalist movement.' In *St. Antony's Papers* 16, ed. Albert Hourani *Middle Eastern Affairs* 3 (1963): 90–105.

——. *The Tijaniyya.* Oxford: Oxford University Press, 1965.

Abu-Rabiᶜ, Ibrahim M. 'Al-Azhar Sufism in Modern Egypt: the Sufi Thought of ᶜAbd al-Halīm Mahmud.' *Islamic Quarterly* 32 (1988): 207–35.

Adams, Charles C. *Islam and Modernism in Egypt.* London: Oxford University Press, 1933.

Ahmad, Aziz. 'Sources of Iqbal's Perfect Man.' In *Studies in Iqbal's Thought and Art,* ed. M. Saeed Sheikh, 107–32. Lahore: Bazm-i Iqbal, 1972.

Ahmad, Feroz. 'Politics and Islam in Modern Turkey.' *Middle Eastern Studies* 27 (1991): 3–21.

Algar, Hamid. 'Some Notes on the Naqshabandi Tariqat in Bosnia.' *Die Welt des Islams* (1972): 168–203.

Amselle, Jean-Loup. 'A Case of Fundamentalism in West Africa: Wahabism in Bamako.' In *Studies in Religious Fundamentalism,* ed. Lionel Caplan, 79–93. Basingstoke: Macmillan, 1987.

Ansari, M. Abdul Haq. 'Ibn Taymiyah's Criticism of Sufism.' *Islam and the Modern Age* (1984): 147–56.

——. 'Shah Waliy Allah's Attempts to Revise *Waḥdat al-Wujūd.*' *Arabica* 35 (1988):197–213.

Arberry, A. J. *Sufism: An Account of the Mystics of Islam.* London: George Allen and Unwin Ltd., 1950.

Ayata, Sencer. 'Traditional Sufi Orders on the Periphery: Kadiri and Nakşibendi Islam in Konya and Trabzon.' In *Islam in Modern Turkey,* ed. Richard Tapper, 223–53. London: and New York: I. B. Tauris, 1991.

Baddeley, John F. *The Russian Conquest of the Caucasus*. London, 1908. Reprint, New York: Russell and Russell, 1969.

Baldick, Julian. *Mystical Islam*. London: I. B. Tauris, 1989.

Baljon, J. M. S. *Religion and Thought of Shāh Walī Allāh Dihlawī 1703–1762*. Leiden: E. J. Brill, 1986.

Bayat, Mangol. *Iran's First Revolution: Shiᶜism and the Constitutional Revolution of 1905–1909*. New York and Oxford: Oxford University Press, 1991.

Bennigsen, Alexandre. 'Muslim Guerrilla Warfare in the Caucasus (1918–1928).' *Central Asian Survey* 2 (1983): 45–56.

—— and S. Enders Wimbush. *Muslims of the Soviet Empire: A Guide*. London and Bloomington: C. Hurst and Indiana University Press, 1986.

——. *Mystics and Commissars: Sufism in the Soviet Union*. Berkeley and Los Angeles: University of California Press, 1985.

Benson, Steven R. 'Islam and Social Change in the Writings of ᶜAlī Sharīᶜatī: His *Ḥajj* as a Mystical Handbook for Revolutionaries.' *Muslim World* 81 (1991): 9–26.

Berkes, Niyazi. *Turkish Nationalism and Western Civilization: Selected Essays of Ziya Gökalp*. London: George Allen and Unwin Ltd., 1959.

Birge, J. F. *The Bektashi Order of Dervishes*. London: Luzac, 1937. Reprint, Luzac Oriental, 1994.

Brenner, Louis. 'Concepts of *Ṭarīqa* in West Africa: The Case of the Qādiriyya.' In *Charisma and Brotherhood in African Islam*, ed. Donal B. Cruise O'Brien and Christian Coulon, 33–52. Oxford: Clarendon Press, 1988.

——. ed. *Muslim Identity and Social Change in Sub-Saharan Africa*. London: Hurst and Co., 1993.

——. 'Muslim Thought in Eighteenth-Century West Africa: The Case of Shaykh Uthman b. Fudi.' In *Eighteenth Century Renewal and Reform in Islam*, ed. Nehemia Levtzion and John Voll, 40–67. New York: Syracuse University Press, 1987.

Broxup, Marie Bennigsen, ed. *The North Caucasus Barrier: The Russian Advance towards the Muslim World*. London: C. Hurst and Co., 1992.

Busool, Assad Nimer. 'Shaykh Muḥammad Rashīd Riḍā's Relations with Jamāl al-dīn al-Afghānī and Muḥammad ᶜAbduh.' *Muslim World* 66 (1976): 272–86.

Chehabi, H. E. *Iranian Politics and Religious Modernism: The Liberation Movement of Iran under the Shah and Khomeini*. London: I. B. Tauris, 1990.

Commins, David. 'ᶜAbd al-Qādir al-Jazā'irī and Islamic Reform.' *Muslim World* 78 (1988): 121–31.

——. *Islamic Reform: Politics and Social Change in Late Ottoman Syria*. New York and Oxford: Oxford University Press, 1990.

——. 'Religious Reformers and Arabists in Damascus, 1885–1914.' *International Journal of Middle East Studies* 18 (1986): 405–25.

Cruise O'Brien, Donal B. and Christian Coulon, eds. *Charisma and Brotherhood in African Islam*. Oxford: Clarendon Press, 1988.

Cruise O'Brien, Donal B. *Saints and Politicians: Essays in the organization of a Senegalese peasant society.* Cambridge: Cambridge University Press, 1975.

——. 'Sufi Politics in Senegal.' In *Islam in the Political Process,* ed. James P. Piscatori, 122–37. Cambridge: Cambridge University Press, 1983.

——. *The Mourides of Senegal.* Oxford: Oxford University Press, 1971.

Daniel, Elton L. 'Theology and Mysticism in the Writings of Ziya Gökalp.' *Muslim World* 67 (1977): 175–84.

Dar, Bashir. *Religious Thought of Sayyid Ahmad Khan.* 2d ed. Lahore: Institute of Islamic Culture, 1971.

Dassetto, Felice. 'The Tabligh Organization in Belgium.' In *The New Islamic Presence in Western Europe,* ed. Tomas Gerholm and Yngve Georg Lithman, 159–73. London: Mansell, 1988.

Davison, Roderic H. 'Jamal al-Din Afghani: a note on his nationality and on his burial.' *Middle Eastern Studies* 24 (1988): 110–12.

de Jong, F. *Ṭuruq and Ṭuruq-Linked Institutions in Nineteenth Century Egypt.* Leiden: E. J. Brill, 1978.

Donohue, John J. and John L. Esposito, eds. *Islam in Transition: Muslim Perspectives.* New York and Oxford: Oxford University Press, 1982.

Escovitz, Joseph H. '"He was the Muḥammad ᶜAbduh of Syria": a study of Ṭāhir al-Jazā'irī and his influence.' *International Journal of Middle East Studies* 18 (1986): 293–310.

Gammer, Moshe. *Muslim Resistance to the Tsar: Shamil and the Conquest of Chechnia and Daghestan.* London: Frank Cass and Co. Ltd., 1994.

Geertz, Clifford. *The Religion of Java.* Glencoe, Illinois: Free Press, 1960.

Gilsenan, Michael. *Recognizing Islam: Religion and Society in the Modern Middle East.* London and New York: I. B. Tauris, 1990.

——. *Saint and Sufi in Modern Egypt: an Essay in the Sociology of Religion.* Oxford: Oxford University Press, 1973.

——. 'Some Factors in the Decline of the Sufi Orders in Modern Egypt.' *Muslim World* 57 (1967): 11–18.

Gohari, Muhammad Javad.' Ibn al-ᶜArabī and Shiᶜism.' Ph.D. diss., University of Leeds, 1996.

Gökalp, Ziya. *The Principles of Turkism.* Translated by Robert Devereux, Leiden: E. J. Brill, 1968.

Hamzeh, A. Nizar and R. Hrair Dekmejian. 'A Sufi Response to Political Islamism: Al-Aḥbāsh of Lebanon.' *International Journal of Middle East Studies* 28 (1996): 217–29.

Hanisch, Ludmila. 'The Denunciation of Mysticism as a Bulwark against Reason – a contribution to the expansion of Algerian reformism 1925–1939.' *The Maghreb Review* Vol. 11, 5–6 (1986): 102–6.

Heyd, Uriel. *Foundations of Turkish Nationalism: The Life and Teachings of Ziya Gökalp.* London: Luzac, 1950.

Hiskett, Mervyn. '*Kitāb al-Farq*: a work on the Habe kingdoms attributed to ᶜUthmān dan Fodio.' *Bulletin of the School of Oriental and African Studies* 23 (1960): 559–72.

——. The *Course of Islam in Africa.* Edinburgh: Edinburgh University Press, 1994.

——. *The Sword of Truth.* London: Oxford University Press, 1973.

Hodgson, M. G. S. *The Venture of Islam*. Vol. 3. Chicago: Chicago University Press, 1974.

Hoffman-Ladd, Valerie J. 'Devotion to the Prophet and His Family in Egyptian Sufism.' *International Journal of Middle East Studies* 24 (1992): 615–39.

Holt, P. M. *The Mahdist State in the Sudan, 1881–1898*. Oxford: Oxford University Press, 1970.

Hourani, Albert. *Arabic Thought in the Liberal Age, 1798–1939*. London: Oxford University Press, 1962.

——. 'Sufism and Modern Islam: Mawlāna Khālid and the Naqshbandī Order.' In *The Emergence of the Modern Middle East*. London: Macmillan, 1981.

——. 'Sufism and Modern Islam: Rashid Riḍa.' In *The Emergence of the Modern Middle East*. London: Macmillan, 1981.

Hunwick, John. 'Sub-Saharan Africa and the Wider World of Islam: Historical and Contemporary Perspectives.' *Journal of Religion in Africa* 26 (1996): 230–57.

Ibn Bishr, ᶜUthmān, ed. *Majmūᶜat al-rasā'il wa'l-masā'il al-najdiyya*. Vol. 1. Cairo, 1928.

Ibrahim, Saad Eddin. 'Egypt's Islamic Activism in the 1980s.' *Third World Quarterly* 10 (1988): 632–57.

Iqbal, Muhammad. *The Reconstruction of Religious Thought in Islam*. Lahore, 1930. Reprint, Lahore: Sh. Muhammad Ashraf, 1977.

——. *The Secrets of the Self*. Translated by Reynold A. Nicholson. Lahore: Sh. Muḥammad Ashraf, 1955.

Jameelah, Maryam. 'An Appraisal of Some Aspects of Maulana Sayyid Ala Maudoodi's Life and Thought.' *Islamic Quarterly* 31 (1987): 116–30.

Kaba, Lansine. *The Wahhabiyya: Islamic Reform and Politics in French West Africa*. Evanston: Northwestern University Press, 1974.

Karrar, Ali Salih. *The Sufi Brotherhoods in the Sudan*. London: Hurst and Co., 1992.

Keddie, Nikki R. *An Islamic Response to Imperialism: Political and Religious Writings of Sayyid Jamal al-din al-Afghani*. 2d ed. Berkeley: University of California Press, 1983.

——. *Sayyid Jamal al-din "al-Afghani": A Political Biography*. Berkeley, Los Angeles and London: University of California Press, 1972.

Kedourie, Elie. *Afghani and ᶜAbduh: an essay on religious unbelief and political activism in modern Islam*. London: Frank Cass and Co., 1966.

Khomeini, Imam. *Islam and Revolution: Writings and Declarations*. Translated by Hamid Algar. London: Kegan Paul International, 1985.

Knysh, Alexander. '*ᶜIrfān* Revisited: Khomeini and the Legacy of Islamic Mysticism.' *Middle East Journal* 46 (1992): 631–53.

Kostiner, J. *The Making of Saudi Arabia 1916–1936: From Chieftancy to Monarchical State*. Oxford: Oxford University Press, 1993.

Kudsi-Zadeh, A. Albert. 'Islamic Reform in Egypt: Some Observations on the Role of Afghani.' *Muslim World* 61 (1971): 1–12.

Lane, E. W. *An Account of the Manners and Customs of the Modern Egyptians*. London, 1836; reprint, London: J. M. Dent and Sons, 1936.

Launay, Robert. *Beyond the Stream: Islam and Society in a West African Town*. Berkeley, Los Angeles and Oxford: University of California Press, 1992.
Lee, J. L. 'Bektashiyya Sufism of Turkey and the Balkans.' Birmingham: Centre for the Study of Islam and Christianity Papers, No. 11, 1994.
Lelyveld, David. *Aligarh's First Generation: Muslim Solidarity in British India*. Princeton, N.J.: Princeton University Press, 1978.
Lewis, Bernard. *The Emergence of Modern Turkey.* London: Oxford University Press, 1961.
Lewis, Philip. *Islamic Britain. Religion, Politics and Identity among British Muslims: Bradford in the 1990s.* London and New York: I. B. Tauris, 1994.
McLoughlin, L. *Ibn Saud, Founder of a Kingdom*. Basingstoke: Macmillan, 1993.
Maḥfūz, Najīb. *Al-Liṣṣ wa'l-Kilāb.* 4th ed. Tunis: al-Dār al-Tūnisiyya li'l-Nashr, 1990. Translated by Trevor Le Gassick and M. M. Badawi, revised by John Rodenbeck. *The Thief and the Dogs*. Cairo: American University in Cairo Press, 1961.
——. *Al-Shaḥḥādh*. Cairo: Maktabat Miṣr, 1965. Translated by Kristin Walker Henry and Nariman Khales Naili al-Warraki. *The Beggar.* Cairo: American University in Cairo Press, 1988.
——. *Al-Summān wa'l-Kharīf*. Cairo: Maktabat Miṣr, 1962. Translated by Roger Allen. *Autumn Quail*. Cairo: American University in Cairo Press, 1985.
Makdisi, George. *Religion, Law and Learning in Classical Islam.* Hampshire and Vermont: Variorum, 1991.
Malashenko, Alexei V. 'Islam and Politics in the Southern Zone of the Former USSR.' In *Central Asia and Transcaucasia: Ethnicity and Conflict,* ed. Vitaly V. Naumkin,109–26. Westport and London: Greenwood Press, 1994.
Mardin, Şerif. 'The Nakşibendi Order in Turkish History.' In *Islam in Modern Turkey,* ed. Richard Tapper, 121–42. London and New York: I. B. Tauris, 1991.
Martin, B. G. *Muslim Brotherhoods in Nineteenth Century Africa.* Cambridge: Cambridge University Press, 1977.
Maududi, Abu'l-A'la. *Islamic Way of Life.* Translated by Khurshid Aḥmad. Damascus: The Holy Koran Publishing House, 1977.
——. *Towards Understanding Islam.* London: U.K. Islamic Mission, 1980.
Mehmet, Ozay. *Islamic Identity and Development.* London and New York: Routledge,1990.
Meier, Fritz. 'Das sauberste über die vorbestimmung. Ein stück Ibn Taymiyya.' *Saeculum* 32 (1981): 74–89.
Metcalf, Barbara Daly. *Islamic Revival in British India, Deoband 1860–1900.* Princeton, N.J.: Princeton University Press, 1982.
Milson, Menahem. 'The Elusive Jamāl al-dīn al-Afghānī.' *Muslim World* 58 (1968): 295–307.
Morsy, Magali. *North Africa 1800–1900: a Survey from the Nile Valley to the Atlantic.* Harlow: Longman, 1984.

Mortimer, Edward. *Faith and Power: the Politics of Islam*. New York: Vintage Books, 1982.
Nasr, Sayyed Vali Reza. *Mawdudi and the Making of Islamic Revivalism*. New York and Oxford: Oxford University Press, 1996.
Niezen, R. W. 'The "Community of Helpers of the Sunna": Islamic Reform among the Songhay of Gao (Mali).' *Africa* 60 (1990): 399–423.
Norris, H. T. *Islam in the Balkans: Religion and Society between Europe and the Arab World*. London: Hurst and Co., 1993.
Ochsenwald, William. 'Saudi Arabia and the Islamic Revival.' *International Journal of Middle East Studies* 13 (1981): 271–86.
O'Fahey, R. S. *Enigmatic Saint: Ahmad Ibn Idris and the Idrisi Tradition*. London: Hurst and Co., 1990.
—— and Bernd Radtke. 'Neo-Sufism Reconsidered.' *Der Islam* 70 (1993): 52–87.
Peters, Rudolph. *Islam and Colonialism*. The Hague: Mouton, 1979.
Piscatori, James P. ed. *Islam in the Political Process*. Cambridge: Cambridge University Press, 1983.
Quelquejay, Chantal Lemercier. 'Sufi Brotherhoods in the USSR: A Historical Survey.' *Central Asian Survey* 2 (1983): 1–35.
Rahman, Fazlur. *Islam*. Chicago: Chicago University Press, 1966. 2d ed., 1979.
Reid, Donald M. *The Odyssey of Farah Antun*. Minneapolis and Chicago: Bibliotheca Islamica Inc., 1975.
Renard, John. '*Al-Jihād al-Akbar*: Notes on a Theme in Islamic Spirituality.' *Muslim World* 78 (1988): 225–42.
Riḍā, Muḥammad Rashīd. *Al-Manār wa'l-Azhar*. Cairo, 1353/1934–5.
Robinson, David. 'Beyond Resistance and Collaboration: Amadu Bamba and the Murids of Senegal.' *Journal of Religion in Africa* 21 (1991): 149–71.
Rodinson, Maxime. *Europe and the Mystique of Islam*. London: I. B. Tauris, 1988.
Ryan, Patrick J. 'Ariadne auf Naxos: Islam and Politics in a Religiously Pluralistic African Society.' *Journal of Religion in Africa* 26 (1996): 308–29.
Said, Edward. *Orientalism*. London: Routledge and Kegan Paul, 1978.
al-Ṣayyādī, Muḥammad Abū'l-Hudā. *Al-Ḥaqq al-mubīn fī ibhāt al-ḥāsidīn*. Cairo, 1310/1892–3.
——. *Tanwīr al-abṣār fī ṭabaqāt al-sādat al-Rifāᶜiyya al-Akhyār*. Cairo 1306/1888–9.
Schimmel, Annemarie. *And Muḥammad is His Messenger*. Chapel Hill: University of North Carolina Press, 1985.
——. *Gabriel's Wing: a study into the religious ideas of Sir Muhammad Iqbal*. 2d ed. Lahore: Iqbal Academy, 1989.
——. *Mystical Dimensions of Islam*. Chapel Hill: University of North Carolina Press, 1975.
Sharīᶜatī, ᶜAli. *Ḥajj*. Translated by ᶜAli A. Behrzadnia and Najla Denny. Houston: Free Islamic Literatures Inc., 1974.
——. *Man and Islam*. Translated by Fatollah Marjani. Houston: Free Islamic Literatures Inc., 1981.

——. *On the Sociology of Islam*. Translated by Hamid Algar. Berkeley: Mizan Press, 1979.

——. *What Is to be Done: The Enlightened Thinkers and an Islamic Renaissance*. Edited by Farhang Rajaee. Houston: The Institute for Research and Islamic Studies, 1986.

Subtelny, Maria Eva. 'The Cult of Holy Places: Religious Practices among Soviet Muslims.' *Middle East Journal* 43 (1989): 594–604.

al-Suhrawardī, Abū'l-Najīb. *A Sufi Rule for Novices (K. Ādāb al-Murīdīn)*. Translated by Menahem Milson. Cambridge, Mass.: Harvard University Press, 1975.

Thanawi, Ashraf ᶜAli. *Perfecting Women. (Bihishti Zewar)*. Translated by Barbara Daly Metcalf. Berkeley: University of California Press, 1990.

Thomassen, Einar and Bernd Radtke. *The Letters of Ahmad Ibn Idris*. London: Hurst and Co. 1993.

Toprak, Binnaz. 'Politicization of Islam in a Secular State: The National Salvation Party in Turkey.' In *From Nationalism to Revolutionary Islam*, ed. Said Amir Arjomand, 119–33. London and Basingstoke: Macmillan, 1984.

Troll, Christian W. *Sayyid Ahmad Khan: A Reinterpretation of Muslim Theology*. New Delhi: Vikas, 1978.

Umar, Muhammad Sani. 'Changing Islamic Identity in Nigeria from the 1960s to the 1980s: From Sufism to Anti-Sufism.' In *Muslim Identity and Social Change in Sub-Saharan Africa*, ed. Louis Brenner, 154–78. London: Hurst and Co., 1993.

Vahid, Syed Abdul, ed. *Thoughts and Reflections of Iqbal*. Lahore: Ashraf Press, 1964.

Voll, John.' Hadith Scholars and Tariqahs: an ulama group in the eighteenth century haramayn.' *Journal of Asian and African Studies* 15 (1989): 264–73.

——. 'Mahdis, Walis and New Men in the Sudan.' In *Scholars, Saints and Sufis*, ed. Nikki Keddie, 367–84. Berkeley, Los Angeles and London: University of California Press, 1972.

——. 'Muḥammad Ḥayyā al-Sindī and Muḥammad b. ᶜAbd al-Wahhāb: an analysis of an intellectual group in eighteenth-century Madīna.' *Bulletin of the School of Oriental and African Studies* 38 (1975): 32–9.

Index

In this index the Arabic definite article ('al-') has been omitted at the *beginning* of an entry.